CALIFORNIA

GETTING STARTED GARDEN GUIDE

**Grow the Best Flowers, Shrubs, Trees,
Vines & Groundcovers**

First published in 2013 by Cool Springs Press, an imprint of the Quayside Publishing Group, 400 First Avenue North, Suite 400, Minneapolis, MN 55401

Cool Springs Press titles are also available at discounts in bulk quantity for industrial or sales-promotional use. For details write to Special Sales Manager at Cool Springs Press, 400 First Avenue North, Suite 400, Minneapolis, MN 55401 USA. To find out more about our books, visit us online at www.coolspringspress.com.

ISBN 978-1-59186-547-6

Acquisitions Editor: Billie Brownell
Design Manager: Brad Springer
Layout: Danielle Smith

Printed in China
10 9 8 7 6 5 4 3 2 1

CALIFORNIA

GETTING STARTED GARDEN GUIDE

Grow the Best Flowers, Shrubs, Trees, Vines & Groundcovers

Bruce & Sharon Asakawa

COOL
SPRINGS
PRESS
Home and Garden Experts™

MINNEAPOLIS, MINNESOTA

DEDICATION & ACKNOWLEDGMENTS

Dedication

For our late parents, Moto and Florence Asakawa and Dr. Harry and Elsie Hashimoto, who not only passed on their love of nature to us, but who raised us to believe that dreams become realities through education and perseverance. For our children, Tasia and Eric Asakawa, and Eric's wife, Stephanie, who nudged and encouraged us to continue our writing. Last, but certainly not least, for our grandchildren Nicholas, Samokai, and Emiko who will, in turn, pass on this love of gardening and the outdoors to others, completing our circle of life for successive generations.

Acknowledgments

The completion of this book is due to many people in particular, our tireless editor—Billie Brownell, who enabled us to get through the revision process with her patience, humor, and tact. She has been, is, and will always be an extraordinary editor and ally. We also value the expertise and staff support of Tracy Stanley and the rest of Quayside Publishing Group and Cool Springs Press. Another grateful acknowledgment goes to horticulture editor and friend, Dee Maranhao, for her conscientious review, constructive corrections, and thoughtful suggestions. A special thank-you to our wonderful listeners who have supported the *GardenLife* radio show, attended our public speaking engagements, and toured with us to wondrous garden sights around the world. Without all of you, this book would not have been completed . . . so good growing everyone!

Bruce and Sharon Asakawa

CONTENTS

WELCOME
TO GARDENING
IN CALIFORNIA

One would have to travel through a number of nations to find the enormous variety of plants, climate, and topography that exist in our 800-mile-long state. Those who have moved here from another part of the United States, or from another country, may be somewhat at a loss when confronted with California's diversity. To begin gardening here, it is best to learn about the unique microclimates, soil conditions, and plant materials.

Not only do growing conditions change dramatically from region to region, but they also change within these regions. The United States Department of Agriculture (USDA) cold-hardiness zone map on page 28 to 31 shows the approximate zones of average minimum temperatures. A zone assigned to an individual plant indicates the lowest temperature at which the plant can be expected to survive. California has eight of the twelve cold-hardiness zones (4 to 11) across its 160,000 square miles . . . more than any other state. The Preferred Zone range assigned to each plant in this book is based partly on the USDA data, but mostly on our many years of experience, taking into account factors such as humidity, wind conditions, soil conditions, and salt tolerance. They represent the area in which a plant will grow best, not the only area in which the plant can grow. (Under the proper conditions, you could grow a lemon tree in the mountains. It certainly would not be the plant's preferred area, however, nor would it be practical.)

In addition to these climate zones, every landscape has microclimates that will enhance or diminish a plant's ability to grow. We recommend that gardeners record the temperature variations in their yards in order to help them make the best plant selections. Consult page 29 to learn how to do this.

Annual average precipitation also varies widely in California, from 2.3 inches in Death Valley to a high of 100 inches or more in certain areas in Northern California.

A Land of Tremendous Diversity

California is a land of astonishing geologic formations. These land forms influence regional climate, soil development, and flora and fauna diversification.

Southern California, for example, is more than Hollywood stars and surfers. It is a geologic area formed by the north-south peninsular mountain ranges to the east and the east-west transverse mountain ranges to the north, offering a Mediterranean climate with subtropical temperatures and lavish vegetation. The Pacific Ocean moderates potential temperature extremes, resulting in an ideal environment for growing both native and imported plants.

To the east of the Peninsular Ranges is the western portion of the Colorado Desert, known as the low desert, where California's sole endemic palm, the California fan palm, flourishes. Travel north of the Peninsular Ranges, across the Transverse Ranges, and you enter the Mojave Desert, known as the high desert, home of the unique Joshua trees and the California Poppy Reserve. This area is subject to severe temperature fluctuations, freezing in the winter and broiling in the summer.

The coastal mountain ranges extend northward from the western end of the Transverse Ranges and parallel to the Pacific Ocean. This is where stands of California live oaks and Monterey pines anchor the sky to the earth. Continuing northward along the coast to the San Francisco Bay area, the influence of the Pacific pushes farther inland as the ocean moisture moves through the delta regions and moderates the extreme temperatures of the vineyard-filled Napa Valley. Farther north, along the coast, grows the majestic redwood forest, filled with California's treasured state trees. An unusual process called fog drip means that coastal moisture condenses on the mighty trees and then accumulates and rains to the ground, creating a moist home for native plants. As you move farther inland towards Redding, on the eastern side of the coastal range of the mountains, the geography is dominated by the southern end of the Cascade mountain ranges, whose soils are of volcanic origin.

The Great Central Valley, which includes Sacramento and the San Joaquin Valleys, is one of the most intense agricultural growing regions in the world, with alluvial soils that make it the most fertile land in California. The Central Valley is bounded on the east by the Sierra Nevada range, and on the west by coastal mountain ranges.

California Gardening: Rewards

A tremendous reward of gardening throughout most of California is the year-round growing season. The nursery industry does not shut down in the fall as it does in other states. This yearlong growing season, coupled with a population that has almost doubled from the 1970 census of just under 20,000,000 to over 38,000,000, has allowed California to become one of the world's leaders in the nursery industry.

Our chapters on Annuals, Bulbs, Citrus, Groundcovers, Lawns, Palms, Perennials, Roses, Shrubs, Trees, Tropicals, Vines, and Waterwise plants include indigenous plants as well as many others from around the world that thrive in California. California may be known for its native plant diversity, but approximately ninety percent of the plant material used for landscaping comes from other parts of the world. Some of the exotic plants have actually displaced some of California's native plants.

You will also find a great variety of succulents, herbaceous plants, and tropical varieties in our state, often growing in the same location without any problem. In many parts of California you can observe fascinating plant combinations while driving down neighborhood streets. It is not uncommon to see a hibiscus from China, a bird of paradise from South Africa, an amaryllis from South America, and a ranunculus from Europe all coexisting in the same landscape.

California Gardening: Challenges

Every entry in this book describes the particular needs of a particular plant. Consulting these pages is the answer to the question: How does a gardener deal with California's horticultural diversity? The countless variations in California's climates and soils bring their share of challenges. There are periods of drought, dry winds, and a scarcity of chill hours in the coastal climates, all conditions that could limit the varieties that can be grown in certain areas. Desert gardeners, in the Mojave for example, have to be particularly mindful to select plant materials that tolerate drought, intense heat, and day-to-night temperature extremes.

The South American Bougainvillea thrives in USDA zones 10–11.

A water-thrifty landscape in bloom is a beautiful sight.

The Planting Techniques & Pruning Tips section following this introduction will enable even the beginner to be successful in the garden.

Today, limited natural resources, changing weather conditions, overpopulation, recycling issues, and the growing movement towards downsizing tempers the state's abundance. As the population increases, the space available for gardening diminishes, and the scale of gardening will become smaller. You will find we address all of these challenges in this book.

Innovations and Trends

In the 1930s, gardeners in California began growing trees in used fruit cans, earning the derisive nickname "Tin Can Growers." Before too long, however, the trend caught on, and today you cannot visit any state where people don't have ornamental landscape plants growing in containers.

After World War II and during the population explosion, Californians popularized indoor/outdoor living with patios and barbecues under sunny skies. In the 1960s, California horticulturists developed what was then called "spaghetti irrigation," an innovative process further improved by the Israelis and now known as "drip irrigation."

Gardeners like color. It may be hard to believe today, but there was a time when plants sold in nurseries were all green. When nurseries began stocking plants in bloom in the late 1970s, parades of flowers appeared in public areas and private gardens. "Selling color" was a major trend that had its beginnings in the Golden State. California was also one of the first states to plant highways and freeways, beginning a trend of beautifying businesses, neighborhoods, and communities that spread across the country.

The most recent innovations, such as the computer, electronic notepad, smart phone, and equally "smart" television, have revolutionized the dissemination of information, including gardening. Today websites, blogs, tweets, YouTube videos, and apps connect California experts with gardeners all over the world. But although the use of technology to transmit valuable gardening information is here to stay, what matters most is what is going on in our own gardens—the successes, failures, the upsides, and the downsides.

Welcome to Our Garden

Bruce and I live in an unincorporated east-to-west stretch of coastal valley in California's southernmost county. Tucked in between three established municipalities, we are about ten minutes north of the U.S.-Mexico border. This is about as rural as a community can be and still be only 15 minutes from the center of California's second most populous city (behind Los Angeles). Each time our community is asked if we would like to be annexed, annexation is voted down. I suppose we like country roads, big trees, and wide open spaces, open enough to raise chickens, ducks, goats, and horses, as well as the more exotic peacocks, ostriches, and buffalo.

A Haven for Wildlife

Our yard is not a manicured landscape—it is more like a habitat we share with Mother Nature's critters, large and small, furry, scaled, and feathered.

On a steep southeast-facing slope in our backyard is a stand of enormous sixty-year-old eucalyptus trees. The tallest tree towers 125 feet above the surrounding landscape, dominating the garden, but several years ago it unfortunately succumbed to an infestation of the eucalyptus longhorned borer. Since it posed no danger to any nearby structure, we let it remain, and the insect infestation attracted a tremendous population of woodpeckers and sapsuckers who have set up housekeeping in our tall sentry, feasting on the insects' larvae.

Over the past several years, another welcome manifestation has been the continuing presence of two magnificent red-tailed hawks. They reside in one of our younger eucalyptus trees, a tall one that reaches skyward as if in anticipation of replacing the canopy of its neighboring dead sentinel. Looking out the dining room window every morning, we see them there perched on the tallest, barest branch, awaiting the early warmth of the sun's rays. Later in the day they gracefully dip and soar, riding the thermal air currents with the greatest of ease. Every year, during the early spring months, they fly back and forth, carrying various-sized sticks and bits of garden frass to build a huge nest in one of the more protected branches of another of our eucalyptus trees. After about 60 days we hear the insistent calling of their offspring and know that, once again, they have successfully hatched a youngster. Sometime during the late summer, just when the fledgling is almost mature, he or she swoops down and lands on our deck or in our vegetable garden and spends a few minutes with us. We like to believe this is the fledgling's way of saying farewell to all that is familiar before it soars away in the next day or two to establish its own home.

In addition to our stand of eucalyptus trees, we have a very old, gnarled cork oak tree cantilevered over the driveway, and next to it is a sprawling pyracantha shrub. When its pale berries transform into fire engine red, they attract flocks of glossy black phainopeplas, buff-colored crested waxwings, jabbering scrub jays, and the brilliant golden orange-and-black hooded orioles. Nestled in the protective branches of the cork oak, the birds test the berries daily until they are to their liking, then, as if there were a public announcement, hundreds of their feathered friends descend on the bush for a berry buffet. It is fun to watch as the insatiable birds establish a "pecking" order, taking turns in a somewhat organized fashion.

More diminutive pollinators, such as the iridescent Anna's hummingbirds, brightly painted swallowtail butterflies, fuzzy bumblebees, and industrious honeybees hover around our butterfly bush, pride of Madeira, blossoming fruit trees, and cutflower garden. Families of coyotes, gray foxes, and an occasional bobcat also traverse our slopes. Resident skunks and opossums use their keen olfactory senses to ferret out tasty morsels like grubs and insects in our garden. Gophers, squirrels, and rabbits tunnel, scurry, and hop by; alligator lizards and rosy boas sunbathe during the warm days; and frogs serenade us at night. We are on the visitation path of a

Red-tailed hawks and Cooper's Hawks (like the one pictured here) can share garden space with many other types of wildlife.

Use a vine-covered morning glory arch as a visual gateway to the view beyond your yard.

trio of juvenile delinquent raccoons who peek in on us on our back deck, scaring our normally mellow Himalayan cat, Miyu. The rascally bandits also periodically treat our pond and its fish as their private sushi bar. In addition to our resident red-tailed hawks, other raptors frequent our trees: kestrels, Cooper's hawks, and the great horned and western screech owls. As well as being home to a varied assortment of citrus, avocado, fruit, and eucalyptus trees and drought-tolerant plants such as rock rose, pride of Madeira, and European olive, the lower portion of our backyard is truly a haven for wildlife.

Understanding the Not-So-Perfect Environment

Over the years we have traveled with fellow garden lovers to horticulturally significant destinations like South Africa, Botswana, Costa Rica, Japan, China, Hawaii, England, Scotland, France, Italy, Canada, the Galapagos, and others, a practice that has increased our tolerance for and heightened our understanding of the "not-so-perfect" environment. One of our most memorable excursions was to the ancient Monteverde Cloud Forest in Costa Rica. Each morning the cloud forest is shrouded in a mystical mist that gently deposits beads of glistening condensation on outstretched leaves reaching towards the shafts of light. As we walked along on the floor of the forest, we were actually strolling through a living laboratory, teeming with wildlife. There were screeching raptors high in the forest canopy, moss-laden two-toed sloths living their slow-motion lives upside-down on borrowed branches, and armies of chewing insects feeding on every leaf, in and out of sight. In fact, there wasn't a single undamaged leaf along the entire walk—and yet every plant seemed perfectly beautiful. In our own gardens, we may fret when we see a single leaf being devoured by a beastly beetle, but in the forest, there is an understanding between provider and consumer.

The Organized Areas of Our Landscape

As is our marriage, our garden is a blend of careful design and carefree habitat, a blend of two different styles that works for us. While allowing a large portion of our yard to be more "natural," we have designated smaller areas for more intensified and organized landscapes. I appreciate my cut-flower garden sprinkled with several roses, bulbs, annuals, and orchids as well as a collection of assorted greenery suitable for flower arrangements. We both enjoy our freshly picked herbs and seasonal fruits and vegetables, and although our resident birds and other wildlife "steal" much of our bounty, it is a small price to pay for their company. In fact, it nudges us to improve the productivity of our harvest so there will be plenty to share with everyone, critters and friends alike. Our love of gardening is based on the observation of such activities as the red-tailed hawks' daily routines and the seasonal changes in our landscape. Gardening slows down our lives so that we can appreciate all the small and large miracles going on in our yard, which brings us to the question, "Why write a revised version of our first *California Gardener's Guide*?"

Why This Book, *California Getting Started Gardener's Guide*?

There have been hundreds of books published on all aspects of gardening, landscaping, and horticulture. So why another publication tilling the soil that has nurtured our interest in the wonders of the natural world? The answer lies in the personal involvement we all experience when tending our gardens. We are individuals, with different personalities and different life experiences that form our individuality, and our gardens reflect this uniqueness. Many, like me, have moved from elsewhere and initially did not know where to begin when it comes to California gardening or even what questions to ask. Others, like my husband Bruce, are native Californians but still have a lot to learn about our diverse state. And still others are just beginning to venture into gardening.

Also it has been 13 years since our first book, *Bruce and Sharon Asakawa's California Gardener's Guide,* was published and as in life, plant varieties, gardening trends, environmental issues, and information tools have changed or come to the forefront. For example, with water usage becoming such a major consideration in our daily lives, it is important to include a chapter on waterwise plants, and because there are a plethora of recent books on California fruits and vegetables, we have limited our coverage to include primarily citrus and other edibles that have ornamental value.

After 50 years in the retail nursery and florist business, over 20 years on the radio, and now, most recently, blogging, tweeting, and writing the weekly online *GardenLife* newsletter as well as hosting the *GardenLife* national radio show, we hope this book will enable you to use our knowledge gathered over these many years from personal and learned experience.

Many Ways to Garden

Whether you are a beginner or seasoned gardener, there are many ways to be successful. Gardens are eclectic; they are expressions of our unique personalities. Hopefully the format of this book will enable you to use the knowledge that is a distilled collection of our life experiences. May it provide you with the information and inspiration to spend more time in your garden.

Now let's get started. Have a great day, and good growing!

Bruce

Sharon

Our "secret garden" with variegated geranium, bearded iris, hanging Haemanthus, and an unused bird cage.

Planting Techniques & Pruning Tips for California

From talking with callers to our *GardenLife* radio show and replying to emails over the years, it is clear that gardening is a common denominator for folks from all walks of life and from all generations. From children to grandparents, from scientists to students, when people get together to chat about their gardens, it's about how to grow the sweetest citrus or successfully maintain the most beautiful roses or when to fertilize their orchids. There are as many opinions about gardening and techniques as there are people who garden, but their ideas and methods are toward the same end: successful gardening.

Fortunately there is never a one-and-only way to achieve this goal. A landscape is an organic, dynamic creation because plants are in a constant state of flux, encouraging us to continually experiment and learn from trial, error, and experience. Challenges and changes are the main reasons people get hooked on gardening and it is also great therapy for the mind and spirit to escape the stuffy confines of indoors for the fresh air and expansiveness of the outdoors. To save you time, money, and effort, here are a few planting techniques to keep in mind.

Planting Pit, Backfill, and Watering Basin Tips for Trees and Large Shrubs

The Planting Pit

Excavate a rectilinear planting pit 1 to 1½ times the plant's original container depth and 4 to 6 times the plant's original container width. In a rectilinear pit, the root system grows through the backfill to the corners, encouraging roots to web more quickly into the native soil.

Pile the excavated earth close by so it can be amended for backfill if needed. Roughen the vertical surfaces of the planting pit with a cultivator. The rectilinear form and the roughened surface will encourage the development of lateral roots. Do not place a layer of gravel at the bottom of the pit because it does not solve poor drainage.

The Backfill

The backfill (soil excavated from the planting pit) should be amended to have a texture halfway between that of the native soil and that of the plant's rootball. Backfill is the material that the plant's new roots will first encounter. When the rootball soil, the backfill, and the native soil are similar in texture, it is unnecessary to amend the backfill. If it's not similar, mix in compost or humus-rich soil amendments and follow package directions to provide a well-draining soil texture. Before planting, tamp the soil in the bottom of the pit to minimize any settling of the rootball. Plant the rootball about 1 inch higher that the surrounding backfill to accommodate any future settling.

The Watering Basin

Build a berm 4 to 6 inches high and 3 to 4 times the plant's original container diameter. Generally 2 inches of surface water gravitates 12 inches in dense, clay soils, so a watering basin that has a 4-inch berm will soak down to 2 feet. In porous, sandy soils, it only takes 1 inch of surface water to gravitate the same 12 inches. Water a newly transplanted plant thoroughly enough to collapse any air pockets in the backfill.

Mulching

Mulching is one of the simplest and most beneficial procedures for the landscape. It saves moisture, moderates soil temperature, reduces soil surface compaction, slows erosion and water runoff, improves soil structure, controls weeds, reduces evaporation, and encourages beneficial microorganisms and earthworms. Mulch the soil surface inside the watering basin with 2 to 4 inches of humus mulch or compost, but keep 2 to 4 inches away from the base of the plant.

Watering Guideline for Basins

The following gives an idea of how much water it takes to fill basins depending on their diameters and berm heights. The volume of water a plant requires is the volume of water that transpires off its canopy and evaporates from the ground.

- 3 ft. diameter, 4 in. berm watering basin takes 20 gallons to fill
- 3 ft. diameter, 6 in. berm watering basin takes 30 gallons to fill
- 4 ft. diameter, 4 in. berm watering basin takes 30 gallons to fill
- 4 ft. diameter, 6 in. berm watering basin takes 50 gallons to fill
- 6 ft. diameter, 4 in. berm watering basin takes 70 gallons to fill
- 6 ft. diameter, 6 in. berm watering basin takes 150 gallons to fill

Soil Texture

Are you soils sandy, silty, or clayey? Sandy soils are porous, free-draining, and often nutrient-deficient. They permit rapid root development if amended to retain moisture and nutrients. Silty soils permit even percolation but often lack moisture-holding capacity unless amended. Clayey soils are the least desirable—they are dense, expansive, and poorly draining. Loam is the ideal soil texture, about 40 percent sand, 40 percent silt, and 20 percent clay—if the soil is moist, this composition permits you to push a shovel into it and withdraw it with relative ease.

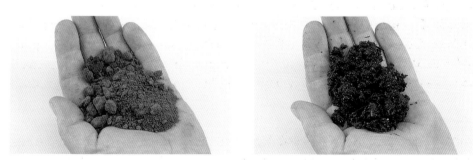

Your soil type may be completely different from your neighbor's; gardens close in proximity often have vastly different soil types, with different colors and textures from the outset.

The root zone should consist of 25 percent air, which is called soil atmosphere; 25 percent water, which is called soil solution; and 50 percent sand, silt, clay, and organic material, which is called soil structure. The root zone is not only home for absorbing, lateral, sinker, and taproots, it is also home to millions of aerobic microorganisms, most of which are beneficial for the plant (anaerobic microorganisms, such as water molds, hinder plant growth or kill the plant).

In simple terms, if the soil is moist and friable enough that you can push a pointed shovel into it and not have a glob of mud stick to it as you pull it out, the soil texture should be porous enough to allow good root development. If there is a glob of mud, amend the soil with compost or humus mulch so that the organic content approaches 20 to 30 percent and add a product rich in humic acid and saponin.

Hands-On Soil Moisture Test

The following helps to determine the wetness or dryness of the soil without using a tensiometer or digging down with a shovel.

- Take a handful of soil and try to form a ball with it. If soil does not form a ball, less than 50 percent of water is available to the soil, and it is time to water (or if soil is gritty and drops through your fingers, it is dry and needs water).
- If the soil forms a ball but does not hold together it indicates 50 to 70 percent of water is available to the soil. Wait to water for another day or two.
- If the soil forms a ball without a shiny surface and crumbles apart, 75 percent of water is available. Wait to water for a few days.
- Another simple test is to let your finger do the talking by pushing your index finger as far into the soil as possible; if it feels dry to the touch, it is probably time to water.

The Soil Reaction (pH) Test

The soil pH, otherwise known as soil reaction, can be acidic, neutral, or alkaline. A reading of 7 is neutral (neither acid nor alkaline), a reading below 7 is acidic, and a reading above 7 is alkaline. When soils are very acidic, elements such as aluminum and manganese become overly available and may become toxic to plants. Soils that are too alkaline may limit the availability of elements such as iron, zinc, and nitrogen, leading to nutrient deficiencies.

It is important to determine the soil pH about twice a year, once in mid-spring and once in early autumn. Take the test samples with a coring tool, at a depth of 10 to 12 inches, from several locations, especially where the topography and growing conditions vary. Use a pH test kit or ask your local garden center if they will test it for you (or have it done at a laboratory by searching online under "soil test labs"). Analog and digital direct reading pH meters are also available, but they are more expensive. In general, most plant species prefer a slightly acidic to neutral soil (6.5 to 7.0).

For overly acidic soil, raise the pH by adding calcium carbonate (lime) following the manufacturer's directions. To lower alkaline readings, add sulfur following the application recommendations or continue to add compost and try not to fertilize with chemicals that are high in salts. Instead, use organic fertilizers such as cottonseed meal.

The Percolation Test

Because poor drainage blocks air from reaching plant roots as well as encouraging the proliferation of anaerobic microorganisms (oxygen-depleting organisms) instead of aerobic microorganisms, it is important to determine the soil's percolation rate by excavating a hole 30 inches × 30 inches. Fill it with water, let it drain completely, then fill it again. The second filling should drain at a rate of 1 inch per hour—in approximately 3 to 11 hours, the water should be gone. If it disappears in that amount of time, then drainage is not a problem, but if the hole is still half full, then the soil drains poorly. Do one of the following:

- Amend and work organic matter into the soil such as humus mulch or compost.
- Excavate planting pits so they are large enough to accommodate the slow percolation rate.
- Remove excess water from the bottom of the planting pit and direct it to a lower elevation by using French drains or perforated PVC drainpipes.
- Build a raised planting area above the planting pit.
- Excavate to a depth where the porosity of the soil will permit free draining.
- Terrace the land if there is a difference in elevation.

Pruning Tips

Pruning doesn't have to be the great mystery it sometimes appears to be. Follow these tips, and don't be afraid to cut!

Pruning Tools

Pruning Tool	Branch Diameter	Blade Type	Use
Hand pruner	¾ in.	bypass	for general pruning
Hand pruner	½ in.	bypass	for thinning
Hand pruner	½ in.	bypass	for cut and hold (flowers and fruit)
Loppers	1½ in.	bypass	for heading back leaders
Hedge clippers	½ in.	bypass	for shearing hedges & groundcovers
Knob cutter Telescoping	1 in.	pinch	for close cutting bonsai pruning
Pole pruner Telescoping	1½ in.	bypass	for pruning branches from the ground
Pole pruner	½ in.	bypass	cut and hold / fruit harvesting
Pruning saw	2 in.	pull	for removing branches
Chain saw	4 in.	gas/electric	for removing scaffolds

General Pruning Tips for Most Plants

- Remove diseased, dead, or interfering wood.
- Prune by thinning or heading.
- Thinning cuts open a plant's canopy to lower a plant's height, reduce the weight on branches, stimulate new growth, and increase flowering and fruiting.
- Heading back (also known as shearing) increases the density of a plant's perimeter, improving its ability to provide shade or screening. It removes current or one-year-old-shoots down to a bud or stub and helps train young trees and shapes flowering trees and hedges.
- Cuts made flush with the surface of the supporting branch (flush cuts) are not recommended.
- Expose the least amount of surface to insect or disease by cutting just outside the branch bark ridge (the wrinkle of bark extending from the "V" at its point of attachment) and the collar (the raised bark below the "V"). Cut up from the lower side of the branch 10 to 20 percent of the diameter and finish by cutting down from the upper side to meet the first cut.

- Do not apply a sealing compound over pruning cuts unless there is insect or disease activity, because it slows down natural compartmentalization (a tree or shrub's method of sealing injured areas).
- If flowering trees bloom in clusters at the ends of branches, do not head back in fall or winter, because you lose the next spring's blooms. Instead, prune shortly after blooms are spent (done flowering).
- Lacing allows light to penetrate the tree's canopy, stimulating new growth, improving air circulation, and controlling pests.
- Prune off suckers that are growing from the lateral surface roots or from the area between a root flare and a bud or graft union.
- After pruning off the sucker, apply a sucker suppressant containing naphthalene acetic acid. If possible, wait until nesting birds have finished raising their young.
- To control the height and shape of pine trees, remove their candles (upright new growth).
- Trees growing in your garden that have branches or roots extending beyond your property line are normally your responsibility.
- Do not prune back a tree's branches when transplanting, because this removes auxins (plant growth hormones concentrated in branch and twig tips that stimulate new root development) and hinders cytokinins (plant growth regulators in the root system that stimulates new canopy growth if it is damaged) from reestablishing the root system.
- When transplanting a tree, reduce moisture loss by pruning off 60 to 90 percent of its foliage.

When pruning a tree, make a first cut about 6 inches from the trunk, cutting the underside of the branch about a fourth of the way through. Then make the second cut, cutting down, all the way through, a few inches out from the first cut. This technique helps prevent the bark from stripping off the tree.

California Fire Department Recommendations for Creating Defensible Space

One of the most critical issues confronting California is making homes fire safe by creating a 100-foot line of defensible space. Plan, and plant, your landscape to be the safest possible. Local fire departments suggest homeowners do the following:

- Clear an area of 30 feet immediately surrounding your home and incorporate low-growing plants with high moisture content.
- For the remaining 70 feet or to the property line create horizontal and vertical spacing between plants depending on slope grades and plant size to prevent fire from spreading.
- It is not necessary to cut down large trees as long as all of the plants beneath them are removed, eliminating vertical "fire ladders."
- Remove all accumulated debris from the roof and gutters.
- Keep tree limbs trimmed 10 feet from chimneys, and remove dead limbs hanging over the home, garage, or other structures.

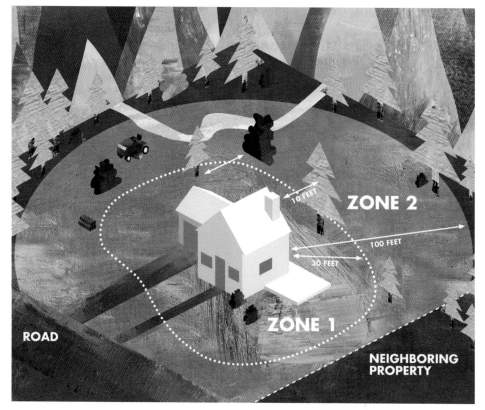

Image courtesy of CAL FIRE, www.readyforwildfire.org

Each entry in this guide provides information about a plant's characteristics, habits, and basic requirements for active growth, as well as our personal experience and knowledge of the plant. Hopefully the pertinent background and facts about each plant will help further an appreciation of California's varied plant palette and ensure a successful gardening experience. A plant's mature height and spread, bloom period, color, fruit period (if any), sun and soil preferences, water requirements, fertilizing needs, pruning and care, and pest information are concisely organized. And because Latin names can be difficult, there is a phonetic botanical pronunciation given for each plant selection as well as another common name (if one applies). Any added benefits such as fall color, drought resistance, edibility, attracts beneficials, or hummingbirds are represented by symbols. To help achieve successful and striking results, we also give you our suggestions for landscape design and companion plants that will work whether you're a beginning or experienced gardener.

Sun Preferences

The range of sunlight suitable for each plant is represented by these three symbols. Full sun means sunlight 8 hours to almost all day. Part sun is 4 to 6 hours of direct sun, preferably in the morning with protection from hot afternoon sun. Part shade is 2 to 4 hours of direct sun per day, primarily in the morning, or all day bright indirect light. Shade is shade about all day.

Full Sun   Partial Sun/Shade   Shade

Added Benefits

The following symbols indicate additional benefits that enhance a plant selection's appeal.

 Native   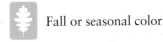 Attracts "good bugs" such as butterflies, bees, and beneficial insects

 Drought tolerant   Fall or seasonal color

 Attracts hummingbirds   Edible

Try These

These include specific species, varieties, or cultivars that we believe are particularly noteworthy based on size, flower color, or other characteristics adaptable regionally or seasonally.

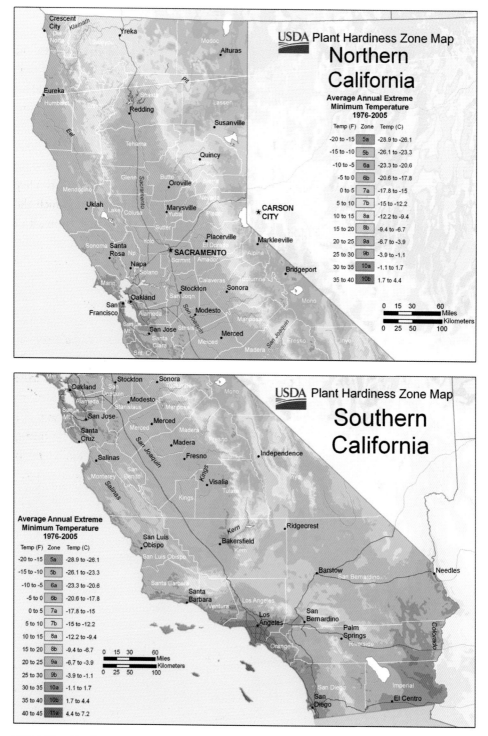

USDA Plant Hardiness Zone Map, 2012. Agricultural Research Service,
U.S. Department of Agriculture. Accessed from http://planthardiness.ars.usda.gov.

USDA Hardiness Zone Map
Preferred Zones

Cold-hardiness zone designations were developed by the United States Department of Agriculture (USDA) to indicate the minimum average temperature for an area. A zone assigned to an individual plant indicates the lowest temperature at which the plant can be expected to survive over the winter. California has an extremely wide zone range, from zone 5 to zone 11. The Preferred Zone range assigned to most plants in this book is based partly on the USDA cold-hardiness zone range, but mostly on our many years of experience. Our Preferred Zone recommendations take into account factors such as humidity, wind conditions, soil conditions, and salt tolerance. They represent the area in which a plant will grow best, not the only area in which the plant can grow. If no zone is noted, then the plant is expected to grow well in all of California's zones.

If you are not sure what cold zone your yard is in, walk or drive around your community and list the plants that have matured by surviving several winter seasons. Consult your plant list, cross reference the plant's cold zone tolerance, and presto!, you will find the applicable cold zone.

Keep in mind that every yard has many microclimates that will enhance or diminish a plant's ability to grow. For example, structures such as fences or walls provide protected areas of protection for frost-sensitive plants; large trees with wide canopies create shaded, sun-protected havens for sun-sensitive plants; pockets of colder temperatures settle near the bottoms of slopes; and warmer temperatures are more common towards the middle and tops of slopes. About once a week, during the coldest and warmest seasons of the year, record the temperature variations in your yard with a high-low thermometer, noting the dates and temperatures in your garden journal.

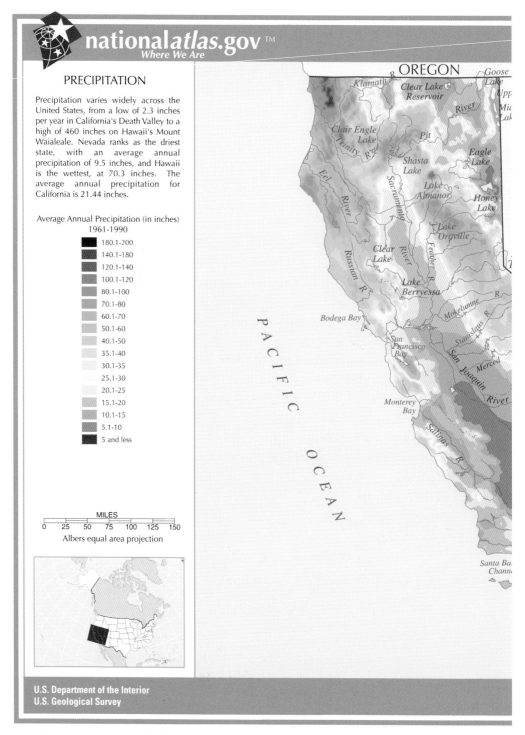

PRECIPITATION

Precipitation varies widely across the United States, from a low of 2.3 inches per year in California's Death Valley to a high of 460 inches on Hawaii's Mount Waialeale. Nevada ranks as the driest state, with an average annual precipitation of 9.5 inches, and Hawaii is the wettest, at 70.3 inches. The average annual precipitation for California is 21.44 inches.

Average Annual Precipitation (in inches)
1961-1990

■	180.1-200
■	140.1-180
■	120.1-140
■	100.1-120
■	80.1-100
■	70.1-80
■	60.1-70
■	50.1-60
■	40.1-50
■	35.1-40
■	30.1-35
■	25.1-30
■	20.1-25
■	15.1-20
■	10.1-15
■	5.1-10
■	5 and less

MILES
0 25 50 75 100 125 150
Albers equal area projection

U.S. Department of the Interior
U.S. Geological Survey

Precipitation varies widely in California, from a low of 2.3 inches per year in Death Valley to a high of over 100 inches in a pocket in Northern California close to the Oregon border. The average annual precipitation for California is 21.44 inches.

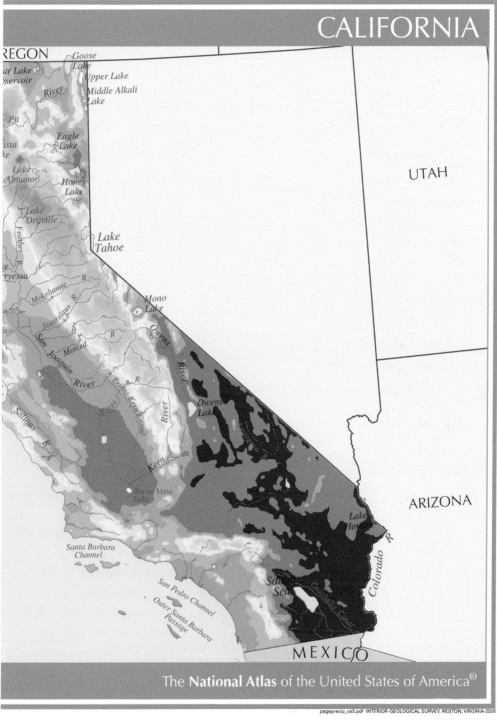

CALIFORNIA

REGON

Goose
Lake
Upper Lake
Middle Alkali
Lake

ar Lake
eservoir

River

Pit

Eagle
Lake

sta
ke

Lake
Almanor

Honey
Lake

UTAH

Lake
Oroville

Feather R.

e
ryessa

Lake
Tahoe

Mokelumne

R.

sco

Stanislaus R.

Mono
Lake

San Joaquin

Merced

R.

Owens

Fiver

Tuolumne-Kern Canal

River

Owens
Lake

Salinas

R.

R.

Kern

Buena Vista
Lake

Lake
Havasu

Santa Barbara
Channel

ARIZONA

Colorado R.

San Pedro Channel

Outer Santa Barbara
Passage

Salton
Sea

Coachella Canal

MEXICO

The **National Atlas** of the United States of America®

pageprecip_ca3.pdf INTERIOR-GEOLOGICAL SURVEY, RESTON, VIRGINIA-2005

(Courtesy www.nationalatlas.com)

ANNUALS
FOR CALIFORNIA

A mixture of annuals with perennials, shrubs, groundcovers, and even fruits and vegetables create an interplay of texture and color, a living orchestra. Permanent plants may require far less care than annuals and they may bloom quite heavily during certain seasons, but most annuals "bloom their heads off" over a very long period.

The Merits of Annuals

Cool-weather annuals such as Iceland poppies, pansy, and stock grow and blossom during winter and spring. When planted in warmer regions in the fall, many cool-weather annuals continue to bloom until the heat and humidity of summer peaks. When they fade, you can replace them with hot-weather lovers such as ageratum, alyssum, and sunflowers. Many are already in flower when you plant them in early spring and they continue to bloom until the first frost in fall.

Some annuals, like California poppy and nasturtiums, are excellent when planted *en masse* for spectacular splashes of garden color. Others, like alyssum, ageratum, and pansies, are well suited for borders and low edging around beds and walkways. Climbing sweet

Edibles are for both culinary and ornamental uses.

peas can be used as quick-growing screens. Many annuals are sources of cut, dried, or edible flowers.

On the subject of edibles: incorporate veggies such as kale, lettuce, and Swiss chard into the mixed flower beds to serve double duty as culinary sources as well as gorgeous ornamentals.

If flower color is the fortissimo in your garden symphony, the diminuendo is the more muted qualities of annual foliage. The fresh, green, rounded leaves of nasturtiums and the variegated foliage of some California poppies make beautiful ornamentals by themselves.

When and How to Plant Annuals

Annuals can be started by seed or from containers. The most economical way is to start from seeds, and it can be very rewarding to see those tiny leaves popping up in flats. Seeds sown indoors are safe from being washed out by torrential rains, eaten by birds, nipped in the bud by frost, or choked to death by weeds. There are some exceptions, such as sunflowers, which do best when sown directly in the garden because of their long taproots.

Instant Color vs. a Longer Season

To add instant color with bedding plants, you can buy them in containers or flats already in flower. If you need a finished-looking garden immediately, buy the plants in flower; for a longer blooming performance, look for smaller plants that have not yet formed flower buds. Since annuals grow fast, buying them small allows the plants to adapt to your garden conditions more easily before expending energy on flowers. You can also start fertilizing earlier, the plants are less likely to be rootbound (which stunts growth), and you can pinch back earlier to promote branching and compact growth.

Do a Little Exploring

To determine which annuals are doing well in your region and which are most attractive to you, visit public and private gardens in your area, consult your local nursery, or ask a University of California Cooperative Extension specialist. There is also nothing wrong with the learn-by-doing method, especially with annuals, since they are relatively easy to grow, inexpensive, and can be replaced two or three times a year. As in life, there are no mistakes in gardening, only learning experiences.

With so many annual varieties, there is bound to be a suitable choice for any purpose—whether to brighten an area around the dark foliage of background shrubs, to fill in flower beds, to overplant bulb beds for color after spring-flowering bulbs are spent, or to bring the outdoors indoors with vases of cutflower bouquets. With just a little effort and planning, you can have a symphony of color from spring through fall (even all year-round in mild-winter regions), amid your stalwart trees, shrubs, perennials, groundcovers, and edible crops. The addition of annuals brings music to all your senses.

Ageratum

Ageratum houstonianum

Bloom Period and Seasonal Color
Blue, lavender, lilac, mauve, pink, and white flowers bloom in summer.

Mature Height × Spread 6–8 in. × 8–10 in.

Botanical Pronunciation
ah-jer-AY-tum hews-tone-ee-AN-um

geratum derives its name from Greek words meaning "not old," perhaps because it was an ancient remedy for ailments associated with old age. Another plausible explanation for the name may be that these plants are such prolific bloomers and are able to retain their color and fresh appearance for a long time, seeming never to age. So who are we to disagree with the ancients? The flowers appear at the ends of short stems and are dense clusters of puffy, button-shaped blossoms that emerge from heart-shaped mounds of crinkled, oval-shaped, matte green leaves. Keep your garden young at heart by planting ageratum (also known as floss flowers) in mixed flower beds, as edging along borders, or toward the front of containers.

When, Where, and How to Plant
Plant from seeds, pony packs, color packs, or 4 in. containers in spring after the last frost, spacing them about 8 in. apart. In mild-winter climates, plant seeds in late winter or early spring, after the garden soil has warmed. Press the seeds gently into the soil, as they need light to germinate. Ageratum prefers a loam soil; if necessary, blend in amendments such as humus mulch, compost, and preplant fertilizer to a depth of 12 in. Apply a root stimulator immediately after planting. They do best in full sun in cooler climates, but will also fare well in light shade, especially where summers are hotter.

Growing Tips
Immediately after planting, soak deeply and thoroughly. For the first week, water daily; thereafter adjust watering frequency and amounts according to climatic and growth conditions. Once their roots are established, fertilize ageratum in spring and summer with a water-soluble organic food or a slow-release granular fertilizer.

Advice and Care
Deadhead regularly to prolong the blooming season. Because it grows so low to the ground, ageratum is a haven for slugs and snails. These pests are easily controlled by handpicking and squishing, or by applying an organic molluscicide such as iron phosphate. Also watch for sow bugs and earwigs. To control them, simply roll up a moistened newspaper and place around your plant in early evening. Sow bugs and earwigs hide in dark, moist places. Come morning, throw the newspaper away in the trash.

Companion Planting and Design
Use ageratum in rock gardens or as a groundcover in mixed flower beds, or as an edging in containers. Ageratum grows well with daylily, lily of the Nile, and shore juniper.

Try These
Ageratum houstonianum 'Blue Horizon' is a taller variety that grows up to 30 in. with blue flowers and looks lovely in the middle of mixed flower beds. For front borders or around the outer edges of a container, choose a dwarf variety (4–6 in.) such as 'Blue Danube'. For bright pink flowers consider 'Swing Pink', or for 9 in. white bloomers, select 'Summer Snow'. Taller varieties also make excellent cut flowers.

Alyssum

Lobularia maritima

Bloom Period and Seasonal Color
White, pink, rose-red, violet, and lilac flowers bloom in spring and summer.

Mature Height × Spread 4 in. × 6–12 in.

Botanical Pronunciation
LOBE-you-lah-ree-ah ma-ri-TEEM-ah

There is quite a lot of confusion about whether alyssum is really the annual *Lobularia*. In the interest of botanical accuracy, sweet alyssum is really *Lobularia maritima*, one of the most popular annuals. In more temperate climates, it reseeds almost continually, making an appearance just about year-round. Multibranched plants with spreading habits, alyssum leaves are erect and grayish green in color. Atop the foliage, from spring to fall, are thick mounds of fragrant, 1–3-in. flower clusters. Their rich nectar provides satisfying nourishment for bees, hummingbirds, and butterflies. Although they withstand short periods of drought, dry wind, heat, and temperatures slightly below freezing, they do best in mild weather with regular irrigation. Because of their tolerance to salt, they can be used in seaside gardens.

When, Where, and How to Plant
Plant in spring from seed or containers spacing them 6–8 in. apart. Alyssum thrives in full sun, in well-drained, evenly moist loamy soil with a pH of 6.8–7.0. If necessary, prepare the flower bed by blending in soil amendments such as humus mulch, compost, and preplant fertilizer to a depth of 12 in. Since alyssum seeds need light to germinate, tap the seeds very gently in the soil so they will not be buried too deeply.

Growing Tips
Immediately after planting, soak deeply and thoroughly. For the first week, water daily; thereafter adjust watering frequency and amounts according to weather and growth conditions. Fertilize once a month during the growing season with a water-soluble food such as liquid kelp or fish emulsion.

Advice and Care
After the first flush of blossoms, clip the plant back by 50 percent to encourage a longer flowering cycle. Alyssum is not susceptible to many diseases or pests, but as is true for so many of our other favorite annual flowers, weekly inspection of the blossoms and foliage is prudent. For chewing insects apply an organic control such as spinosad and for sucking insects, apply a suffocant such as a horticultural grade of canola oil.

Companion Planting and Design
Use alyssum in rock gardens, creating floral rivers of white or blue flowing down through the boulders; as groundcover in mixed flower beds; and as edging in containers. Sweet alyssum grows well with shore juniper, daylily, lily of the Nile, and wallflower.

Try These
Lobularia maritima 'Royal Carpet' is fragrant, with very dark blue flowers. 'Pastel Carpet' grows to diminutive 3 in. tall but spreads to 12 in., blooming in soft shades of rose, pink, violet, blue, white, and creamy yellow. 'Carpet of Snow' is a compact grower in bright white. 'Snow Crystals' has extra-large white blooms, is taller to 10 in., and trailing. 'Clear Crystal' is mounding in habit and comes in rose, pink, lavender, peach, white, and violet. *Lobularia* 'Basket of Gold' grows 6 in. tall, spreads to 18 in. wide, and is covered with bright, golden-yellow blooms.

Angelonia

Angelonia augustifolia

Bloom Period and Seasonal Color
Rose, plum, blue, lavender, white, combination stripes, and bicolors bloom from spring to autumn.

Mature Height × Spread 18–36 in. × 18 in.

Botanical Pronunciation
an-jel-oh-NEE-ah ah-GOOS-tih-fo-lee-ah

Often referred to as a summer snapdragon, this native of Mexico and the West Indies can be treated as a perennial in mild-winter areas, but should be considered an annual where extended winter freezes are common. Its miniature snapdragonlike, two-lipped flowers arranged on spires of stems with narrow, pointed, rich green leaves grow particularly vigorous when temperatures warm up in the late spring and summer months. While other flowering plants wilt in summer's heat and humidity, angelonia flourish. They also do well in cutflower arrangements, lasting for about ten days when fresh water is added daily with a floral preservative. And they add a slight, grape soda–like or apple fragrance to the bouquet. Once established, it requires very little maintenance and care.

When, Where, and How to Plant
Angelonia can be planted from seed, but the hybrids are commonly sold in 4–6-in. pots. Since angelonias are heat lovers, it is best to plant in mid-spring or later, even during the typical midsummer hot spells. Although they tolerate clayey soils, they do best in well-draining soil, amended with compost or humus. Ideally, plant in full sun for optimum bloom production. It will not bloom as profusely but will tolerate partial shade conditions.

Growing Tips
Once established, allow the plant to dry out a bit before watering again. Apply a granular organic food every four to six weeks during the growing season in beds, but in containers, supplement with an additional treatment of liquid kelp in between the granular applications.

Advice and Care
Deadheading is usually not necessary, but an occasional errant or floppy flower spike can be easily snipped off. If chewing insect or snail and slug damage is extensive, use spinosad to control the chewing insects and an iron phosphate molluscicide for snails and slugs. For powdery mildew, spray leaves off with a stream of water; if it's persistent, spray with a horticultural-grade canola oil.

Companion Planting and Design
Because it remains beautiful, tough, and vigorous from spring until frost, angelonia is a wonderful low-maintenance annual for containers or mixed flower beds no matter where you live, provided there is full sun and enough summer warmth. Their upright, bushy habit contrasts well with softer, more cascading flowers such as petunias or calibrachoa, as well as the white-textured foliage of dusty miller or lamb's ear.

Try These
There are many hybrids that are improved versions of the standard angelonia. Some refer to the hybrids as angelonias on steroids, with bigger blossoms, stronger plants, and increased resistance to disease. Proven Winners' Angelface® hybrids are perfect in mixed borders or in containers and come in blue, dark violet, Wedgewood blue, and white colors. The growers from Ball offer the Angelmist™ hybrid series in white, lavender, purple, and pink.

Calibrachoa

Calibrachoa hybrids

Bloom Period and Seasonal Color
Yellow, orange, red, pink, purple, terracotta, and white blooms from spring to fall.

Mature Height × Spread 6–12 in. × 6–12 in. depending on variety/cultivar.

Botanical Pronunciation
CAL-ih-bra-ko-ah

Many consider Yasayuki Murakami to be the father of the *Calibrachoa* hybrid, which is native to Brazil and Peru but now available to gardens worldwide. He began crossing *Calibrachoa* species to create a more floriferous and disease-resistant hybrid, eventually creating a heat-tolerant and practically nonstop blooming garden staple known as Million Bells. There are now other calibrachoa series besides Million Bells, which differ in color range and patterns, but all share certain characteristics. Covering itself with hundreds of blossoms, calibrachoa resemble miniature petunias, but without the sticky texture. And unlike their larger petunia cousins, their flowers do not collapse in the rain, nor do tobacco budworms relish them. There is no need to deadhead, as most hybrids are self-cleaning, self-branching, heat loving, and drought tolerant!

When, Where, and How to Plant
Plant in full sun in well-draining, acidic soil. Calibrachoa will do well planted in the ground, but good drainage is a must. Add humus mulch and cottonseed meal in bedding areas to improve drainage and to acidify the soil. In containers, use a potting soil mix and add 20 percent perlite to create a loose, less compact medium. Space plants 8–12 in. apart.

Growing Tips
Water only when the soil surface feels dry to the touch—too much water can contribute to root rot. Feed with an organic water-soluble fertilizer about once a month in ground plantings and about every two weeks in containers.

Advice and Care
To increase branching, stimulate fresh growth, and promote compact fullness, give the plants a slight trim before planting and periodically thereafter. Calibrachoas can also be cut back after winter to return in the spring for continuous bloom from mid-April through mid-November. There are few disease and pest problems, except aphids and chewing insects. Wash off aphids with a strong stream of water and spray with spinosad for chewing insect control.

Companion Planting and Design
Because of their need for a well-draining medium, *Calibrachoa* are ideally suited to containers: hanging baskets, window boxes, pots, and so on. Combine with dusty miller, marguerite daisies, or use to fill in spaces between roses in a landscape. Avoid planting with petunias because they may overwhelm the smaller calibrachoa.

Try These
There are several Million Bells® varieties, including the mounding and trailing types such as 'Terra Cotta', which are 12–15 in. tall with a 20 in. spread and look perfect in all types of containers. 'Bouquet Pink' is more upright in habit, with an 8–12 in. height and 12 in. spread that not only does well in containers, but also in the landscape. Like Million Bells®, Superbells® are fast growing and disease and heat resistant, producing hundreds of self-cleaning blooms cascading over hanging baskets and other containers in an extensive color palette that includes 'Red', an eye-popping red with contrasting purple veins and a yellow eye.

California Poppy

Eschscholzia californica

Bloom Period and Seasonal Color
Orange flowers bloom in spring.

Mature Height × Spread 8–12 in. × 8–12 in.

Botanical Pronunciation
esh-SHOL-zee-ah KAL-ih-for-ni-kah

The Antelope Valley California Poppy Reserve, located on the high desert southwest of the bustling town of Mojave, is one of our favorite places to visit in spring. Near the end of the rainy season, a carpet of greenish blue, finely dissected, fernlike foliage emerges from a seemingly barren desert floor. Within weeks the poppies grow, mature, and display a profusion of cup-shaped blooms that blanket the carpet of foliage with an overlay of brilliant orange. After the crepe-textured flowers have been pollinated, the petals fall and the next season's seeds are dispersed. Native California poppies thrive in somewhat dry conditions and cool, sunny temperatures, but they quickly die back during extended periods of drought; hot, dry winds; and high temperatures.

When, Where, and How to Plant
Plant from pony packs or 4-in. pots in spring or broadcast seed before fall rains. California poppies prefer prefer full-sun areas of warm, dry, sandy loam, and well-drained soils with a pH of 6.8–7.2, but will tolerate denser textures. If needed, blend in soil amendments such as humus mulch, compost, and preplant fertilizer (2–10–6) to a depth of 8 in.

Growing Tips
If planting from pony packs or 4-in. pots, soak deeply and thoroughly after planting. Water daily the first week; thereafter adjust watering according to weather and growth conditions. If seed is sown, don't begin regular watering until seedlings are visible. Fertilize monthly during the growing season with a water-soluble food. Do not overfertilize established plants.

Advice and Care
Leave the spent flowers alone for seed production and dispersal. Once you have successfully grown California poppies in a particular area, they will continue to reestablish themselves. Thin out crowded seedlings and keep the area free of weeds for optimum growing conditions. Unless damage is extensive, simply handpick and squish snails and slugs.

Companion Planting and Design
You can replicate this desert growth cycle in your own landscape and enjoy a field of brilliant orange or hybridized versions in shades of yellow, scarlet, creamy white, copper, or pinkish red each spring. Grow *en masse* in expansive areas near edges of lawns, on sunny slopes, or naturalized in rock gardens. They make attractive but short-lived cut flowers if picked in the early morning while tightly budded. Plant with other California natives or water-thrifty plants, or bird of paradise, shore juniper, and silverberry.

Try These
Eschscholzia californica 'Mission Bells' has double and semidouble flowers. Also try *E. californica* 'Milky White', with single cream-colored flowers with orange centers. 'Wrinkled Rose' has semidouble and double flowers that are crinkly petaled in rose-red shades. 'Thai Silk Mix' has distinct gray finely cut foliage with semidouble blooms in bright jewel tones with yellow centers. *E. californica* 'Red Chief', with bright red blooms, interplanted with orange poppies, puts on a dazzling, fiery show.

Icelandic Poppy

Papaver nudicaule

Bloom Period and Seasonal Color
White, yellow, orange, or red flowers bloom in spring.

Mature Height × Spread 8–12 in. × 10 in.

Botanical Pronunciation
PA-pa-ver NEW-dih-kaw-lee

In ancient times, poppy flowers, seeds, and sap were used for cooking and as a narcotic. Because of its toxic qualities, this plant was often associated with death. Even now, artificial poppies are handed out as a remembrance of those who have died while serving their country. Icelandic poppy has 3-in. saucer-shaped flowers ranging in colors from bright red to hot pink to brilliant orange to soft salmon to sunny yellow and greenish white. The ciliated, deeply indented, moss green leaves form a thick circle of foliage from which thin, leafless stems emerge, bearing spectacular, delicately fragrant, crepe paper–textured flowers. Strictly speaking, the Icelandic poppy is a perennial, but you will have younger and stronger growth if you treat it as an annual or biennial.

When, Where, and How to Plant
Plant in fall from pony packs, color packs, or 4-in. pots, spacing 6–8 in. apart. Although they tolerate extremely cold temperatures, they dislike drought; hot, dry winds; and intense heat. It is best, therefore, to use them during the cooler months. Where summers are hot and humid, select a spot with morning sun and afternoon shade; in cooler areas, full sun is preferable. An evenly moist, well-drained loam soil with a pH of 6.8–7.0 is best. Blend in amendments such as humus mulch, compost, and preplant fertilizer to a depth of 12 in. After the flower petals fall, remove the seed capsules to extend the blooming season. You can also extend the blooming season by planting at successive intervals of every three to six weeks. If planting from seed, tamp lightly and cover completely with soil, as darkness promotes better germination.

Growing Tips
Soak deeply after planting. Water daily the first week; thereafter water according to weather and growth conditions. Fertilize monthly during the growing season with a water-soluble food such as liquid kelp.

Advice and Care
There are few disease or insect problems, but spinosad and a horticultural oil are effective controls for chewing insects and many fungal diseases.

Companion Planting and Design
Poppies grow well with pansies, phlox, and rock rose. Use as an ornamental in mixed flower beds, as a border plant, and as an excellent cut flower. Cut when the flower petals are just beginning to open, then burn the ends with a flame or immerse in boiling water for a few seconds to prevent the loss of latex and avoid flower wilt. Before arranging, set in cold water for several hours.

Try These
Papaver nudicaule 'Garden Gnome' hybrids are dwarf, compact, and have yellow and pink flowers. 'Meadow Pastels' have large petals with blooms in soft pastel shades reaching 24–30 in. tall. Buy *P. nudicaule* seed in bulk for home meadows. For coverage of up to 1,000 ft., just one-quarter pound of seed will create a lovely blanket of color.

Kale

Brassica oleracea

Bloom Period and Seasonal Color
Pink, rose, creamy yellow, magenta, white, and variegated foliage.

Mature Height × Spread
12–24 in. × 12–24 in.

Botanical Pronunciation
BRA-sih-kah oler-aye-CEE-ah

A relative of cabbage, flowering kale is know for its brightly hued, ornamental foliage, which is becoming a mainstay in the fall through early spring garden. It is a plant that is popular at garden centers in the fall. As long as they have been grown organically without chemical fungicides or insecticides, they are also edible. Whether a traditionally ornamental, curly, or flat-head variety, all belong to the Brassica family that also include other cruciferous vegetables such as cabbage, collards, broccoli, and Brussels sprouts. Kale is rich in calcium; iron; vitamins A, C, and K; and antioxidants, making it the superstar in the ornamental and edible garden. Alongside other cool-season plants such as Swiss chard, asters, chrysanthemums, and pansies, kale is a good companion.

When, Where, and How to Plant
In late summer or early autumn, sow seeds directly in garden soil that has been amended with humus mulch or compost and thin according to the packet directions. Seedlings started indoors can also be set outdoors and spaced about 1½–3 ft. apart. From color packs, plant 18–24 in. apart in full sun in moist, cool soil. Kale is typically planted in the late summer to early fall for a winter display, but where summers are cool, it can also be planted in early spring for a summer crop. Most varieties are hardy down to 10 degrees Fahrenheit, and light frost actually sweetens the flavor, but in hot climates, the leaves taste bitter.

Growing Tips
Water every seven to ten days when the soil feels dry to the touch to encourage deep roots. To prevent mold or fungus, avoid splashing leaves when watering. Fertilize every three to four weeks with liquid kelp or fish emulsion.

Advice and Care
There are few pest and disease problems, but if caterpillars, snails, or slugs appear, simply pick and squish. Spray with a horticultural-grade canola oil for persistent mildew problems. Since kale produces new leaves from the center, harvest the outer leaves. Pick young leaves for a lighter taste and more mature leaves for a more pungent, bold taste.

Companion Planting and Design
For fall and winter color, ornamental kale is beautiful as edging in mixed flower beds, as a focal point in containers, in rock gardens, or combined with alyssum and lobelia. They are also stunning in cut-flower arrangements.

Try These
Besides ornamental kale, why not try edible varieties that are decorative and nutritious such as 'Dick's Picotee', also known as 'Kosmic Kale'? With blue-green leaves ruffled and edged in creamy white, it grows as a perennial in most climates. 'Petit Posy' is a cross between kale and Brussels sprouts, standing upright like sprouts, but with frilly edged, purple, green, and bicolored rosettes resembling kale. Children love 'Lacinato' kale, aka dinosaur kale, because it grows to 2–3 ft. tall with large, bluish green, deeply puckered (like dinosaur skin), and lance-shaped foliage.

Lettuce

Latuca sativa

Bloom Period and Seasonal Color
Red, green, yellow, speckled foliage almost year-round.

Mature Height × Spread
Depends on cultivar/variety.

Botanical Pronunciation
lah-TOO-ka sat-EE-va

Native to Asia Minor, leaf lettuce has been cultivated for two thousand years and head lettuce for five hundred years. Butterhead, crisphead, loose-leaf, romaine, and stem are considered the main lettuce categories: butterhead tend to be small, loose-headed, and known for tender leaves and a sweet taste; crisphead are the iceberg varieties commonly available at grocery stores; loose-leaf is the most widely planted salad vegetable, with crisp leaves loosely arranged on its stalk; and romaine or cos develops an erect, elongated head. Since iceberg types of lettuce are readily available at supermarkets, require the most care, and are low in nutrients, this section will focus on prettier, easier to grow, and more nutritious varieties. Besides being nutritious, most have decorative leaves and look beautiful in the ornamental garden.

When, Where, and How to Plant
Plant leaf, romaine, and butterhead seeds in the spring when the soil is workable in full sun (part shade in the summer) in amended, well-draining soil. Seeds barely need to be covered with soil, about ¼ in. deep in single, double, or triple rows 12–18 in. apart. Sow seeds at two-week intervals for a continuous supply. Planting can also begin in late summer for autumn through winter harvest. In winter, lettuce withstands moderate frost conditions, but where summers sizzle, select varieties that are slow to bolt (such as heat-tolerant loose-leaf types) and provide some protective shade. Where summers are short, sow lettuce seeds indoors and transplant them outdoors after the last frost.

Growing Tips
Water every five to seven days and fertilize with a liquid food every two to three weeks. Make sure the soil has good drainage and the plants are spaced apart for proper air circulation to help minimize foliage rots, common during hot or wet seasons.

Advice and Care
Cut off outer leaves as needed rather than the entire head to prolong the harvest. Control slugs and snails with an iron phosphate bait, and wash off aphids with a stream of water.

Companion Planting and Design
Lettuce makes a beautiful ornamental in mixed borders and containers and a lovely filler between other plants. Don't confine lettuce to a strictly kitchen garden—use it as an edible, decorative border plant to outline a flower bed. Lettuce also does well grouped in a pot with other salad greens.

Try These
'Dark Lollo Rossa' is a curled loose-leaf variety with serrated and frilly magenta-red leaves. 'Forellenschluss' (meaning "speckled like a trout") is a romaine with maroon-speckled leaves. 'Val D'Orges' is a light green French butterhead perfect for overwintering in mild climates. 'Australian Yellow' is a gorgeous loose-leaf lettuce painted in chartreuse with a 12–16-in.-diameter head that grows rapidly and is slow to bolt. 'Tom Thumb' butterhead produces apple-sized heads of sweet, succulent leaves and its Lilliputian size makes it ideal for growing in containers or even bordering a flower bed.

Nasturtium

Tropaeolum majus

Bloom Period and Seasonal Color
Yellow, orange, and red flowers bloom in spring and summer.

Mature Height × Spread 4–10 in. × 4–6 ft.

Botanical Pronunciation
TROPE-a-oh-lum MA-jus

Nasturtiums flourish on a slope in our garden, their cheerful red, orange, and golden-spurred flowers making a beautiful display of spring and summer color against a backdrop of lilypad-like, fresh, green leaves. In most temperate areas of Southern California, nasturtiums may act like perennials, but in other areas they die back after the first frost. Nasturtiums do not like excessive summer heat, frost, drought, or dry winds, preferring cool, even temperatures. Individual flower stems or lengths of blooming vines can be cut for fun, informal bouquets. Gather in the early morning when the buds are still tight but showing color and they will last up to five days in water. Organically grown nasturtium flowers and leaves add a peppery flavor to mixed salad greens and sandwiches.

When, Where, and How to Plant
Plant anytime of year in frost-free zones or after the last frost in colder areas. Nasturtiums do best in full sun except in areas where summers are hot and dry—then plant them in partial sun. They prefer well-drained, loose-textured soil with a pH of 7.0. Make the soil a loam texture by adding amendments such as humus mulch, compost, and a pre-plant fertilizer to a depth of 12 in. Nick the seeds with a file or knife and soak them overnight to speed germination; plant ½ in. deep, sowing them 4–6 in. apart for bush varieties, 8–10 in. apart for vine varieties.

Growing Tips
Soak deeply and thoroughly after planting. Water daily the first week; thereafter water according to weather and growth conditions. Using a water-soluble food, fertilize container plants twice a month during the leafy growth period, and after that only if the foliage begins to turn yellow. Fertilize only once a month if the plants are directly planted in the ground, and do not water excessively or you may be rewarded with lush foliage, but few flowers.

Advice and Care
Keep dried undergrowth cleared to discourage families of rodents, such as mice, from setting up habitats. Few pests and diseases except snails, slugs, and sucking insects such as aphids. If damage is extensive, use spinosad as a remedy against chewing insects and a horticultural oil for sucking insects. Control snails and slugs with iron phosphate, an organic molluscicide; otherwise, resort to the tried-and-true organic method of "pick and squish." Rabbits, gophers, groundhogs, and deer seem to dislike the peppery, spicy flavor.

Companion Planting and Design
They make lovely trailing or climbing accents in containers on patios or decks, and look beautiful planted *en masse* on slopes, or tumbling over raised flower beds or rock gardens. Ideal companion plants are California lilacs, roses, geraniums, Shasta daisies, and persimmon trees.

Try These
'Amazon Jewel' has variegated leaves and is excellent for camouflaging spent bulb beds. 'Whirlybird' is early blooming in bright jewel tones and is a compact grower.

Pansy

Viola × wittrockiana

Bloom Period and Seasonal Color
Violet, lavender, blue, purple, yellow, and orange flowers bloom fall, winter, or early spring.

Mature Height × Spread 8–10 in. × 6–10 in.

Botanical Pronunciation
VI-oh-la WIT-rok-ee-an-ah

You might think pansies are simple flowers, but on closer inspection you will find that they come in such a dazzling array of patterns, colors, and shapes that it is difficult to adequately describe them. There are single- to double-flowered hybrids in colors ranging from violet, lavender, wine purple, lilac blue, bronze, yellow, and orange. Some have dark, velvety faces that offer a contrasting color to the surrounding five petals, and some come in single hues. Their leaves are varied, running the gamut from rounded, lobed, and toothed to heart-shaped. Depending on climate, they bloom in the fall, winter, or spring, but because they are cool-weather annuals, they die out in hot-summer areas. Pansies tolerate cold temperatures and wind, but do not tolerate drought or high temperatures.

When, Where, and How to Plant
Plant in early autumn from pony packs, color packs, or 4-in. pots, spacing 6 in. apart. Plant from seeds in midsummer in mild climates, but in hot-summer areas, wait until early to mid-fall. They do best in full sun but will also grow in partial shade. Provide rich, moist, well-drained loamy soil, pH 6.7–7.0. If necessary, blend in amendments such as humus mulch, compost, gypsum, and preplant fertilizer (2–10–6) to a depth of 12 in. Cover seeds with 1/8 in. of soil, then with a newspaper or piece of black plastic, for they need darkness to germinate. Be sure to remove the covers immediately after germination.

Growing Tips
Soak the soil after planting. Water daily the first week; thereafter water according to climatic and growth conditions. Fertilize monthly during the growing and blooming seasons with a water-soluble food, 12–55–6.

Advice and Care
Deadhead regularly to extend the blooming cycle. Damping off, a soilborne fungus, is one of the few serious disease problems. It is quickly identified when the main stems deteriorate at ground level, eventually falling over. Remove the diseased plants, and solarize the soil by covering the area with 4- or 6-mil clear plastic, weighing down the edges with 2 × 4s or bricks. Leave in place for four to six weeks; the heat that builds up underneath the plastic should suppress the fungus. Although the problem will not be completely eradicated, solarization will keep it under control.

Companion Planting and Design
Pansies are fantastic in containers or mixed flower beds. They grow well with wallflower, candytuft, ageratum, alyssum, and phlox.

Try These
'Majestic' and 'Matrix Morpheus' have very large, tricolored flowers. The 'Bolero' series offers a startling array of knock-your-eyes-out pansies. 'Bolero Blue with Black Top', 'Golden', 'Nerone', 'See Me', and 'Soft Light Azure' are multicolored, ranging from bright true blue, deep purple and black petals outlined in crisp white, to powderpuff soft yellow, pink, and lavender classic blooms. 'Fizzy Lemonberry' has ruffled flowers and the spreading 'Plentifall Mix' is lower growing, fragrant, and spreading to 16–18 in.

Petunia

Petunia hybrids

Bloom Period and Seasonal Color
Multitude of colors, picotee, and bicolors from spring through fall.

Mature Height × Spread
6–20 in. × 6–20 in. depending on cultivar

Botanical Pronunciation
peh-TOON-yah

Would you believe that a plant belonging to the potato family is one of the signature flowering annuals for the summer months? Especially popular where summers are dry and sunny, the genus *Petunia* is comprised of many species native to Central and South America, but modern breeders now focus on hybrids offering a cornucopia of color, bloom size, and plant habit. They are sticky-leaved annuals with single, funnel-shaped flowers or double, ruffled ones ranging from petite 1-in. selections to giant 6-in. varieties. Since the development of the prolific and vigorous trailing types such as the Surfinia series, petunias are even more in demand for window boxes and hanging baskets. And some, such as the Supertunia series, spread so effectively that they make ideal seasonal groundcovers.

When, Where, and How to Plant
Plant from color packs in humus-rich soil with 6.0–6.8 pH. Petunias thrive in full sun planted in rich, amended, and well-draining soil. Depending on the plant size, space them in the garden 12–18 in. apart and follow the directions for a controlled-release fertilizer at planting time. Planting from seed is challenging because of its tiny size, fine texture, and requirement for light to germinate. For this reason, it is recommended to use potted plants. Single-flowered types tolerate alkaline soil if it's well draining.

Growing Tips
Apply a controlled-release fertilizer at planting time and supplement every one to two weeks with an organic water-soluble food such as liquid kelp. Water every seven to ten days.

Advice and Care
For compact, new growth and more flowers, pinch back 50 percent toward the end of the bloom cycle and continue to pick off dead flowers. Botrytis, a gray mold that attacks flowers and stems, can be a problem in humid climates, so select more resistant varieties. Control geranium budworm with an organic insecticide such as spinosad.

Companion Planting and Design
Trailing or cascading petunias look particularly lovely in a hanging basket, provided it is located in a wind-protected area. For the "wow" factor, try planting a spreading variety as an eye-popping groundcover. For pots, looks for dramatic-colored petunias that have a more mounding habit.

Try These
With its spreading habit, Supertunia® 'Vista Bubblegum' makes a fantastic groundcover that is smothered in pink flowers. For large, ruffled, fragrant flowers in hanging baskets, try the Doubles series. In hot, humid areas plant Surfinia® hybrids because they are more resistant to botrytis. To visit the dark side and to pair with any color combination, 'Black Velvet' is the world's first black petunia. The 'Phantom' is also black, but with a stunning yellow star pattern in the center and 'Pinstripe' is a deep, dark purple with a creamy star pattern. So many new series and varieties come out each year, be sure to consult the latest plant catalogues, websites, and your local garden center to find the petunia that best suits your garden needs.

Snapdragon

Antirrhinum majus

Bloom Period and Seasonal Color
A rainbow of colors (except blue) and bicolors from winter to spring.

Mature Height × Spread 10–36 in. × 6–24 in.

Botanical Pronunciation
ANT-er-hin-um MA-jus

The ancient Greek philosopher Theophrastu claimed naming rights to the *Antirrhinum*, meaning noselike, but who put the "snap" in snapdragon? Possibly it is because children have fun gently pinching the sides of the flower, forcing its floral lips to open wide before letting go as if to snap at prey. In the garden, snapdragons are bushy, erect plants with lush green, lance-shaped foliage that contrasts nicely with floriferous spikes. The flowers tend to open in succession starting from the bottom of the spike to the top. Don't think of this plant as old-fashioned. Newer snapdragons have been developed including the azalea-and-bell-shaped blooms and the double flowered, plus they now come in all sizes: tall, intermediate, and dwarf, and different growth habits besides erect, the trailing and cascading varieties.

When, Where, and How to Plant
Amend the soil with humus or compost to create a well-draining and rich soil. Seedlings and color packs can be planted outdoors in the fall for winter and spring blooms. Space them about 6–24 in. apart depending on the specific variety. You can also start seedlings indoors by pressing the seeds lightly on the potting soil surface; when they have developed six true leaves, pinch off the top stem for better branching and a fuller plant. Transplant the seedlings outdoors as early as a couple of weeks before the last frost date. Snapdragons thrive in the cooler temperatures of spring and early summer, but where winters are mild or summers are hot, they bloom best in winter and spring.

Growing Tips
Water once a week or more during dry period and fertilize with a water-soluble food every two weeks.

Advice and Care
Deadhead regularly to extend blooming. For areas that are damp and humid, plant rust-resistant varieties.

Companion Planting and Design
Snapdragons are beautiful in cutflower gardens, borders, or in large containers as vertical accents; dwarf selections are perfect in rock gardens and pots. Companions like baby's breath and larkspur are ideal. Pastel varieties blend well into a mixed border filled with hotter pink, purple, and red-hued plants.

Try These
For tutti-fruity fragrance, hot sunset colors, double flowers, and statuesque beauty, the 3-ft.-tall 'Double Azalea Apricot' takes the grand prize of all snapdragons and stands tall as a vertical accent toward the back of a mixed border or in the middle of a large pot. Intermediate-sized specimens, such as 'Coronette Mix', reach 1–2 ft. tall and look wonderful toward the middle of a bedding area or in the center of a medium-sized container. The Chinese Lantern series make great trailing or cascading accents in hanging baskets and containers and the rust-resistant Rocket series grow 30–36 in. tall. 'Magic Carpet' is a dwarf variety standing only 6–8 in. tall; it needs no staking and makes a beautiful edging along rock gardens or raised beds.

Stock

Matthiola incana

Bloom Period and Seasonal Color
Pink, red, purple, lavender, blue, yellow, cream, and white blooms from winter to spring.

Mature Height × Spread
12–36 in. × 10–16 in.

Botanical Pronunciation
MAT-thee-oh-la IN-kan-ah

The genus *Matthiola* was named after the sixteenth-century Italian botanist and personal physician to Emperor Maximillian of Austria, Pietro Andrea Matthioli, and the species name *incana* means hairy or gray-white, referring to the plant's foliage. Whatever its namesake, few flowers are as perfect planted close to the house, bordering a vegetable garden, or peeking out of any corner where its spicy, clovelike fragrance can be appreciated. Native to the Mediterranean region, the original species are rarely cultivated today. Instead there are many hybrid strains that grow on upright stems clothed with ciliated, grayish green leaves and highly scented flowers, including singles and doubles, that bloom in tight clusters in a rainbow of colors from late winter to spring. Although it's a biennial or perennial, it is grown as an annual.

When, Where, and How to Plant
Find a sunny location and plant color packs or 4-in. to 1-gallon pots in richly amended soil such as humus or compost, to ensure good drainage. Space them 8–12 in. apart depending on the variety. For mild-winter areas plant from seed or color packs in early fall, but where winters dip to freezing, plant in early spring. Since stock seeds need light to germinate, press lightly into the seed-starting planting mix so that they are barely covered. Keep the temperature between 60–65 degrees Fahrenheit for germination to occur within seven to twenty-one days. Where winter rainfall is heavy, it is best to plant stock in raised beds or containers for adequate drainage. Although tolerant of light frost, the flower buds will not set if there are prolonged periods of chilly nights. Once hot weather arrives, stock stop blooming.

Growing Tips
Water thoroughly after planting. Thereafter keep the soil moist, but not soggy, because stock is susceptible to root rot. Feed with an organic granular or water-soluble fertilizer once a month during the growth and bloom cycles or use a slow-release fertilizer to last the entire season.

Advice and Care
Deadhead spent flower spikes to keep the plants neat and tidy. To cut for flower arrangements, pick when half of the flowers on the stalk are open. There are few insect problems, but if fungal leaf spot is pervasive, pull out the infected plants and throw them away in the trash to prevent spreading to other healthy stock plants. For areas with deer problems, stock is deer resistant.

Companion Planting and Design
Stock plants are ideal for the cottage and cutflower garden. To appreciate their spicy perfume, place them close to walkways, window boxes, and toward the front of borders. Combine with nemesia, pansies, sweet peas, and other cool-season bloomers.

Try These
M. bicornis grows to 12 in. with modest, purple blossoms, but they are marvelously fragrant at night and should be planted under a window for Mother Nature's aromatherapy. For a taller cultivar, plant the double-flowered, 2-ft.-tall 'Legacy' series.

Sunflower

Helianthus annuus

Bloom Period and Seasonal Color
Yellow, cream, red, orange, multicolors, and bicolors bloom from summer to fall.

Mature Height × Spread 2–16 ft. × 2 ft.

Botanical Pronunciation
HE-lee-an-thus AN-ue-us

Sunflowers and summer are synonymous. With new varieties and hybrids introduced yearly, there are myriad choices, from 10–15-ft. tall giants to knee-high varieties, pollen-bearing to pollenless, and single to multiflowered. It is magical to watch it grow practically before your eyes. Plus they produce bundles of cut flowers, and seeds that can be roasted, used for oil extraction, fed to birds, and, if ground up, make excellent flour. Bees love the nectar and its leaves are even used for animal forage. However, it is not entirely true that sunflowers follow the sun—only the immature flower buds track the sun across the sky; once mature, the flowering heads remain fixed, typically pointing in an eastern direction.

When, Where, and How to Plant

Sow seeds directly in the ground in well-amended soil at the seed packet's recommended spring date, depth, and spacing and make sure it is a sunny location. Another option is to start seeds indoors several weeks before the last frost date, but keep moist and provide bright, indirect light until ready to transplant outdoors. For the giant, tall sunflower plants, however, plant directly in the ground because of their long taproots. Soil temperature should be at 50 degrees Fahrenheit or more because if the soil is too cold, the seed will go dormant and delay germination. Provide a sturdy support for statuesque or large-headed varieties.

Growing Tips

Add a slow-release or organic fertilizer at planting and select a site that is protected from strong winds. Although drought tolerant, water when top 2 in. of soil surface is dry for optimum bloom production. Fertilize with liquid kelp every one to two weeks.

Advice and Care

Loosely cover freshly planted seeds with netting or plastic berry cartons to protect against birds, but remove when plants emerge.

Companion Planting and Design

Use as a temporary "living fence" in the garden or plant smaller cultivars for a stunning cutflower garden or toward the back of an informal border. Create a sunflower house by sowing seeds of tall varieties such as 'Skyscraper' or 'Kong' along a 9 ft. × 6 ft. rectangle, keeping one side open for a doorway. Once the flower buds appear, attach twine and crisscross over the top so morning glories or other summer viners can climb up the more established sunflower stalks and form a ceiling supported by the twine.

Try These

The mahogany 'Red Velvet Queen' and golden yellow 'Sunbeam' have 4–6-in. flowers do not shed indoors. 'Sunzilla' at 12–16 ft. is one of the tallest sunflowers, with thick stalks providing more support and stability than some of the other giants. For a dramatic mix of 6-in. orange, yellow, bronze, and red flowers on 7-ft.-tall stems, plant 'Autumn Beauty'; for containers, plant the 2–3-ft.-tall 'Teddy Bear'.

Sweet Peas

Lathyrus odoratus

Bloom Period and Seasonal Color
Blue, pink, white, purple, red, and bicolor flowers bloom in spring through summer.

Mature Height × Spread 4–6 in. (vining)

Botanical Pronunciation
LATH-er-us O-do-rah-tus

With their bush or vining habit, sweet peas are always at an ideal height for children and for adults to breath in their fragrant, butterfly-shaped flowers. Since sweet peas were originally found in cool wooded areas, along riverbanks, in mountainous regions as high as 6,000 ft., and even along seashores, it is easy to see why they do best in temperate to cool weather and bloom less in hot, dry climates. Sweet peas usually have three winglike petals per flower, with five to seven flowers on a single stem in warm hues of blue, lavender, rose-pink, white, salmon, and orange. Their leaves divide into feathery leaflets, with curly tendrils that wrap around supports of string, wires, trellises, and tree branches.

When, Where, and How to Plant
Sow 1 in. deep in rows in early spring, spacing about 2 in. apart. In colder zones, plant seeds as soon as you can work the soil. Nick seeds with a file or knife and soak overnight to speed germination. In mild-winter areas, sow directly in the ground in late summer for late-winter or early-spring blooms; otherwise, plant in late winter and early spring for late-spring and early-summer blooms. They need full sun and well-drained soil with a pH of 6.0–7.2. Give the soil a loam texture by adding amendments such as humus mulch, compost, and preplant fertilizer to a depth of 12 in. We have been successful using a planting trench 18–20 in. long with a 4–5-in. cover of organic material. After blooming is over, save seeds in airtight containers in a cool, dry place for sowing the next year.

Growing Tips
Soak thoroughly after planting by providing a gentle stream of water, similar to a gentle rain to keep seeds from displacing. During the first week until the seeds germinate, water so the ground stays evenly moist. Thereafter, water according to climatic and growth conditions. Fertilize with an organic, granular food once seedlings sprout six to eight leaves. After that, fertilize monthly with a water-soluble fertilizer.

Advice and Care
Anchor the trellis or the weight of the vines will topple it. Keep sweet peas flowering and prevent from going to seed by deadheading spent flowers. Protect tender seedlings from birds with netting and control snails and slugs with iron phosphate bait.

Companion Planting and Design
Use bush sweet peas as a border in the annual or perennial bed, where their sweet scent will reward passersby. Cover a trellis or arbor with vines of sweet peas or allow them to ramble freely, cottage garden–style.

Try These
Interplant the fragrant 'Sweet Dream' with mixed colored blooms and 'High Scent' that have white flowers with lavender edges. 'Saltwater Taffy Swirls' have long stems in pastel colors, but for beds and borders, the knee-high 'Explorer', at 2½ ft., needs no support.

Swiss Chard

Beta vulgaris subspecies *cicla*

Bloom Period and Seasonal Color
Red, green-and-white, burgundy, and green leaves year-round where winters are mild.

Mature Height × Spread
18–24 in. × 18–24 in.

Botanical Pronunciation
BAY-tah VOOL-gah-rus SIK-la

Swiss chard is related to the beet family, but instead of harvesting its roots, people grow it for its leaves and stalks. Despite its name, chard comes from the Mediterranean region and is not native to Switzerland. Swiss chard is prized for its decorative, glossy, ribbed, and crinkly leaves, with stalks in hues of green, yellow, orange, pink, purple, and white. So why not plant it amid your flowering annuals and perennials? Besides its ornamental value, chard is one of the easiest vegetables to grow for the home gardener with a long harvest season, and is one of the top leafy superstars when it comes to nutrition: high in vitamins A, K, and C as well as powerful antioxidants, minerals, protein, and dietary fiber.

When, Where, and How to Plant
Swiss chard seeds germinate indoors, but if there is no frost in your area, plant them ½ inch deep directly in the ground. Sow seeds in full sun in amended, well-draining soil from spring through summer. Apply a preplant fertilizer before planting. Space thinned-out seedlings 12 in. apart. Where winters are mild, sow also in late summer for a fall-winter through spring crop. If plants bolt and go to seed in summer's heat, just pull them up and start more seeds in a cooler, partially shaded part of the garden before moving them to a sunnier locale after summer's heat wave is over.

Growing Tips
Water every five to seven days depending on weather conditions and growth. Provide an additional feeding of a balanced organic vegetable fertilizer once during the growing season in spring or summer and twice if also growing in the autumn.

Advice and Care
Chard is ready to harvest about two months after sowing. Cut outer leaves as needed when plant is 12–18 in. tall since new leaves grow from the plant's center. If leafminer larvae leave tunneling markings in the foliage, spray with organic spinosad and apply every ten to fourteen days until the infestation is remedied. Control the garden brown snail and slugs in Southern California with decollate snails, but in Northern California apply an iron phosphate bait. Keep browsing deer away with a motion-activated water sensor, such as the scarecrow, or olfactory repellents.

Companion Planting and Design
There is no rule against interspersing vegetables among ornamental plantings, especially when there is insufficient room or sunshine for a separate edible garden. Include Swiss chard in mixed flower beds, as a border, and in containers.

Try These
'Swiss Chard' has white stalks, but 'Bright Lights' have green leaves with stalks shaded in neon pink, white, purple, yellow, burgundy, green, and orange. For a green form, 'Lucullus' and 'Fordbrook Giant' are longtime favorites.

BULBS, CORMS, RHIZOMES, AND TUBERS

FOR CALIFORNIA

When we kneel down in the cool autumn soil, scoop out holes, and plant our brown parchment–wrapped bulbs, we are acting on an optimistic gardening belief that from such plain, often ugly vessels will emerge breathtaking blossoms of every shape, size, form, color, and fragrance, transforming our garden into a shimmering tapestry of springtime magic. And with just a little effort, we truly can have bulbs that put on a radiant color show celebrating spring's beginning and winter's end.

Plan Your Bulb Showcase

Plan your design on paper and keep it simple, especially if you are a novice. Use two or three colors, or select just a few varieties of bulbs, picking out at least twelve of each kind, and group them in clusters or scatter in drifts.

One of the most important considerations when developing a bulb showcase is knowledge of heights and bloom times of the plants. Place the taller plants at the back or middle of the bed and plant the shorter ones in front. For maximum visual impact, select bulbs that bloom at the same time. If early-, mid-, and late-flowering varieties are mixed together, the look will be less dramatic, but the succession of blooms will make the season last longer. Daffodils come in a range of early- to mid- to late-season varieties; ranunculus flower later than daffodils and extend the bloom time after the others fade.

Once the spring buds peak, begin planting clusters of lilies, dahlias, gladioli, and tuberoses in anticipation of the warm summer months.

Don't forget that the adage about nice things coming in small packages applies to bulbs like grape hyacinth and miniature forms of cyclamen and daffodils.

Not All Bulbous Plants Are True Bulbs

The term "bulb" is often used loosely, as many bulbous plants are technically not true bulbs. True bulbs have pointed tops, short underground stems on basal plates, and new growths, called bulblets, that form from offshoots of the parent bulbs. Amaryllis, grape hyacinth, Oriental lilies, and daffodils are considered true bulbs, because they grow from enlarged buds with modified leaves called scales.

Included in the family of "bulbous plants that are not true bulbs" are those produced from corms, rhizomes, and tubers. Corms are similar to bulbs, except that each summer a new corm grows on top of the original one. As the parent corm disappears, the roots of the new corm grow downward into the hole left by the decayed corm. Gladioli and freesias grow from corms that divide by growing small corms, called cormels, around the base of the parent bulb.

Unlike corms, which grow upward, rhizomes are specialized stems that spread horizontally, underground, or on the surface with adventitious roots, and they sprout stems, leaves, and flowers from the rhizomes' upper sections. Bearded iris and tuberoses grow from rhizomes and are propagated by cutting out a section of their spreading layers.

Dahlias and ranunculus grow from tubers, which are swollen rhizomes that produce pulpy (instead of scaly) stems. Tubers normally grow just below the surface of the soil and, like bulbs, store food for the plants. The buds on tubers become stems, leaves, and flowers, and clusters of roots form at the base. They multiply by division, and as they divide, the parent tuber deteriorates.

Whether bulbous plants derive from a true bulb, corm, rhizome, or tuber, there is a flowering bulb to suit every taste and to serve every garden purpose. And when it comes time to do the actual planting, choose the biggest, plumpest bulbs that are clean, solid, and free from scars. With faith in the magic of nature, bulbs bring forth spring, summer, and autumnal jewel-like colors in perennial borders, rock gardens, and random drifts in lawns or along slopes.

Dazzling dahlias are easy to grow.

Amaryllis

Hippeastrum × hybrid

Bloom Period and Seasonal Color
Red, orange, yellow, pink, green, white, and bicolored blooms in spring.

Mature Height × Spread 1–2 ft. (clumping)

Botanical Pronunciation HIP-ee-ae-strum

Zones 10–11

Marketed during the winter holiday season as *Amaryllis* (from South Africa), the long-stemmed plants with colorful clusters of tubular-shaped flowers are really *Hippeastrum* (from South America). They have been forced to bloom in the winter, but their natural bloom cycle is in spring. Every autumn we put our potted "hippies" to bed under our deck, allowing their yellowed foliage to die back. In late winter they awaken with the arrival of winter and spring rains. Thick, hollow, leafless stems emerge bearing two to six enormous flowers measuring 4–6 in. across, followed by the appearance of deep green, straplike leaves in the spring. They reward our seasonal routine with colors ranging from velvety red with a white star in its center, to bright orange with green stripes, to delicate pinks and whites.

When, Where, and How to Plant
Plant in fall from bulbs, spacing them 18 in. apart in full sun in well-drained soil, pH 6.7–7.0. Prepare a flower bed by adding a preplant fertilizer (2–10–6) and, if needed, a soil amendment such as compost or humus mulch. Make sure the top third of the bulb is above soil level. If planting in a pot, use potting soil, add a preplant fertilizer, and allow a 1–2-in. space between the bulb and the pot perimeter (they prefer cramped quarters). Keep away from small children and pets, because the bulbs are toxic if ingested.

Growing Tips
Water sparingly at first. Adjust frequency and amount according to weather and growth conditions. In the late summer or early fall, stop watering when the leaves have yellowed and withered, then forget them until early spring. Remove spent flowers; the foliage needs the energy to return to the bulb rather than to be expended on the production of seed. Fertilize once a week during the growth cycle with a water-soluble food and continue to fertilize until no new leaves emerge and the mature leaves discontinue their growth. Remove damaged foliage and any mealybugs or aphids by hand, because many remedies such as Neem oil may damage the flower buds.

Advice and Care
For winter holiday forcing in pots, use a well-draining potting soil, then transplant outdoors in the spring. Where winter freezes are common, it is best to dig up the bulbs in late autumn; store in a protected, dark place; and plant in the early spring after the danger of frost has passed.

Companion Planting and Design
Prostrate natal plum, dwarf jade plant, and Transvaal daisy grow well with amaryllis.

Try These
Hippeastrum hybrid 'Apple Blossom' has pinkish white flowers. 'Kalahari' has large, solid-red flowers. 'Exotic Star' is quite glamorous, with orchid-shaped blooms that have raspberry petals with ivory margins and green highlights. 'Picotee' is candy-cane bright white edged in red. 'Ambiance' is creamy ivory with bold red stripes. 'Summertime' is a deep watermelon pink with a luminous green center.

Bearded Iris

Iris germanica hybrids

Bloom Period and Seasonal Color
A rainbow of hues and bicolors bloom in late spring to summer; some repeat in autumn.

Mature Height × Spread 8–36 in. × 18–20 in.

Botanical Pronunciation
EYE-ris JER-man-ih-ka

Count bearded iris among our favorite plants because of its elegant, classic beauty with three upright petals (standards), three pendulous petals (falls), and the bristly hairs (beard) extending from the base of the flower's throat. Although its beauty appears ethereal and fragile, bearded iris is one of the easiest plants to grow, with very little maintenance. The showoff blooms open in succession and display themselves on sturdy stems that emerge from bluish green, sword-shaped foliage. There are several types, including miniature dwarf (8 in. or less) all the way up to tall (28–48 in.). It is a hardy, long-lived perennial able to flourish in a wide range of soils and climates. Known to be fast and vigorous growers, many have a sweet fragrance and some rebloom.

When, Where, and How to Plant
Add a 2–4-in. layer of humus mulch or compost and loosen the soil down 10–12 in. before planting the rhizomes in a sunny area from midsummer to early fall. Although iris adapts to a variety of soil types, it needs to drain well. Plant at or slightly below the soil surface and space the rhizomes 12–24 in. apart depending on the variety. If planting directly from a container, set the rhizome at the soil surface. Container-grown iris can also be planted in the spring.

Growing Tips
Fertilize with a liquid or granular organic food when growth begins and again after the bloom season. Water immediately after planting and begin watering every seven to fourteen days when new growth appears. For spring bloomers, decrease water in the summer, but continue watering in the summer for rebloomers. Divide rhizomes every three to four years after flowering by pruning down the leaves by two-thirds, digging up the clump, washing it off, and cutting rhizomes apart so each section has a minimum of one healthy fan of leaves and firm, white roots. For a mass of color, plant at least three rhizomes (spaced 8–10 in. apart) or plant undivided clumps; point each fan of leaves away from the center of the group. Space clumps 18 in. apart.

Advice and Care
In areas with hot climates, plant iris where there is afternoon shade. Rhizomes tend to rot in clayey soils, so amend with organic material and keep the top of the rhizome slightly above soil level. Where soils are sandy, rhizomes can be buried completely with a thin layer of soil. If winter freeze is common, apply a 2–3-in. layer of mulch to protect the rhizomes.

Companion Planting and Design
Irises are standouts in mixed borders, containers, and cutflower or cottage gardens. Combine with cushion chrysanthemums, Shasta daisies, and even succulents.

Try These
Remontant varieties such as the white 'Immortality' and pink 'Beverly Sills' bloom in the spring and rebloom in the fall. For fragrance, try the purple-ruffled 'Indigo Princess' or multicolored 'Trillion'.

Cyclamen

Cyclamen persicum

Bloom Period and Seasonal Color
Red, white, pink, or purple flowers bloom
in winter.

Mature Height × Spread 8–12 in. × 10 in.

Botanical Pronunciation
SYKE-la-men per-SEE-cum

Zones 8–11

We can never have enough cyclamen nestled in the shady spots of our garden and as holiday décor in our home. When few plants are blooming in our winter garden, purple-tinged magenta flowers on 6-in. stems burst forth from nests of deep green, heart-shaped leaves marbled with silvery streaks. *C. persicum* is the florist's cyclamen, with large, sweetly fragrant flowers composed of five upright, twisted petals in colors of white, pink, magenta, and red. They flower from spring to summer or in winter if weather conditions are mild. When their blooms are spent, stalks of straight seed capsules emerge, signaling the beginning of a rest period, usually during midsummer. During dormancy they tolerate drought, wind, and heat, but they cannot withstand such conditions during growth.

When, Where, and How to Plant
Plant these Mediterranean natives in the ground in early spring as long as the climate is temperate and frost free. They require shade or dappled light in a frost-free location and a well-drained, slightly alkaline soil, pH 6.8–7.2. If the soil does not drain freely, amend with compost, peat moss, or humus mulch. Space 4–6 in. apart and make sure the tuber tops are just above the soil surface.

Growing Tips
Soak deeply after planting. Water daily the first week; thereafter, adjust frequency and amount to weather and growth conditions. During the growth period, water around the edges of the tuber to avoid water settling in the tight mass of leaves and buds,

which can cause rot. Reduce frequency when the growth cycle ends, and gradually extend the dry period for about two to three months. Afterwards, repot or restart the growth cycle by watering regularly. Fertilize during the growing and blooming season about twice a month with an organic water-soluble food. Remove spent flowers from tubers to prevent root rot. Be on the lookout for snails, slugs, sowbugs, and cyclamen mites. If damage is severe, use an organic iron phosphate snail bait or the pick-and-squish method of control. For mites, use a Neem oil or chemical miticide.

Advice and Care
In cooler regions, plant in spring after the last frost or cultivate in containers (preferably clay pots, not plastic) and provide winter protection.

Companion Planting and Design
Plant in a shady location with other shade-lovers, such as camellias, azaleas, clivias, and impatiens.

Try These
'Winter Ice' has clear, crisp, white blooms atop large, silver, patterned leaves. The 'Tianis' series offers bright red, magenta, light purple, rose, salmon, and white cultivars. *C. neapolitanum* is a miniature cyclamen with fragrant pink, white, or rose flowers from July through autumn. The flowers are followed by angular leaves marbled with silver that remain until May, then die back. *C. cilicium* are hardy cyclamen (zones 5–9) and do well in full shade. Fall flowers are rose pink, fading to pale pink with spotted foliage.

Dahlia

Dahlia × hybrid

Bloom Period and Seasonal Color
Red, orange, yellow, pink, white, and bicolored flowers bloom in late spring through summer.

Mature Height × Spread 2–7 ft. × 2–4 ft.

Botanical Pronunciation DAHL-ee-ah

Zones 8–11

Whenever someone who claims to be "green-thumb impaired" pleads for a flowering plant that is easy to grow, we suggest dahlias, named for Swedish botanist Andreas Dahl. Once their tubers are correctly planted, they do well throughout California. With a minimum of effort, they reward you with spectacular, almost limitless shapes, sizes, and colors. Hot reds, oranges, yellows, pastel pinks, salmons, lavenders, rich magentas, bronzes, purples, and apricots are available in single, double, or multicolored dahlia varieties that show off atop stems from 2–6 ft. in height. The foliage ranges from gray-green and bright green to bronze. Depending on the variety, they bloom from late spring and die back when the weather cools. Their only real enemies are drought, frost, and blustery winds.

When, Where, and How to Plant
Plant in spring from tubers, 6–8-in. pots, or 1-gallon containers, spacing 2½ ft. for larger varieties, 2 ft. for pompons, and 12–18 in. for dwarf hybrids. Dahlias need full sun and rich, well-drained loam soil with a pH of 6.7–7.0. Before planting, prepare a flower bed 8–12 in. deep and blend in a preplant fertilizer. When new growth is about 4 in. tall, thin out, leaving only the three strongest stems; cut any other shoots back to ground level. Repeat throughout the growth cycle, allowing only three stems to flourish. Although disbudding is not necessary for dwarf or shorter varieties, it encourages larger blooms and thicker stems on taller forms. When the first flower buds emerge, keep only the central bud. Just below the first group of buds are smaller flower buds that should also be removed, as well as any foliage. Deadhead spent flowers to keep dahlias from seeding and shortening the bloom cycle.

Growing Tips
Soak deeply after planting and thereafter adjust frequency and amount to weather and growth conditions. Except for dwarf varieties, staking may be necessary to keep dahlias upright. Do not fertilize during the growth cycle. Because dahlias are susceptible to mildew and rust, good air circulation is important; spray with a horticultural-grade canola oil as a control.

Advice and Care
In frost-free areas you can leave the tubers in the ground, but in colder regions, dig them up, clean, and dry, then store in a cool, dry place in the fall, and replant in the spring. Where winters are mild, prune stems back to 4–6 in.

Companion Planting and Design
English ivy, foxglove, delphinium, and lavender are ideal companion plants.

Try These
Dinnerplate 'Babylon Red' dahlias have 8-in. blooms sitting atop tall 4-ft. stems. 'Tahiti Sunrise', a semicactus dahlia, has smaller 6-in. blooms with bright yellow centers progressing to red and purple tips on 30-in. stems. The miniature ball form 'Talisman' grows to a more diminutive 4 ft. with 3-in. perfectly round, purple flowers.

Freesia

Freesia hybrid

Bloom Period and Seasonal Color
Red, orange, yellow, pink, and white flowers bloom in spring.

Mature Height × Spread 1–1½ ft. (clumping)

Botanical Pronunciation
FREEZ-ee-ah

Zones 9–11

This is our favorite late-winter to early-spring flower for bouquets, because they cultivate easily, naturalize in mild climates, and bear prolifically. The flower's elegant form, myriad array of colors, and delicate perfume are the first signs of more scents and colors to come into our warm-season garden. Fans of erect, narrow, iris-like leaves bear spiked stems. Along one side of each stem, five to seven trumpet-shaped flowers gather single file and politely wait to open one at a time. In single or double forms, these spikes of sweetly scented flowers are painted in solid colors or two-toned combinations of pale white, cream, yellow, pink, mauve, lilac, and lavender-blue, or in brilliant orange, crimson, and dark blue. Freesias dislike excessive heat, freezing temperatures, persistent winds, and drought.

When, Where, and How to Plant
Where winters are mild, plant freesias in the early fall for winter and spring blooms; where freezing temperatures prevail, plant in the late spring for summer flowering. They need full sun and average, well-drained soil, pH 6.7–7.0. Prepare a flower bed or container, sprinkle the bottom of the hole with a preplant fertilizer, and place the corms pointed ends up 2–3 in. deep and spaced 3 in. apart.

Growing Tips
Soak deeply after planting, then adjust frequency and amount according to weather and growth conditions. Water regularly during the growth cycle. Decrease watering when foliage yellows, and stop when the leaves dry. In late winter or spring (depending on the climate zone), resume watering as new growth appears. Fertilize once a month beginning in spring or earlier, when new growth appears, with an organic water-soluble food like liquid kelp. It is not necessary to prune or deadhead. With good air circulation, and if you respond immediately to the first signs of insect infestation, fungal and insect problems will be minimal. Try horticultural-grade canola oil or wash with a stream of water to keep problems at bay.

Advice and Care
If in a temperate climate, allow the corms to remain in the bed—otherwise, lift the corms out after the foliage is dead; store in a cool, dry place during winter; and replant in spring after the last frost. Containers may be stored, corms and soil, in a cool (not freezing) dry place until fall, then resume watering. Do not move freesias while they are in their growth cycle, because they do not like having their roots disturbed.

Companion Planting and Design
Mass in rock gardens, along borders, and in containers, or overplant with candytuft, wallflower, and Transvaal daisy.

Try These
'Antique Freesia' is extremely fragrant and naturalizes in Mediterranean climates. 'Aphrodite' has double, soft pink to red flowers. 'Uchida' has semi-double flowers with yellow throats. Make a sweeping show and buy in bulk with clear, single-colored packs of 'Double Blue' and 'Double White'.

Gladiolus

Gladiolus × hybrid

Bloom Period and Seasonal Color
Flowers in red, orange, yellow, pink, white, and other colors bloom in late spring and summer.

Mature Height × Spread 1–4 ft. (multiplying)

Botanical Pronunciation
GLAD-ee-oh-lus

Zones 9–11

At Cape Town's world-famous garden Kirstenbosch, we saw massive plantings of so many different gladiolus species and hybrids that it is easy to understand why they are classified into groups by height, flower size, and shape. Gladiolus comes from the Latin word *gladius*, meaning "sword," referring to the sword-shaped foliage. Stiff spikes with funnel-like florets arise, facing one way, splashed with hues of white, green, yellow, orange, red, maroon, salmon, pink, mauve, or purple, but not blue—some are striped, streaked, or splattered with contrasting tints. Some flowers have ruffled or hooded petal segments; others have a flatter habit. Some stems are dainty at 18 in. tall; others reach just under 5 ft., and many have fragrances similar to honey, plums, or spicy carnations.

When, Where, and How to Plant
Plant from corms in spring after the last frost, or in fall where winters are mild. With adequate moisture, most hybrids flourish where there is winter rainfall and summer heat. Except for some of the smaller hybrids, they need protection from wind and freezing temperatures. Provide full sun, evenly moist, well-drained soil with a neutral to slightly alkaline pH, 6.5–7.0. Prepare a flower bed, blending in a preplant fertilizer, and set the corms 2–4 in. deep and space 6–8 in. apart, depending on their size. Cut off spent flowers, but leave as much green foliage as possible.

Growing Tips
Soak deeply after planting, then adjust frequency and amount depending on weather and growth conditions. In hot, dry summer months, water roots and leaves generously. Fertilize monthly with an organic water-soluble food. The organic product spinosad effectively controls thrips and other chewing insects. Spray in the late afternoon or early evening when any nearby bees have returned to their hives.

Advice and Care
In temperate zones, you can plant from January to July, but in colder regions wait as late as May, after the last frost. After flowering, the corms can remain in the ground in zones 8–10. It is best to dig them up, clean them, and store in a cool, dry, dark place with good air circulation for the winter in colder regions. Fungal diseases and insect infestations may be a problem in warm, humid conditions, but if you remove debris (a breeding ground for disease and pests), and keep a watchful eye out for symptoms before they have a chance to proliferate, you will be rewarded with vigorous plants and spectacular blooms.

Companion Planting and Design
Perfect in cottage gardens. Plant with dahlias, ivy geraniums, lilies of the Nile, and canna lilies.

Try These
'Glamini' mix offers smallish, 24-in. glad stems in rainbow colors. Rainbow mixes stretch to 60 in. Reported as true blue, 'Blue Isle' is a rare beauty. Byzantine gladiolus (*Gladiolus communis* ssp. *byzantinus*) is a species that stands 2–3 ft. tall and bears bold, magenta-hued flowers.

Narcissus

Narcissus × hybrid

Bloom Period and Seasonal Color
Orange, yellow, or white flowers bloom in late winter and spring.

Mature Height × Spread 1–2 ft. (multiplying)

Botanical Pronunciation
NAR-sis-us

We are ashamed to admit it, but there is a narrow strip of ground in front of our star jasmine that rarely receives any care. Yet just before Valentine's Day, like clockwork, stems of fragrant, golden yellow narcissi lift their heads to wave hello. These are perfect bulbs that can grow under the most neglected conditions and flourish beautifully. Whether they are jonquils, daffodils, or narcissi, all belong to the genus *Narcissus*. Generally speaking, the flowers have cups or trumpets known as coronas, most are surrounded by six petals or corollas, and emerge from a base of erect light green leaves. Provided there is adequate moisture during the growth and bloom cycles, narcissi tolerate wind, heat, and cold, and when dormant, tolerate drought and freezing temperatures.

When, Where, and How to Plant
Keep bulbs in a cool, dark, dry place until ready to plant. In warmer climates, plant in fall from bulbs, spacing 4–8 in. apart in the ground or crowding them even closer in a pot (18–24 bulbs may be grown in a 14–16-in. pot). They need full sun or partial shade and moist, well-drained, sandy loam soil and a pH of 6.7–7.0. Prepare a trench 2–12 in. deep, depending on the size of the bulb, and add a preplant fertilizer at the bottom. Once in the ground, they can remain undisturbed for about five years, and can be dug up for division when dormant in the summer.

Growing Tips
Immediately after planting, soak deeply and thoroughly to collapse any air pockets in the soil, then adjust frequency and amount according to weather and growth conditions. Water more lightly during fall and winter and more heavily during the spring growing season, and discontinue in the summer. Fertilize monthly during the growing and blooming seasons with a water-soluble kelp or fish emulsion. Remove only diseased or damaged foliage while in the growth cycle—the leaves are needed to manufacture food for current and future seasons.

Advice and Care
Where deer, rabbits, and gophers are prevalent, narcissus are excellent repellents because of their toxic alkaloids.

Companion Planting and Design
To make any kind of display, plant at least three to six bulbs in a cluster. If you want your bulbs to naturalize in grassy or woodland areas, throw out the bulbs and plant them where they fall, in a free-form or random pattern. For a long bloom cycle, plant a mixture of early-, mid-, and late-blooming types. In containers or flower beds, overplant with violas, pansies, nemesia, and freesias and plant around shrubs and trees, such as pink Indian hawthorn and magnolia.

Try These
'Ziva' paperwhites are very fragrant with pure-white petals and cups, but many find its perfume overwhelming if brought indoors. 'Bethlehem' and 'Israel' have milder perfumes. For forcing indoors, try the mild-scented 'Inbal' or *N. tazetta* 'Grand Soleil d'Or'.

Oriental Lily and Orienpets

Lillium hybrids

Bloom Period and Seasonal Color
White, pink, yellow, and red blooms from midsummer to fall.

Mature Height × Spread 3–5 ft. × 1–3 ft.

Botanical Pronunciation
lil-EE-um

Zones 5–10

For eye-popping flowers in the plant world, few can compete with the 3–5-ft.-tall Oriental lilies, hybrids primarily from Japanese species with large—some up to a plate-sized 9 in.—often perfumed flowers in white or pink, and frequently speckled in red or streaked with red or gold on the center of each petal. They look like giant orchids! Orienpets are the result of recent crosses between China's trumpet lilies and Japan's Oriental lilies. The result is a lily that gardeners consider to be even better than either of the parents: more disease resistant, and heat-, humidity-, and cold-tolerant. Many have subtle, sweet perfumes blended with hints of citrus, and come in bold red, orange, burgundy, and gold, as well as pastel pink peach, yellow, cream, and white.

When, Where, and How to Plant
Plant two-and-a-half times as deep as bulb's diameter and space 1 ft. apart. Although Oriental lilies can be planted in full sun or morning sun, it is best to plant the Orienpets in dappled sun or partial shade. Avoid areas that are windy or exposed to the hot afternoon sun. Often the bulbs are the size of fists and need 4–6 in. of soil to properly cover them. From pots, transplant and set at the same soil level as its original container. Plant in slightly acid, well-draining soil.

Growing Tips
Water year-round. Decrease water after leaves yellow, but don't allow roots to dry out completely. Use an organic granular or liquid fertilizer when growth occurs and when budded flowers are showing color.

For alkaline soils, fertilize with cottonseed meal to help acidify. Stake maturing, budding plants to keep them from toppling. Apply a 2–3-in. layer of mulch to conserve moisture and to keep their "feet" cool. Protect from gophers by planting in wire baskets.

Advice and Care
Orienpets have been known to adapt to late frosts and have been successfully grown in many different zonal conditions, but where temperatures reach 90 degrees Fahrenheit or more, plant the bulbs where there is afternoon shade. If soil is clayey, plant them in a raised bed or large container for improved drainage.

Companion Planting and Design
For greater impact, plant in groups of three to five and place in between shrubs to support their mature stems and to camouflage their yellowing foliage after summer's bloom. Ferns, hellebores, and other low-growers help keep the soil moist and cool around the lilies. In mixed borders, combine them with cleomes and salvias. With their large, perfumed blooms, plant close to pathways for all to enjoy. If cutting the flowers for arrangements, select partially open buds and remove the stamens to prevent their pollen from staining the flower and you.

Try These
Alabaster white 'Casablanca' and rose-red with white margins 'Stargazer' are magnificent Oriental lilies. Crimson pink and white 'Silk Road' and deep rosy-red with creamy margins 'Scheherazade' are Orienpet must-haves for the summer garden.

Peruvian Lily

Alstroemeria aurantiaca

Bloom Period and Seasonal Color
Pink, lavender, yellow, orange, and bicolors bloom in spring and summer.

Mature Height × Spread 2–3 ft. (clumping)

Botanical Pronunciation
al-STRO-mir-ee-ah OW-rahn-tee-ah-ka

Zones 9–11

The elegant spring- to summer-flowering Peruvian lilies look so graceful in the rectangular terracotta pots placed as highlights in our backyard. Once their handsome flowers are spent, the wind and visiting birds disperse the seeds. Come spring, we find their volunteer seedlings growing among rosebushes, in other mixed-flower pots, standing tall in a mass of ivy and geraniums, and in the middle of our raised vegetable plot. Gray-green lance-shaped leaves line tall flower stalks that hold several trumpetlike blossoms in hues of bronze, orange, yellow, purple, pink, red, and cream, and may be bicolored, multicolored, streaked, striped, spotted, or marbled. They dislike hot, dry conditions such as drought and blustery winds, and do not tolerate freezing temperatures, but thrive in temperate regions with adequate moisture.

When, Where, and How to Plant
Plant alstroemeria in spring after the last frost from seed, from rhizomes, or from 4–8-in. pots or 1-gallon containers. They need full sun and rich, well-drained, sandy soil with a neutral pH, 7.0. Space them 4–12 in. apart depending on the size of the rhizome or container. Amend the flower bed with compost or humus mulch if the soil does not drain freely.

Growing Tips
Soak deeply after planting. Water three times the first week; thereafter adjust frequency and amount to weather and growth conditions. Fertilize monthly during the growing and blooming seasons with a water-soluble organic food. Clip off the spent flowers if you do not want any seed production. When plants go dormant, do not water unless there are no winter rains. If you notice premature yellowing of leaves, this may be the nefarious work of thrips; if you see chewed-off leaves, you know they have been "slimed" by snails or slugs. When damage is extensive, use a molluscicide or squish the slimy pests by hand, and apply an organic remedy like spinosad for thrips.

Advice and Care
If the area has high temperatures, plant in partial shade to avoid the fading of flower color. For cut flowers and to encourage the development of more blooming stems, yank the entire stem up and out of the plant.

Companion Planting and Design
They serve as dramatic garden accents in the middle of borders and mixed-flower beds, as container plants, or along a warm, sheltered wall. Coreopsis, candytuft, and Shasta daisy make ideal planting companions.

Try These
'Dover Orange' has tall flowering stems and deep orange flowers. 'Lutea' has yellow flowers marked with red. New hybrids are being bred for more heat and cold tolerance. 'Princess Fabiana', is a dwarf type, growing to just 10 in. with clear white blooms, that is more tolerant of heat. Cold-tolerant 'Freedom' has peachy-red blooms and 'Inca Ice' comes in muted shades of apricot, pink, cream, and yellow, reaching 3 ft. tall and wide.

Ranunculus

Ranunculus asiaticus

Bloom Period and Seasonal Color
A rainbow of colors, plus Picotee and bicolors, bloom in late spring and summer.

Mature Height × Spread
12–24 in. (multiplying) × 12–24 in.

Botanical Pronunciation
ra-NUN-kew-lus A-SEE-at-ick-us

Zones 7–11

Acres of ranunculus (Persian buttercup) blossoms can be seen in April at the famous Flower Fields in Carlsbad, California. The colorful beauties are living examples of the truism "You can't judge a book by its cover," because their tubers look like pint-sized bunches of brown bananas with fuzzy berets. From such a homely embryo Mother Nature hatches another of her miracles. Feathery foliage, pale green in color, emerge on long stalks. Soon saucer-shaped, 3–5-in.-diameter flowers with tight bundles of stamens in their centers unfurl in the warmth of the spring sun. Persian buttercups do not tolerate frost, high temperatures, cold winds, or drought; they do best where winters are mild and autumns are warm during the days and cool during the evenings.

When, Where, and How to Plant
Plant in fall where winters are mild or in spring after the last frost where winters are cold, from tubers, 4–6-in. pots, or 1-gallon containers. They need full sun and rich, fast-draining soil with a pH of 6.5–7.0. Prepare a flower bed, add a preplant fertilizer, and amend the soil with humus mulch, peat moss, or compost if needed. Before planting, soak the tubers in water for 30–45 minutes, but not much longer or they may rot. Bury the tubers "toes down," spacing them 4–6 in. apart; if from 4-in. or larger containers, plant 6–10 in. on center in the ground.

Growing Tips
Soak deeply after planting. It should not be necessary to water again until the leaves appear, as long as the soil remains moist but not soggy. Once the root systems are established, adjust watering frequency and amount to weather and growth conditions. Fertilize monthly with a water-soluble food such as liquid kelp or fish emulsion. Deadhead the spent flowers. Other than mildew resulting from airborne fungi spores and the ubiquitous snails and slugs, few diseases or pests pose a problem. You might protect the immature, tender leaves with netting or chicken wire, because birds love to feed on them. For humans, however, all parts of ranunculus are poisonous.

Advice and Care
Ranunculus will die back during the heat of the summer and awaken in fall. Leave the bulbs in the ground in mild climates, but dig them up and put away for winter storage in colder areas.

Companion Planting and Design
They are fabulous in borders or containers in a solid mass or mixed with Icelandic poppies, alyssum, pansies, Shasta daisies, cotoneaster, and narcissus.

Try These
New hybrids have double or semidouble buttercup-like flowers painted in hues of green, yellow, orange, red, rose, pink, cream, and white; some are edged with a darker color while others are bi- and tricolored. 'Pauline' is a brilliant eggplant purple. Try 'Tecolote' series for huge, colorful, cabbage-roselike flowers on 18–14-in. stems.

CITRUS

FOR CALIFORNIA

Citrus are plant nomads brought to California from China, southeast Asia, and other parts of the world, resulting in hundreds of varieties and subspecies. They have taken root and made themselves at home in the welcoming warmth of our Golden State.

The Virtues of Citrus

Citrus trees are handsome evergreens and are ideal additions to orchards and mild-climate gardens. They are very ornamental with their lustrous green foliage, large clusters of intensely perfumed, creamy, pink, or purplish blossoms, and mature bright nuggets of sunshine. The crops of tasty fruits are a bonus, particularly in winter when other trees are dormant. Many varieties are available both as standard 20 foot and dwarf 6 to 10 foot trees. Most citrus trees sold at nurseries are grafted, meaning their rootstocks differ from their tops (scions) to improve fruit quantity and quality and to increase resistance to pests, diseases, or less-than-optimum soil conditions.

Select a Healthy Tree

Select well-grown one- or two-year-old trees, because older trees may be rootbound and won't establish as quickly. A healthy, vigorous tree should have large, uniformly green leaves, free from pest damage. The branching should be symmetrical, and the bark should be bright and clean with a healed graft union that is 6 in. above the ground.

Grow a Variety for Your Climate

Growing tasty fruit begins with selecting a variety that suits your climate. Lemons and limes require less heat and produce good fruit near the coast, but the Valencia orange needs higher temperatures and produces quality fruit from the coast to the desert. Navel oranges, mandarins, and tangelos require even more heat and do best in inland valleys. Grapefruit need prolonged periods of high heat to develop peak flavor and grow best in the desert, although recent hybrids such as 'Oroblanco' have a lower heat requirement. Yuzu, Satsuma mandarin, and Nagami kumquat, are the most cold tolerant.

Provide Proper Care

In addition to a suitable climate, successful citrus cultivation depends on year-round care. Proper irrigation is very important. All citrus need well-drained soils—if allowed to stand in water, the roots will be prone to disease. Where drainage is a problem, plant citrus in raised beds filled with commercial potting soil and mulch. Do not plant lawns

Dwarf citrus trees make ideal container plants.

or other shallow-rooted plants underneath citrus, because their watering needs differ (the soil will be too moist for citrus).

Add 2 to 4 inches of mulch under the tree, 6 inches from the trunk and extending out to the drip line (the canopy of the tree) to prevent weeds, modulate temperature fluctuations, and absorb excess salts from the water. Fertilize with an organic, complete citrus food in late winter after the fruit has set and again in early summer. If new leaves are turning yellow, iron deficiency (known as iron chlorosis in plants) may be the problem. Apply an iron chelate or spray foliage with liquid kelp. Zinc deficiency causes yellow mottling or blotching of green leaves and can be remedied with chelated zinc as a foliar spray or as a soil application.

Keep Pruning to a Minimum

Prune citrus after harvesting fruit, but keep pruning to a minimum for shape and to remove dead wood, broken or damaged limbs, water sprouts, and suckers. Protect the inner branches from sunburn by painting with whitewash or latex paint.

"June drop" and insect infestations are common citrus maladies. June drop is the sudden shedding of immature fruit, which is nature's way of adjusting the crop size to the tree's capability to produce good fruit. To control persistent insect or snail and slug infestations, select methods that are preferably organic or appropriate for the particular pest and locality.

More than Fruit Factories

Whether displayed as an ornamental or grown in an orchard, citrus trees are more than fruit factories: they are handsome shade, hedge, container, and specimen trees. But to be perfectly candid, they are probably one of our favorite plants because of their fruits, which feed us and sweeten our days.

Australian Finger Lime

Microcitrus australasica

Bloom and Fruit Period
Spring bloom, fall to winter fruit.

Mature Height × Spread 4–9 ft. × 4–6 ft.

Botanical Pronunciation
MI-cro-sit-rus AUS-tray-la-sih-ka

Zones 10 and above

Who could predict that finger-shaped fruits nestled among small, pointed, thin leaves on thorny branches would appeal to citrus lovers? Native to Queensland as an understory plant, this citrus hits the top of the "super cool" meter and is often referred to as citrus caviar. Chefs prize the 3–7-in. tapered fruits because the juice vesicles burst out when they are sliced widthwise and resemble caviar or tapioca balls. The translucent orbs range from pale green to dark berry and the unique tangy, refreshing, lime-tasting fruits are used as garnish, spooned over oysters on the half shell, in salads, soups, jams, sauces, Thai curries, or eaten plain for a zesty, crunchy munch. Because of its rangy (and very thorny) habit, grow it away from pathways.

When, Where, and How to Plant
Transplant one- to two-year-old trees in 8–12-in. containers. Fill with a well-draining commercial potting soil. Three-year-old trees with trunks at least ½ in. in diameter can be transplanted in a 12–14-in. container, or directly in the ground in full sun in mild winter or coastal areas during spring, and spaced 12 ft. apart. If farther inland where it is very hot, provide afternoon shade. When planting in the ground, construct a 6-ft.-diameter watering basin and cover with 3 in. of mulch or compost, leaving a 6-in. space away from the trunk to avoid fungal rot or insect problems. Where frost is common, plant in containers and move to more protected areas during extended freezing periods. See page 63 for more planting information.

Growing Tips
Water deeply and regularly every ten to fourteen days, depending on growth and weather conditions. If in containers, it may be necessary to water more frequently, every seven to ten days or more during hot, dry weather conditions. Fertilize with an organic citrus food twice a year (late winter and early summer).

Advice and Care
Wrap copper bands around the trunk to keep snails out of the tree's canopy. Control scale with an organic horticultural-formulated canola oil and watch out for citrus leafminer. The larvae leave distinctive tunneling marks in the foliage. Control future damage with spinosad, but spray during the late afternoon when the bees have returned to their hives. Once spinosad has dried, it is no longer harmful to beneficials such as bees. There are also systemic products specifically formulated for citrus trees.

Companion Planting and Design
Plant in a container or where winters are mild, directly in the ground with other citrus or as a visual screen.

Try These
'Yellow' is aptly named for its bright yellow skin and very large juice vesicles, while 'Collette', with shiny purplish-black skin and a dark lime green to deep yellow pulp, has been highly rated by chefs. To add to a collection of unusual citrus, consider *C. medica* 'Buddha's Hand' with fruit shaped like fingers, or 'Ertog'; both are used to perfume rooms.

Blood Orange

Citrus sinensis

Bloom and Fruit Period
Flowers early spring, fruits November to June depending on variety.

Mature Height × Spread
12–15 ft. × 12–15 ft.

Botanical Pronunciation SIT-rus si-NEN-sis

Zones 10–11

The red flesh and juice make blood oranges particularly interesting. It is not only dramatic in looks but has rich flavor with hints of raspberry. Its pulp coloration will vary depending on variety, location, and fruit maturity; some even exhibit a reddish blush on the rind that is light related and can vary from year to year. The juice is used in sauces and desserts and can also be sliced for salads or garnish. What causes the "blood" coloration? It's all about anthocyanins, pigments that are produced where summers are hot and dry and winters are cold, but not freezing, resulting in the deepest internal color and richest flavor. 'Moro' and 'Sanguinelli' have the most consistent internal color, with 'Moro' darkening after December.

When, Where, and How to Plant
To transplant in the ground, dig a planting hole in spring that is twice the size of the rootball. Fill the hole halfway with soil amended with humus mulch or compost, set the tree into the hole, add preplant fertilizer, and fill, but make sure the graft is about 1 in. above its original soil level. Tamp the soil to eliminate air pockets. Water thoroughly. If in a colder zone, below USDA 9, it is best to plant it in a container that can be moved indoors or to a more protected area during the winter months. If it's in a container, repot every two to three years and prune about one-third of its roots before replanting in fresh, well-draining commercial potting soil.

Growing Tips
After planting water thoroughly and continue to water about every three to four days for two more weeks. Once new growth emerges, water every seven to ten days depending on weather and growth conditions. Feed with an organic citrus fertilizer every three to four months. During bloom and fruit development, supplement with liquid kelp every two to three weeks.

Advice and Care
Prune only for shape or to cut out any dead or interfering branches before bloom or after fruit has set. Also remove any suckers that emerge from below the graft.

Companion Planting and Design
Use the blood orange as a small to medium-sized shade tree in a citrus orchard, or as a landscape accent near a pathway where its fragrance and fruit color can be appreciated. Avoid planting in lawns, because water and fertilizer needs differ between lawns and citrus. 'Tarocco' blood orange makes a great espalier.

Try These
The most popular for the California home garden, 'Moro' bears its deep red– to dark purple–fleshed fruit from early winter-spring. Its fruit are usually seedless, easy to peel, and grow on medium-sized trees. 'Sanguinelli' has lighter-colored flesh, but its peel is often cherry red; it needs more heat than 'Moro' and does best in inland California. 'Tarocco' fruit ripens in between 'Moro' and 'Sanguinelli' and is sweet with hints of berry taste but thrives best in California's inland valleys.

Calamondin

Citrofortunella microcarpa

Bloom and Fruit Period
Flower and fruit almost year-round.

Mature Height × Spread 6–10 ft. × 6–8 ft.

Botanical Pronunciation
Sit-ROE-fore-tune-el-lah MY-kroe-karp-ah

Zones 10–11

In China, calamondin is known as Sechi Chief, meaning "four seasons," an appropriate appellation since it bears fruit practically year-round. On a mature tree, hundreds of fruits bearing at the same time make it a spectacular sight. This shapely evergreen tree grows upright with a columnar habit. Covering the delicately textured, almost thornless branchlets are small, glossy green, oval-shaped leaves. The petite 1½-in. spherical fruits have reddish orange rinds; tender, bright orange pulp; and few seeds. The organic or residually chemical-free grown calamondin makes excellent marmalade, refreshing drinks when sweetened with sugar, and flavorful additions to foods. Calamondins are also used as culinary substitutes for lemons and lime. They tolerate heat if there is sufficient humidity and water but do not like drought or wind.

When, Where, and How to Plant
Plant in spring after the last frost from 5- or 15-gallon containers, spacing them 12–15 ft. apart. Calamondin prefers full sun in porous, well-drained soil that has a pH of 6.7–7.0. Construct a watering basin 6–10 ft. in diameter and cover with 2 in. of organic material such as humus mulch or compost.

Growing Tips
Immediately after planting, soak the soil deeply and thoroughly. During the first week, water twice; thereafter adjust watering frequency and the amount according to weather and growth conditions. Fertilize in late winter or early spring and early summer with a granular citrus and avocado food. In the coastal areas of Southern California

and the coastal valleys of Northern California, calamondins are harvested from winter through fall. In Southern California's inland regions, they are picked from winter through midsummer. The harvest season lasts from early winter to late summer along California's central valleys, but only lasts from early winter to early spring in the desert areas.

Advice and Care
Prune for shape and remove dead wood between two of the harvest cycles. Snails can happily spend most of their lives in the dense canopy of the calamondin. Remove them by hand and feed them to your ducks, or use the foot-stomp method of eradication. Watch out for aphids, particularly when tender growth emerges in the spring; as the weather warms, inspect for mites. An organic canola-based oil is an effective biodegradable control.

Companion Planting and Design
Calamondin is a wonderful ornamental background or shade tree in the landscape and a perfect indoor or outdoor container plant as long as there is sufficient light, humidity, and moisture. Because it is somewhat cold hardy, it grows where many other citrus are either unavailable or cannot be grown.

Try These
Variegated calamondin is attractive with variegated leaves, and petite green-and-yellow striped fruit that ripens to bright orange. It is a great edible in the California landscape. Philippine lime is a prolific producer with zesty acid juice. Its compact growth habit makes it perfect for containers.

Grapefruit

Citrus paradisi

Bloom and Fruit Period
Blooms March to April, fruits April to January depending on variety.

Mature Height × Spread
10–20 ft. × 20–20 ft.

Botanical Pronunciation
SIT-rus PEAR-ah-dis-eye

Zones 10–11

E ven without their large yellow or pink-blushed fruits that grow so extravagantly in grapelike clusters near the outside of the trees, these would be handsome evergreen ornamentals. Their shiny, dark green leaves provide a lush background for their equally impressive fruits. There are two types of grapefruit: white-fleshed and pigmented. The latter need long periods of heat to color, but there is no flavor difference between the two. There is a difference, however, between seeded and seedless varieties—the former tends to be more flavorful and separates into segments easily. If organically grown or free of chemical residuals, then use them as you would oranges in freshly squeezed juice; in salads, especially paired with avocado; and as marmalade, candied peel, and sorbet.

When, Where, and How to Plant
Plant in spring from 5- or 15-gallon containers, spacing at least 15–20 ft. apart for large varieties and closer for smaller ones. They require full sun in rich, well-drained soil with a pH of 6.7–7.0. Although tolerant of strong sunlight and gusty winds, there will be some sun and wind damage. Build a watering basin 10–12 ft. in diameter and cover with 2 in. of organic material such as humus mulch or compost. Grapefruit have the highest heat requirement among all citrus. Where winters are warm and summers are long and hot, such as in the California low desert, the fruits ripen in nine to twelve months; in cooler coastal regions they may need a year or more, but their rinds will be thicker and their juice tarter in flavor. Allow the fruits to hang on the tree for up to eighteen months,

but do not leave them on too much beyond that time because it diminishes the flavor. For the juiciest fruits at their peak prime, pick those that are heavy, smooth, and thin-skinned, and avoid those that have sandpaper-like, puffy rinds.

Growing Tips
Immediately after planting, soak deeply and thoroughly. During the first week, water three times and thereafter adjust the frequency and the amount according to weather and growth conditions. They are sensitive to drought. Fertilize in late winter or early spring and early summer with a granular citrus and avocado food.

Advice and Care
Prune only for shape and to remove dead or interfering wood. Giant whitefly and mites are common problems that are controlled by an organic canola-based oil or Neem oil.

Companion Planting and Design
They make ideal background, ornamental, or shade trees in the landscape and are great outdoor container plants.

Try These
'Marsh' is the popular white-fleshed variety, but requires sustained heat. 'Oroblanco' is a pummelo–grapefruit hybrid that bears sweet, seedless, white-fleshed fruit in the cool coastal areas of California. Another pummelo–grapefruit hybrid, 'Melogold', also performs well with less heat, but is bigger and thinner-skinned.

Kumquat

Fortunella japonica

Bloom and Fruit Period
Flowers in midsummer, fruits fall to winter.

Mature Height × Spread 6–15 ft. × 6–15 ft.

Botanical Pronunciation
four-TOON-el-lah jah-PAWN-ih-kah

Zones 9–11

Often called the "little gems of citrus," kumquats are unique in that they do not belong to the genus *Citrus* and their fruit is eaten whole. We like to pick the small orange fruits, gently press and roll them between our fingers, pop them in our mouths, and savor the combination of the peel's sweet flavor with the pulp's tart taste. They are attractive, symmetrical, compact evergreen trees that are covered with tiny, lustrous, dark green leaves during the growing season. Kumquat trees don't begin their growth cycle until the onset of warm weather, and don't bloom until midsummer. In the California desert, the fruits are large but a bit more acidic in flavor; in the coastal regions, the fruits are smaller but juicier.

When, Where, and How to Plant
Plant in spring after the last frost from 5- or 15-gallon containers, spacing them 10–15 ft. on center. They require full sun in rich, well-drained soil with a pH of 6.7–7.0. Construct a watering basin 6–10 ft. in diameter and cover with 2 in. of organic material such as humus mulch or compost.

Growing Tips
Immediately after planting, soak deeply and thoroughly. Water three times during the first week; water regularly and deeply every ten to fourteen days, but also adjust watering frequency and amounts according to weather and growth conditions. Fertilize in late winter or early spring and early summer with a granular citrus and avocado food. They produce the sweetest and juiciest fruit where summers are hot and humid, but they can

adapt to other zones. Because they stay dormant in the cooler fall and winter months, kumquats withstand temperatures below 20 degrees Fahrenheit with little damage to their foliage. However, provide protection against extended periods of drought and wind.

Advice and Care
Prune as needed for shape and to remove dead wood. Few diseases affect kumquats, but citrus red scales and brown soft scales can be a problem. A horticultural oil is an effective treatment for these sucking insects if you follow the manufacturer's directions. Avoid harmful pesticides, fungicides, and herbicides (unless formulated for citrus) if you want to use the kumquat as an edible.

Companion Planting and Design
With their brightly colored fruit, they are prized as ornamentals, make excellent foundation shrubs and plants for terrace and patio containers, and can even be planted in bonsai containers. They are also used as decorative centerpieces with dainty foliage clipped and jeweled fruits attached.

Try These
'Nagami' is an oval-shaped kumquat and is the variety most used in cooking sauces, marmalades, and piquant preserves because its peel is sweet and its flesh is sour. It has a better harvest and sweeter taste where summers are hot. 'Meiwa' is a round fruit with a spicy-sweet flavor—peel and flesh—best for eating fresh. This one does well where summers are cool.

Lemon

Citrus limon

Bloom and Fruit Period
Year-round in coastal areas.

Mature Height × Spread
10–15 ft. × 12–15 ft.

Botanical Pronunciation
SIT-rus LEE-mone

Zones 9–11

Where temperate conditions prevail, we think every garden should have a lemon tree, because there is nothing more satisfying than being able to pick fresh fruits anytime you need them. It is a necessary luxury. We have always believed that "when life hands you lemons, make lemonade," as well as marinade, Hollandaise sauce, pie filling, sorbet, pudding, and preserves—provided, of course, you have grown your lemons organically or with chemicals formulated specifically for citrus. These are attractive, vigorous, upright trees, with light green leaves that are tinged with purplish red when immature, highlighting their bright yellow fruit. Like most citrus, a lemon tree (probably a hybrid of *C. medica* × *C. aurantifolia*) does not tolerate drought or wind.

When, Where, and How to Plant
Plant in spring after the last frost from 5- or 15-gallon containers, spacing 10–20 ft. on center. Lemon trees require full sun in loam-textured, well-drained soil, pH 6.7–7.0. Build a watering basin 6–10 ft. in diameter and cover with 2 in. of organic material such as humus mulch or compost. Lemons do not need too much heat for fruit to ripen, but may suffer frost damage when temperatures dip below 30 degrees Fahrenheit.

Growing Tips
Soak deeply after planting to collapse air pockets. Water twice the first week; thereafter water deeply and regularly every ten to fourteen days, but adjust watering frequency and the amounts according to weather and growth conditions. Fertilize

in late winter or early spring with a citrus and avocado food.

Advice and Care
If left alone, standard-sized lemon trees often become too tall, rangy, and unsightly. Trees that are regularly pruned every year or two are more productive and the fruits are easier to harvest. Lemon trees are prone to mite infestations that result in a condition called russeting or silvering, a blemishing of the rind. Since this does not destroy the quality of the lemons, do not intervene unless the infestation becomes severe. If necessary, you can introduce predacious mites from agricultural insectaries, or apply a horticultural canola or Neem oil.

Companion Planting and Design
Lemon trees can be pruned into espaliers or planted as ornamental or background trees. They are also desirable in containers for terraces and patios.

Try These
'Improved Meyer' in the only Meyer lemon sold in California; *improved* refers to its disease-free attribute. The Meyer lemon is very hardy. It has a round shape with a thin, yellowish orange rind. It's juicy and less acidic in flavor than other lemons, and favored among cooks. As a dwarf, it is an excellent container plant, growing 6 ft. tall. 'Variegated Pink' (aka 'Pink Lemonade') bears green-and-white foliage, and green stripes on young fruit, with pale pink flesh. It does not require heat to develop its color. 'Eureka' is the lemon sold at supermarkets and 'Ponderosa' bears enormous, 1- to 2-pound fruits.

Lime

Citrus aurantiifolia

Bloom and Fruit Period
Spring to summer blooms; fruit year-round, but primarily winter.

Mature Height × Spread 8–12 ft. × 10 ft.

Botanical Pronunciation
SIT-rus ow-RAN-tee-fole-ee-ah

Zones 10–11

Limes are another excellent citrus, with sensitivity to cold ranging from moderate to zero tolerance. For frost-free areas, limes are an excellent choice, but where frosts are common, plant them in containers and move them to more protected areas in the winter. Mexican lime, Key lime, or bartender's lime is a round, thorny, shrubby tree with a wiry, open habit, and is very sensitive to cold temperatures. Its dark green, seeded, and aromatic fruit's flavor develops best in areas where summers are hot and humid. Persian or Tahiti limes do well in Southern California and are a few degrees hardier than Mexican limes. They are more compact trees with larger, juicy, flavorful fruits that are less seeded, less fragrant, and need less heat to ripen.

When, Where, and How to Plant
Plant in spring from 5- or 15-gallon containers, spacing 8–10 ft. apart. Limes prefer full sun and well-drained loam soil, pH 6.7–7.0. Build a watering basin 8–10 ft. in diameter and cover with 2 in. of organic material such as humus mulch or compost.

Growing Tips
Immediately after planting, soak deeply and thoroughly. During the first week, water three times; thereafter water every ten to fourteen days, adjusting frequency and the amount according to weather and growth conditions. Fertilize in late winter or early spring and early summer with a granular citrus and avocado food. Although it bears fruit year-round, the main harvest occurs in winter. Limes can be picked when they are green to yellow.

Advice and Care
Prune for shape and to remove dead wood during late winter or early spring. Few disease or insect problems affect these trees, but keep a watchful eye out for spider mites, citrus woolly whitefly, and snails. If damage is extensive, apply Neem or horticultural canola oil for mites, spinosad for whitefly, and an iron phosphate molluscicide. Only use a chemical pesticide if it is formulated for edibles such as citrus.

Companion Planting and Design
A lime tree is a great container plant as well as a foundation plant. If you want to plant only one type of lime tree, we would recommend the Tahiti or Persian lime because it is a much more attractive ornamental, and it bears larger fruits that are about as juicy and flavorful as the Mexican lime.

Try These
'Bearss Lime' is a seedling of Tahiti lime, the most popular lime for California gardeners. Our 'Bearss Lime' produces almost year-round, bearing juicy light yellow fruits when ripe with minimal disease or insect problems. The leaves and juice of 'Makrut' Thai lime, commonly called Kaffir lime, are used in Thai, Cambodian, and Indonesian culinary delights. Kaffir is also a good choice for containers. 'Palestine Sweet' is popular in Middle Eastern, Latin American, and Indian cuisine. It is ready to pick fall to winter and has little acid in its fruit.

Mandarin

Citrus reticulata

Bloom and Fruit Period
Spring to fall flowers, fruit December to January.

Mature Height × Spread
10–15 ft. × 12–15 ft.

Botanical Pronunciation
SIT-rus re-TIK-ooh-lah-tah

Zones 10–11

M andarins are alternate bearing, yielding a large crop of small fruit one year, followed by a less prolific crop of large fruit the next year. The foliage is dark green, with fruit borne on the outside of the canopy. One of our favorite pleasures is plucking the perfectly ripe mandarins from our garden, zipping off their rinds, and eating them out of hand. Mandarins are somewhat frost hardy, tolerating short temperature dips as low as 28 degrees Fahrenheit. Although early-maturing varieties do better in cold climates, most cannot survive sustained frost. In hot, inland desert areas, protect mandarin trees from hot, dry winds. They flourish best in subtropical regions where high heat in the late stage of ripening and adequate moisture produces the sweetest and juiciest fruit.

When, Where, and How to Plant
Plant in spring from 5- or 15-gallon containers, spacing 10–15 ft. apart. These evergreens prefer full sun in well-drained loam soil with a pH of 6.7–7.0. Construct a watering basin 10 ft. in diameter and cover with 2 in. of organic material such as humus mulch or compost.

Growing Tips
Immediately after planting, soak deeply and thoroughly. Water three times during the first week; thereafter water every ten to fourteen days, adjusting frequency and amount according to weather and growth conditions. Fertilize twice in late winter or early spring and early summer with a granular citrus and avocado food.

Advice and Care
Prune just after the fruits set to even out alternate-bearing fruit production and to remove any dead or interfering wood. Also, if you thin the trees' interiors, it will help prevent pest and disease infestations by promoting good air circulation. Washing the foliage weekly with a strong stream of water will help keep the insect population down. Pick mandarins when they are heavy with juice, and avoid puffy, lightweight fruits that have soft spots. If left too long on a tree, the fruits will become dry and bland. To avoid tearing off the rinds around the stems when harvesting, use clippers to snip off the fruits.

Companion Planting and Design
Most mandarins are pollinated by bees, but a few varieties, such as 'Fairchild' and 'Clementine,' need cross-pollinators that bloom during the same time, normally a different type of mandarin or tangelo.

Try These
'Owari-Satsuma' has exceptionally sweet, nearly seedless, medium to large fruit with easy-to-peel skin that ripens early (early autumn–December) and is a good choice for colder climates such as the California foothills. Standard trees grow 10–15 ft., while dwarf trees are suitable as 6-ft. shrubs. The University of California has introduced several patented varieties, including 'Gold Nugget', a seedless, easy-to-peel, small- to medium-sized fruit that ripens from late winter to spring. 'Page' is a hybrid between 'Clementine' mandarin and 'Minneola' tangelo that bears very sweet, small fruit from fall to winter and is not only wonderful eaten fresh but also makes delicious juice.

Pummelo

Citrus grandis

Bloom and Fruit Period
Fruit April to June except inland and desert
December to April.

Mature Height × Spread 10–15 ft. × 12 ft.

Botanical Pronunciation
SIT-rus GRAND-is

Zones 10–11

Closely related to the grapefruit, but sweeter, less acidic, and larger, pummelo is used like a grapefruit. We like the evergreen one because its shelled segments taste so good. Some are small with moundlike canopies, others are about the same size as grapefruit trees. Some have a drooping habit while others are large, open, and spreading. Fruit color and flavor varies, and there are seeded and seedless, thorny and thornless varieties. Most have thick branches covered with distinctively wide, winged leaf stems that bear large, thick blossoms. Because the fruit rind is thick, they are a bit hardier to cold than grapefruit. They grow best in warm tropical regions close to the sea in sheltered areas, and dislike extended periods of drought, wind, or freezing temperatures.

When, Where, and How to Plant
Plant in spring from 5- or 15-gallon containers, spacing 15–20 ft. Plant in full sun in rich, well-drained soil, pH 6.7–7.0. Construct a watering basin 10 ft. in diameter and cover with 2 in. of organic material like humus mulch or compost.

Growing Tips
Soak deeply after planting. Water three times the first week; thereafter water regularly and deeply every ten to fourteen days, adjusting frequency and amount to weather and growth conditions. Fertilize in late winter or early spring and early summer with a granular citrus and avocado food.

Advice and Care
Encourage strong branching by pruning out spindly, damaged, or interfering branches before spring growth, because pummelo fruits are hefty. There are few diseases, but citrus red scale, brown soft scale, and citrus woolly whitefly can cause problems, particularly during the warm, growing seasons. Horticultural canola oil or Neem oil are effective controls. For chemical pesticides or fungicides, use only those that are specifically formulated for citrus and follow directions. For maximum sweetness, ripen a freshly picked pummelo at room temperature for ten to fifteen days or until its skin is a deep yellow and it has a heavy fragrance.

Companion Planting and Design
In Asia, it is believed that this fruit is a symbol of prosperity and that good fortune happens to those who eat it. They are in great demand during Chinese New Year celebrations; if you want to create a stir at your next dinner, set out a few of these giants as table decorations.

Try These
'Chandler' is juicy, pink-fleshed, often seedless, and has an acid-sweet flavor. It does best in warm inland regions and is the most popular in home gardens. The slightly larger 'Reinking' is white-fleshed, seeded, and not as sweet as 'Chandler', and thrives in warm inland areas. Pummelo (also classified as *C. maxima*) 'Sweetie' is a newer hybrid developed at the University of California. The flesh is pale yellow, mild, and sweet, retaining some green even when ripe. *C. maxima* 'Siamese Sweet' is a dwarf type that is acidless, mild flavored, and sweet.

Sweet Orange

Citrus sinensis

Bloom and Fruit Period
Flowers and fruit depending on variety.

Mature Height × Spread 8–20 ft. × as wide

Botanical Pronunciation
SIT-rus SIN-en-sis

Zones 10–11

There are three major types of sweet oranges: navel, common, and blood oranges. The navel orange has a sweet, rich flavor and develops a secondary fruit at the blossom end that creates a small protrusion resembling a navel. Navels are best for eating fresh because they are seedless, easy to peel, and have the perfect blend of sweetness and acidity. They flourish where summers are warm and the nights are cool, in the subtropical interior regions. Common oranges do not have navels, are seedier, and harder to peel, but they are perfect juicing oranges and can be fresh or frozen. Because common oranges adapt to most citrus-growing regions (except frost areas), they are grown worldwide. Blood orange has been described separately; see page 65.

When, Where, and How to Plant
Plant in spring from 5- or 15-gallon containers, spacing them 10–15 ft. apart. Navels prefer subtropical interior regions where the summers are warm and the nights are cool. Common oranges adapt to most citrus-growing regions, except frost areas. Sweet oranges do not tolerate windy locations or extended periods of drought. These evergreens prefer full sun in rich, well-drained soil with a pH of 6.7–7.0. Build a watering basin 10 ft. in diameter and cover with 2 in. of organic material such as humus mulch or compost. The bark and fruit of citrus are sensitive to sunburn, especially in arid areas of California. As a preventive, plant your trees in an easterly exposure, paint the trunk with a white latex paint or whitewash or use a tree wrap, available at your local garden center.

Growing Tips
Immediately after planting, soak deeply and thoroughly. Water three times the first week; thereafter water every ten to fourteen days, adjusting frequency and amount according to weather and growth conditions. Fertilize in late winter or early spring and early summer with a granular citrus and avocado food.

Advice and Care
Prune for shape or to remove dead wood as needed. Protect from ants by using ant baits, where ants take it to the nest, destroying the entire colony. Control infestations of aphids, mealybugs, and citrus red scale with Neem oil or horticultural oil when necessary.

Companion Planting and Design
If you have the space and live in a frost-free area, plant a 'Washington Navel' and a 'Valencia' orange and you will have fresh oranges for about ten months out of the year. 'Washington' and 'Valencia' are available as standards (20–25 ft.) and dwarfs (8–12 ft.). Use as background trees or in large containers.

Try These
'Valencia' are tall trees with vigorous growth and are the best common oranges for the California gardener, with juice-making fruit available in summer. 'Washington Navel' is the most widely grown navel, with large, thick-skinned fruits, few seeds, and a sweet taste from early winter to midwinter. 'Cara Cara' is a navel with reddish pink flesh and a rich, sweet taste.

Tangelo

Citrus × tangelo

Bloom and Fruit Period
Spring flowers, late fall to winter fruits depending on variety.

Mature Height × Spread 10–15 ft. × 12 ft.

Botanical Pronunciation
SIT-rus TAN-jel-oh

Zones 10–11

At the edge of our orchard, we are growing a mature, 12-ft. tall 'Minneola' tangelo that continues to bear generous crops, particularly on the southwest side of the tree where the warmth of the late-winter and early-spring sun ripens the fruits. An 'Owari-Satsuma' mandarin is nearby. Because the trees are relatively sheltered from prevailing winds, the honeybees industriously cross-pollinate the two citrus trees. Other varieties adapt to hot climates if there is sufficient humidity and moisture available. Some also adapt to cooler weather, but their flavor will be more tart. A tangelo's cold hardiness generally falls between that of a grapefruit and an orange, or intermediate between its parents' tolerance to cold. Like our 'Minneola', most tangelos are sensitive to wind, freezing temperatures, and drought.

When, Where, and How to Plant
Plant trees in spring from 5- or 15-gallon containers, spacing them 10–15 ft. apart. Build a watering basin 10 ft. in diameter and cover with 2 in. of organic material such as humus mulch or compost. These evergreens prefer full sun in well-drained soil with a pH of 6.7–7.0. For containers, use a well-draining commercial potting soil. Whether planting in ground or in a container, make sure the graft is above the soil level. If soil drains slowly, plant in a raised bed for best results.

Growing Tips
Soak deeply after planting. Water two or three times the first week; thereafter water every ten to fourteen days, adjusting frequency and amount according to weather and growth conditions. Fertilize in late winter or early spring and early summer with a granular citrus and avocado food.

Advice and Care
After harvesting fruit, prune to remove damaged, twiggy wood, and to cut off suckers that emerge below the graft line. Also, prune off any errant growth for a balanced shape. Control leafminer, giant whitefly, and citrus woolly whitefly with an organic product such as spinosad. Harvest when fruits are heavy and full of juice because, as with most citrus, sweet oranges do not ripen off the tree.

Companion Planting and Design
Because tangelos do not cross-pollinate with each other, cross-pollination with a mandarin will usually produce a more prolific crop. Tangelos make excellent orchard or foundation trees in the landscape.

Try These
'Minneola' is a cross between a Duncan grapefruit and a Dancy mandarin that bears ripe fruit from mid-to-late winter. It has slightly elongated, deep orange fruit with knoblike formations at the stems, peels and segments easily, and tastes similar to a mandarin. 'Orlando' has the same parents as 'Minneola' except its light orange, flattened fruits mature earlier, the tree is more resistant to cold, and its rind doesn't separate from the flesh. 'Wekiwa' resembles a small grapefruit, but tastes like a mandarin, ripens late autumn to winter, and is a hybrid between a grapefruit and a tangelo. It's often sold as 'Lavender Gem' because of its purplish cast in hot climates.

Yuzu

Citrus ichangensis × *C. reticulata*

Bloom and Fruit Period
Late winter to spring bloom, late summer to winter fruit.

Mature Height × Spread 8–10 ft. × as wide

Botanical Pronunciation
SIT-rus EYE-kan-jen-sis ×
SIT-rus re-TIK-ooh-lah-tah

Zones 8–11

It's not a lemon or an orange, but its fruits sell for $16–$40 per pound; culinary connoisseurs are beginning to use yuzu (YOO-zoo) to highlight their specialty dishes. Cultivated for more than a thousand years, the small, rough-textured, and seedy fruits have a unique flavor and fragrance: tart like a grapefruit with hints of mandarin orange combined with the perfume of lime or lemon flowers. Not very juicy or beautiful, it is the aromatic outer rind that is particularly prized by the Japanese, who use it in ponzu sauce, soups, syrups, vinegar, syrups, sweets, liquors, and even plopped into hot baths. Because of its relation to *C. ichangensis*, yuzu is also one of the cold-hardiest citrus and grows where winters dip as low as 10 degrees Fahrenheit.

When, Where, and How to Plant
Plant from spring to fall, except in cold climates plant in spring. Yuzu can be planted directly in the ground as long as winter temperatures are above 10 degrees Fahrenheit with a minimum of 6 hours of sunshine in winter and summer. Protect from wind, and, because of its thorns, allow enough space to walk around it safely. For clayey soil, amend with at least 2 in. of humus mulch or compost so that the soil drains well. Dig a hole about twice as wide and as deep as the rootball. Fill the hole halfway, place the tree in the hole, spread its roots, and add remaining soil, but keep the graft slightly above the soil level. Tamp soil and water thoroughly to remove air pockets.

Growing Tips
Water deeply and regularly every ten to fourteen days, depending on growth and weather conditions. Fertilize with a complete organic citrus food twice a year (late winter and early summer) and supplement with liquid kelp if foliage yellows between the green veins (often a sign of iron deficiency). Apply a 2–3-in. layer of mulch out to the drip line (as far as the tree canopy), leaving a 4–6-in. space away from the trunk.

Advice and Care
Prune for shape if desired and remove dead, diseased, or damaged wood and suckers as needed. Compared to less hardy citrus, yuzu is resistant to many diseases and pests such as scale. Wrap copper bands around the trunk to keep snails away.

Companion Planting and Design
Yuzu forms an upright, slow-growing shrub shape, and can be planted as a backyard tree in an orchard setting, in a large container, or situated toward the back or middle of a mixed bed so that its hefty thorns can do no harm.

Try These
Another small-fruited, acidic citrus variety, Sudachi is a hybrid between *C. ichangensis* and *C. reticulata* and its greenish fruits are smaller than yuzu, less seedy, and juicier. It is used in soft drinks and alcoholic beverages and sliced in wedges to serve with a main course. It's hardy in USDA zones 10–11.

GROUNDCOVERS
FOR CALIFORNIA

G roundcover is a carpet for the earth beneath your feet. A less poetic definition of groundcover is this: any dense, low-growing plant that covers an area when planted *en masse*. To be worthy of the name it must grow quickly, and it is often fiercely aggressive by nature.

How to Grow

For successful cultivation, prepare the planting area by turning over the soil, raking it free of weeds, and adding 25 percent organic amendments. Whether bare root, in containers, or in flats, the spacing of the plants is determined by variety and mature size. A groundcover normally requires one to two years to cover an area, unless the plants are spaced farther apart than recommended—then allow an additional twelve to twenty-four months. Cuttings are usually spaced 8 to 10 inches apart on center (measuring from the center of one plant to the center of the next). After planting, water well and add 2 inches of organic mulch. Pull out any weeds or use a pre-emergent product until the groundcover has filled in sufficiently.

Maintaining a Groundcover

Maintenance of an established groundcover is much less demanding than that of a lawn. Some groundcovers, like vinca minor and Algerian ivy, tolerate partial shade, and most others consume less water, fertilizer, and pesticides than do lawns to keep them looking their best. Fertilize once a year during the growth cycle, water during extended periods of drought or high heat, and rake off leaves and debris from the top of a planting.

Woody plants such as dwarf coyote bush, kinnikinnick, and shore junipers need only selective pruning to remove dead wood or to reduce their size if they are beginning to cover a walkway. For vining or trailing groundcovers, carefully use an edger in areas around the base of a tree to avoid nicking it. Set the lawnmower 6 in. high and mow dwarf coyote bush once a year to improve its appearance and keep it low. Any groundcover that has undergone intense heat or cold will also be rejuvenated by a lawnmower trim, which stimulates fresh growth and removes damaged foliage.

Keeping a Groundcover Under Control

The yin and the yang of groundcovers is that many of them cover a large area so quickly and thickly that they become unwelcome invaders of other garden areas. To effectively tame their wild nature, first observe how they grow. Plants like Algerian ivy that have holdfasts or suckers have a reputation for swallowing anything immobile, but they can be controlled if their new growth is regularly cut back. Groundcovers that spread by rhizomes can be stopped with metal or vinyl edging or other physical barriers placed directly into the ground. Others that spread by runners or stolons, like red apple, beach strawberry, rosea iceplant, trailing African daisy, and vinca minor, can run over edging and settle on the other side—they can be curtailed by trimming their young runners several times a year.

Ground-Level Dimensions

Whether in a sunny spotlight or shadowy shelter, groundcovers soften a landscape, hide bare soil in all seasons, stabilize soil, and provide fire-retardant buffers. Red apple, beach strawberry, rosea ice plant, trailing African daisy, and vinca minor provide a broad expanse of vibrant color. Hall's honeysuckle adds sweet perfume to summer landscapes and beneficial bees and hummingbirds love its nectar. The berries produced by dwarf coyote bush, kinnikinnick, and shore juniper are not only attractive but are also food sources for wildlife. Kinnikinnick, dwarf coyote bush, rosea ice plant, and shore juniper are handsome groundcovers suitable for many different garden designs, including xeriphytic, Mediterranean, and woodland. Beach strawberry, Japanese honeysuckle, and shore juniper are excellent choices for seashore plantings or rock gardens. While trees allow us to touch the sky and shrubs capture the "middle" world, floral and foliar carpets encourage us to enjoy the ground-level dimensions of our gardens.

A low path can remove the job of hand trimming and make mowing an easier task.

Algerian Ivy

Hedera canariensis

Bloom Period and Seasonal Color
White blossoms appear in late spring or early summer, on adult growth only.

Mature Height × Spread 8–12 in. × spreading

Botanical Pronunciation
HEAD-er-ah KAN-air-ee-en-sis

Zone 11

Pepper trees, peach trees, and Victorian box shade a long slope that parallels a meandering brick path in our backyard. The trees provide a perfect shelter for migrating birds, but covering such a long expanse of slope is a challenge. We finally decided to plant Algerian ivy, commonly used in California, because of its ability to carpet an area quickly and its tolerance for shade. Despite its reputation for swallowing anything motionless, when properly tended it is a beautiful groundcover for shady slopes, underneath trees, and around bushes. It is also an effective climber for silhouetting pillars and walls. Whether stabilizing steep banks, tumbling over ledges, hiding unsightly foundations, or providing a fresh green scent after a spring rain, Algerian ivy is an excellent choice, particularly in frost-free regions.

When, Where, and How to Plant
Plant anytime from flats, spacing 10–14 in. apart in well-drained soil with a pH of 6.5–7.2. These plants prefer semishade or shade, but will tolerate full sun in mild climates.

Growing Tips
Soak deeply after planting. During the first week, water daily; thereafter, water every seven to ten days, adjusting frequency and amount according to weather and growth conditions. Fertilize in fall and early spring with a complete organic granular food. Algerian ivy does not tolerate extended periods of frost or drought, but it can withstand high temperatures and dry winds if there is sufficient moisture.

Advice and Care
Prune after the bloom cycle but just before the fruits ripen in December. Confine growth to specific garden areas by regularly cutting away from walls, trees, or other climbing surfaces and edging the ivy's borders. Since its leaves are toxic and its sap can irritate skin, wear gloves when handling. To remove ivy from its tight grip of "holdfasts" on trees, houses, and walls, snip it off at the base, wait a few weeks for remaining material to die, then remove it. Although its flowers attract bees, and birds enjoy the protected safety of its dense branches, Algerian ivy is also a haven for slugs, snails, and rodents. Control the slimy marauders with an iron phosphate molluscicide, or, if you live in a county that allows decollate snails, colonize these beneficials in your groundcover—they will prey on small and medium-sized brown garden snails without harming your mature plants. Use manual traps for rodents.

Companion Planting and Design
Camellias, clivias, lilies of the Nile, and golden mirror plants are ideal companions.

Try These
Variegated Algerian ivy 'Gloire de Marengo' has dark green leaves with gray-green marbling, preferring cooler, part-shade locations. *Hedera helix*, commonly known as English ivy, has smaller leaves and is less aggressive than Algerian ivy. There are many variegated types. *H. helix* 'Baltica' has white-veined leaves and is considered the hardiest English ivy. *H. colchica*, common name Persian ivy, has large 7 in. × 10 in. leaves.

Beach Strawberry

Fragaria chiloensis

Bloom Period and Seasonal Color
White flowers appear in spring.

Mature Height × Spread 4–6 in. × spreading

Botanical Pronunciation
fra-GAR-ee-ah CHIL-oh-en-sis

Zones 10–11

While walking toward the beach on a summer family vacation just beyond Santa Barbara, we noticed a groundcover that seemed to be flourishing between some otherwise desolate sand dunes. It was a low-growing, evergreen mat of glossy green strawberry leaves that supported a white frosting of blossoms. Once the flowers fell to the ground, deep red fruits resembling elfin strawberries took their place. Although not as sugary as hybrid strawberries, these fruits smell just as sweet and deserve their Latin name *fraga*, which means "sweet smelling." The name *chiloensis* refers to Chile, one of this plant's native habitats (California is another). Whenever we include beach strawberry in a landscape design, it conjures up the sights and aromas of that family seashore vacation as if it were yesterday.

When, Where, and How to Plant
Plant in fall or spring from flats, spacing 8–14 in. apart. It does best in cool, temperate areas and tolerates some foot traffic, but try to plant it where there are no regular pathways. The plants require full sun in coastal regions, partial shade in inland areas. Plant in well-drained, porous soil, pH 6.7–7.2.

Growing Tips
Soak deeply after planting. Water daily during the first week; thereafter, adjust frequency and amount according to weather and growth conditions. This 4–6 in. tall, silky-leafed groundcover needs regular watering. It tolerates some heat and dry wind if there is adequate moisture but cannot withstand extremely high temperatures or extended periods of drought. Fertilize in early spring and early summer with a complete granular organic food or apply a slow-release fertilizer once during the growing season. To treat yellow leaves, use chelated iron.

Advice and Care
If mowed in early spring, this rapidly spreading plant forms a more compact and dense mat. Few serious disease or insect problems affect beach strawberry, except rust and other fungal infestations. Consult your local garden center or county agricultural department for correct identification and appropriate remedies. If planted in your landscape in dappled shade, slugs and snails may also cause problems. Control the slimy marauders with a molluscicide, or, if you live in a county that allows decollate snails, colonize these beneficials in your groundcover—they will prey on small- and medium-sized brown garden snails without harming your mature plants.

Companion Planting and Design
Because beach strawberry spreads by means of offsets, it is excellent for rock gardens, as a substitute for lawns, as attractive groundcovers in woodsy or beachfront areas, in front of shrubs, and around trees. California lilac, Japanese mock orange, and New Zealand Christmas tree make ideal companion plants.

Try These
F. vesca is the woodland strawberry that is native to open woodlands. It has softer textured foliage. Variety *F. v. crinita* is smaller and grows in open rocky areas west of the Cascades.

Dwarf Coyote Bush

Baccharis pilularis 'Twin Peaks'

Bloom Period and Seasonal Color
In summer, pale creamy yellow flowers bloom, the nutlike fruits follow.

Mature Height × Spread 12–24 in. × 6–10 ft.

Botanical Pronunciation
BACK-ahr-is PIL-oo-lahr-is

Zones 8–11

One of our friends lives on a hillside that offers privacy and a spectacular view. The good and bad news is that her priceless view and solitude come with steep terrain and tinder-dry brush. To make matters worse, the groundcovers she planted as erosion controls and fire-retardant buffers were quickly devoured by salad-aficionado rabbits, rodents, and other wildlife. We suggested the dwarf coyote bush, a low, prostrate, woody shrub growing 1–2 ft. tall and spreading to 10 ft. wide. Because its evergreen leaves have sharp, serrated edges and a sticky surface, it is not very palatable for most herbivores, but it is an excellent fire-retardant plant and stabilizes banks with deep roots that go down 4–6 ft.

When, Where, and How to Plant
Plant in early fall or winter where climates are mild or in spring after the last frost in full sun in sandy, well-drained soil with a pH of 6.0–7.0. Plant dwarf coyote bush from 1-gallon containers spacing them 3–6 ft. apart or closer if planting from flats. Be careful about planting too close to each other because they may grow into each other as they compete for light. If this happens, they will become woody underneath. So plant them farther apart for denser foliage. Adaptive to a variety of conditions, dwarf coyote bush is found from high deserts to coastal areas. It tolerates heat, drought, dry winds, and salt spray, but does not withstand foot traffic.

Growing Tips
Soak deeply after planting. Water twice during the first week; thereafter, adjust frequency and amount according to weather and growth conditions. After the first year, dwarf coyote bush should be established enough to survive on moisture from average rainfall, with occasional supplemental watering during summer. It will appreciate an occasional misting to clean its foliage. Fertilize about once a year in the early spring with a complete organic granular food or feed after cutting back.

Advice and Care
As it matures, the dwarf coyote bush tends to get woody and lumpy; prune for shape and appearance before new growth emerges, in late winter or early spring. If it is clipped back to new green growth once a year, light and improved air circulation can reach the lower leaves, encouraging lush growth. Regular pruning prevents any buildup of dead or damaged wood. Few disease or insect problems affect it except for black sooty mold and aphids. If the conditions persist, apply Neem or horticultural-grade canola oil.

Companion Planting and Design
Ideal companion plants are butterfly bush, California sycamore, white birch, and crimson bottlebrush. Plant dwarf coyote bush around entryways, as borders, and along sidewalks.

Try These
'Pigeon Point' stays low and clean at 1 ft. tall and spreading to 12 ft. wide; it's good for large slopes.

Hall's Japanese Honeysuckle

Lonicera japonica 'Halliana'

Bloom Period and Seasonal Color
Small whitish yellow flowers appear spring to fall.

Mature Height × Spread 15–24 in. spreading

Botanical Pronunciation
LAWN-ih-sare-uh ja-PON-ih-kah

Zones 4–11

For a challenging area where grass and other plants have struggled, Hall's Japanese honeysuckle is the perfect choice. It has a rampant growth habit and a reputation for engulfing fences, walls, and sheds, as well as covering banks and slopes in just one or two seasons. It is also an aromatherapy factory. In fact, once you inhale the sweet perfume from the showy, whitish yellow flowers, you may have to stand in line, because it is also a nectar buffet for birds, bees, and butterflies. The most common honeysuckle for gardens, it is a reliable country garden standby and hardy in a wide variety of USDA zones, from 4–11. Best of all, this honeysuckle is not too fussy about growing conditions or soils.

When, Where, and How to Plant
Because of its rapid growth, honeysuckle is an economical selection to cover large areas quickly. Plant from containers or flats in full sun and space about 5 ft. apart or 3 ft. apart for faster coverage. It will grow in partial-sun areas but will not bloom as profusely. It tolerates poor soils but does best in well-draining, evenly moist soil. Once established, it is drought resistant.

Growing Tips
Keep freshly planted honeysuckle moist until signs of new growth emerge, then water regularly every seven to ten days for its first growing season to establish an extensive root system. Once established, extend the watering intervals to about every fourteen days or more depending on weather and growing conditions. Feed with an organic granular general fertilizer for flowers every four to eight weeks during growth and blooming periods or use an application of a controlled-release fertilizer every six to twelve months.

Advice and Care
To control rampant growth, thin out scraggly, leggy, or woody growth cut to the ground before spring growth, and, if necessary, prune again after blooms are spent in the late summer or early autumn. It's resistant to most pests, but if aphids are a persistent problem, wash them off with a strong stream of water or spray with an organic canola-based oil. Also look for ants, because they farm and harvest the aphids' honeydew (sooty mold resulting from aphid excretions). Control the ant population with baits that they take back to their nests.

Companion Planting and Design
Can be used as a shrubby groundcover or vine. It adds delicious fragrance to summer gardens, and its sweet nectar attracts hummingbirds and bees. Hall's Japanese honeysuckle can be planted to cover fences, walls, slopes, and other large areas. It's excellent for cottage gardens, erosion control, fire-retardant buffers, and seacoast plantings.

Try These
Since birds spread the seeds and because it is the most vigorous variety, Hall's Japanese honeysuckle can become invasive. For similar positive qualities, but less aggressive behavior, plant *L. periclymenum*—it looks like its more rambunctious cousin but grows 10–20 ft. tall and behaves much better in a mixed garden setting.

Kinnikinnick

Arctostaphylos uva-ursi 'Point Reyes'

Other Name Manzanita

Bloom Period and Seasonal Color
Small white flowers appear in spring.

Mature Height × Spread 1 ft. × 3–6 ft.

Botanical Pronunciation
ARK-toe-staf-ih-lose OO-vah ur-SEE

Zones 8–11

Native Americans call it kinnikinnick, but its botanical name is of Greek derivation, from *arctos*, meaning "bear," and *staphyle*, meaning "a cluster of grapes." *Uva-ursi* translates as "the bear's grapes." This cumbersome and almost unpronounceable name simply means that bears enjoy noshing on this species' berries and that the berries resemble grapelike clusters. It's a prostrate, low-growing plant with wide-spreading, woody branches covered with inch-long, leather-textured, deep green, teardrop-shaped leaves. In the fall and winter months, its leaves turn a brilliant reddish bronze color, coordinating perfectly with its red berries. By spring, its leaves regain their green luster and provide a lush background for minuscule, urn-shaped white flowers tinged with a blush of pink. After the flowers are spent, grapelike clusters of glossy green berries emerge.

When, Where, and How to Plant
Plant in fall from 4-in. pots to 1-gallon containers, spacing 36–48 in. apart. It needs full sun in well-drained, sandy loam soil. Apply a 2–4-in. layer of mulch in between the plantings to control weeds until the plants become established.

Growing Tips
Soak deeply after planting. Water regularly twice a week, adjusting frequency and amount according to weather and growth. After the first year, where summers are hot, water once a month, but where summers are cool, water less, once or twice during the summer. Fertilize in fall and early spring with cottonseed meal to help acidify the soil. It withstands some foot traffic

and tolerates prevailing winds, salt spray, high temperatures, drought, and below-freezing temperatures.

Advice and Care
Prune only for errant growth and dead wood; to encourage a more compact habit and more branching, pinch back young spring growth. Few serious disease or insect problems affect kinnikinnick if planted in full sun, but the woody growth and low-creeping habit can be a shelter of choice for rodents. If there are no hunting cats in the neighborhood, a manual trap or bait is the next-best remedy.

Companion Planting and Design
A native to California's coastal region, use this prostrate low-grower for water-thrifty and erosion-resistant landscapes on steep slopes, in rock gardens, along seashores, and in natural or informal landscapes. Trees such as magnolias, bronze loquats, and European olives are ideal companions.

Try These
'Vulcan's Peak' has the same growing characteristics as those of 'Point Reyes' but with pink flowers. 'Massachusetts' is very cold hardy. It is 1 ft. tall and spreads up to 10 ft. with clusters of pink 2 in. blooms followed by red berries persisting into winter. 'Woods Red' is ground hugging, only growing to 2–3 in. but spreading 15 ft., with clusters of 2 in. blooms followed by red berries and red foliage in autumn. *A. coloradoensis* has cinnamon-red exfoliating bark and shell-pink blooms in spring, followed by red berries in the fall. It grows 1 ft. tall and spreads to 6 ft. wide in zones 5–8.

Red Apple

Aptenia cordifolia

Bloom Period and Seasonal Color
Pink flowers bloom in spring, summer, and fall.

Mature Height × Spread 8 in. × spreading

Botanical Pronunciation
ap-TEEN-ee-ah KORE-dih-foe-lee-ah

Zones 8–10

A blanket of red apple covers our north slope next to a grizzled, weeping California pepper tree. Only a few inches tall, but spreading to 4 ft., this green-lacquered groundcover bears a profusion of reddish pink flowers. At the bidding of their queen, regiments of industrious bees teem over all the blossoms, intent on harvesting every last drop of precious nectar. Our apricot, cherry, pomegranate, orange, lime, tangerine, and grapefruit trees are nearby, and they benefit from these buzzing pollinators. Whenever we cut back the succulent creeping stems of glossy leaves, we share our cuttings with friends and neighbors—because red apple grows so easily, our original patch has spread throughout the neighborhood. Instead of Johnny Appleseed, perhaps Bruce will become known as the Red Apple man.

When, Where, and How to Plant
Plant from spring to fall from cuttings or flats in full sun in well-draining soil with a pH of 6.0–7.0. Space them 12–24 in. on center. In desert climates, provide afternoon shade. From cuttings, cut 2–4-in. stems and allow to callus over for 24–48 hours. Remove leaves from the lower portion of the cut stems, place cuttings in a commercial cactus mix, and soak deeply after planting. Return to a partially shaded area and keep cuttings moist, but not soggy. Transplant when roots are about 1 in. long. Once established, red apple requires little maintenance. It tolerates dry winds and heat if there is adequate moisture, as well as short periods of drought, but it does not hold up well in temperatures below 40 degrees Fahrenheit.

Growing Tips
Water regularly while establishing, but once mature, decrease intervals to ten to fourteen days. During periods of drought or high temperatures, water more frequently. Fertilize twice, in late winter or early spring and fall, with a complete organic granular food or a slow-release fertilizer once or twice a year.

Advice and Care
Since red apple spreads by way of creeping stems, give them plenty of room to run, or thin them out once every two or three years. Except for slugs and snails, there are few serious disease or insect problems. Control slimy marauders by handpicking and squishing, or by applying a molluscicide. If your county allows decollate snails, colonize these beneficials in your groundcover—they will prey on small- and medium-sized brown garden snails without harming your mature plants.

Companion Planting and Design
In addition to covering small to medium areas, red apple looks wonderful cascading over planters or nestling in rock gardens. Because red apple is such a bee magnet, plant it with fruiting trees or shrubs, such as peaches, plums, nectarines, citrus, avocado, and apricots that benefit from pollination.

Try These
'Variegata' is smaller at 4 in. tall and spreading to 24 in. It has variegated crystalline leaves edged in creamy white and red to bright pink blooms in autumn. Hybrid 'Red Apple' has brighter red flowers.

Rosea Ice Plant

Drosanthemum floribundum

Bloom Period and Seasonal Color
Pink flowers bloom in summer.

Mature Height × Spread 6–10 in. × spreading

Botanical Pronunciation
DROE-san-thih-mum flor-ih-BUN-dum

Zones 10–11

As California's most spectacular carpet-maker, rosea ice plant thrives with a minimum of water and very little attention. We planted rosea ice plant along our barren southern-exposure slope and within a year, not only did it cover the bank, it also provided a vista of intense pink outside our dining room window. From April to June, hot-pink daisylike flowers with sun-yellow faces emerge from fleshy needlelike leaves. These long-blooming evergreen plants reach 6–12 in. high, with 1½ in. blossoms resting on semisucculent foliar pillows. It blankets an unsightly slope, improves our spring-season view, and serves as an erosion control and fire retardant. Wherever the climate is sunny, hot, and dry, the rosea ice plant will show off its dense mat of gray-green leaves and glistening blossoms.

When, Where, and How to Plant
Plant in spring or fall from flats, spacing 12–18 in. apart. Rosea ice plant does best in full sun in a sandy, well-drained soil with a pH of 6.5–7.0. Try cultivating rosea ice plant if you have sandy soil and experience difficulty establishing a groundcover. It will grow where few other plants survive, but plant where there is no foot traffic. Rosea ice plant tolerates short periods of frost, drought, prevailing winds, and high temperatures.

Growing Tips
Soak deeply after planting. Water daily during the first week; thereafter, adjust frequency and amount according to weather and growth conditions. Fertilize in early spring and fall with a complete organic granular food.

Advice and Care
After the plant matures, thin out its woody undergrowth. Propagate by cuttings anytime of the year, except winter, and keep fairly dry until roots develop. Except for slugs and snails, few serious disease or insect problems affect rosea ice plant if it is planted in full sun. Control the slimy marauders by handpicking and squishing them, or by applying an iron phosphate molluscicide. If you live in a county that allows decollate snails, colonize these beneficials in your groundcover—they will prey on small- and medium-sized brown garden snails without harming your mature plants, but do not apply a molluscicide if you're colonizing decollate snails.

Companion Planting and Design
Because rosea ice plant attracts bees, plant it near fruit trees that benefit from pollination, such as sweet oranges, mandarins, and avocados. Other suitable companion plants are California lilac, dwarf coyote bush, and silverberry.

Try These
Drosanthemum striatum grows a bit taller at 18 in. and spreads 30 in. It has frosted foliage, blooming a bit earlier in spring with ¾-in. flowers that cover the foliage. Other plants commonly called ice plants are *Delosperma* species, also drought tolerant with a low spreading habit, growing in zones 5–7. *D.* 'Fire Spinner' has brilliant pink centers surrounded by bright orange petals. *D.* 'Lesotho Pink' is hot pink. 'Lavender Ice' is pale lavender to pink. Yellow-flowering ones are *D.* 'Gold Nugget' and *D. nubigenum*.

Shore Juniper

Juniperus conferta

Bloom Period and Seasonal Color
Shore junipers are conifers that produce cones, providing a summer and fall buffet for birds, squirrels, rabbits, deer, and other wildlife.

Mature Height × Spread 6–12 in. × 3–6 ft.

Botanical Pronunciation
JUNE-ih-per-is KON-fert-ah

Zones 6–11

S hore juniper is a dense horizontal plant that stands about 6–12 in. tall and spreads to 6 ft. wide. Its needlelike leaves are green and prickly to the touch; when wet, they release a pleasing resinous scent. Native to the misty coastal areas of Japan, it has adapted very well to the diverse temperature zones of California. Hardy to -10 degrees Fahrenheit, it is drought and wind resistant and survives high temperatures if there is adequate moisture. Few plants can challenge its ability to survive in the face of adversity, even growing near seaside bluffs, exposed to the ocean wind, misty mornings, and an occasional gull roosting on its branches. The only significant weaknesses are that it cannot tolerate foot traffic and is slow growing.

When, Where, and How to Plant
Plant in spring or fall from 1- or 5-gallon containers. Shore juniper prefers full sun but tolerates partial shade. Plant in well-drained soil that has a pH of 6.5–7.0, and space plants 3–4 ft. apart.

Growing Tips
Soak deeply after planting. Water twice during the first week; thereafter water every seven to ten days until established, then decrease watering frequency to about once a month during hot weather. Fertilize in spring and fall with a complete organic granular food. Until junipers fill in, apply a 2–4-in. layer of mulch between plants to keep soil cool and to control weeds.

Advice and Care
Because it is a slow-growing groundcover, prune selectively for shape or to remove dead or damaged wood. Except for slugs and snails, few serious disease or insect problems affect this hardy groundcover when it is planted in full sun or dappled shade. Control slugs and snails by handpicking and squishing, or by applying an organic iron phosphate molluscicide. Shore juniper is subject to occasional attacks from juniper tip moths and twig girdlers, but they are easily controlled with a systemic insecticide containing imidacloprid.

Companion Planting and Design
Shore juniper is a perfect choice for sunny slopes because it is strong-rooted and thrives on dry conditions caused by water runoff. Use shore juniper as a substitute for lawns, as an erosion control on moderately steep slopes, as plantings in front of trees and shrubs, and in rock and seashore gardens. It is also a popular choice for bonsai. Ideal companion plants are Hollywood twisted juniper, rock rose, and dwarf jade plant.

Try These
'Blue Pacific' is a slow grower to 1 ft. × 7 ft. Cold hardy to zone 5, it has beautiful blue-green needlelike foliage and is more heat tolerant. *Juniperus horizontalis* is low growing, ranging from 1 ft. wide and spreading up to 10 ft. *J.h.* 'Blue Chip' has a low mounding growth and spreading habit with silver-blue foliage. *J.h.* 'Lime-glow' is vase shaped and spreading with bright chartreuse foliage.

Trailing African Daisy

Osteospermum fruticosum

Bloom Period and Seasonal Color
White, pink, purple, yellow, blue, and bicolor flowers intermittently spring to winter.

Mature Height × Spread 1 ft. × spreading

Botanical Pronunciation
OST-ee-oh-sperm-um FRUIT-ih-koe-sum

Zones 10–11

This is another plant species from South Africa that has adapted easily to diverse regions throughout the world. They are commonly seen spreading their oval-shaped light green leaves all along freeway embankments from coastal to inland areas, and along northern to southern byways. They are also used as soil stabilizers for steep slopes, as groundcovers for difficult-to-reach berms and terraces, as salt-tolerant seashore plantings, and as a low-maintenance alternative to a flower garden. From early spring to fall they show off a glistening blanket of white or lilac daisylike flowers that poke through a 12 in. thick evergreen mattress. Although somewhat fire retardant and able to withstand short periods of cold as low as 30–40 degrees Fahrenheit, they cannot withstand foot traffic.

When, Where, and How to Plant
Plant in spring or autumn from flats. Trailing African daisies prefer full sun in moderately rich loam soil, but they tolerate other soils as long as they are well drained, with a pH of 6.5–7.0. Space plants 12–20 in. apart. To save time, use an auger to dig the planting holes.

Growing Tips
Once established, trailing African daisy is drought, wind, and heat tolerant, but supplemental watering in the summer months is best for optimum growth and appearance. Soak deeply after planting. Water daily the first week; thereafter, adjust frequency and amount according to weather and growth conditions. Fertilize in fall and late winter or early spring with a complete organic granular food.

Advice and Care
Prune back trailing stems as they overgrow their borders. If you thin old growth, light penetration and air circulation will be increased, initiating new growth and improving the plant's appearance. If growth becomes too rangy, either cut back or mow during summer. Propagate by cuttings in spring or fall. Except for fungal diseases such as damping-off, and slugs and snails, few serious disease or insect problems affect trailing African daisy when planted in full sun or afternoon shade. Fungal diseases result from too much moisture and poor soil drainage, so water judiciously. Control slugs and snails with a molluscicide or by handpicking and squishing.

Companion Planting and Design
Often taken for granted as "those freeway daisies," they are excellent soil stabilizers for steep slopes, groundcovers for difficult-to-reach terraces, and salt-tolerant seashore plantings. Canna lilies, angel's trumpet, and pride of Madeira are ideal companions.

Try These
'African Queen' has deeper green foliage with rich, purple flowers. 'Whirligig' has distinctive, deeply cut petals with blue, lavender, and white blooms with blue centers. 'Seaside' has white and light pink blooms. 'Burgundy' has purple blooms growing a bit taller than the species. Many hybrid osteospermum are available with varied habits, including mounding forms in the Symphony series that are heat tolerant with blooms that stay open on overcast days and at night.

Vinca

Vinca minor

Other Name Minor periwinkle

Bloom Period and Seasonal Color
Lilac, blue, or white flowers bloom in spring
and summer.

Mature Height × Spread 6 in. × spreading

Botanical Pronunciation VEEN-kah MY-nor

Zones 6–11

On our long strolls through the neighborhood we pass many gentle slopes blanketed with the vinelike groundcover vinca. Its trailing tendrils are covered with small, dark green, oval-shaped leaves that glisten in the sun. In the spring, miniature five-petaled flowers in shades of lilac-blue, blue, or white stretch their faces out of the low, green undergrowth; they put on a less profuse show in the fall. The plant's size and leaves are smaller than those of V. *major*, growing to about 4–6 in. high with long, slender, foliar fingers that spread and root at every knuckled node. Because their tough runners (survives down to -10 degrees Fahrenheit) bind the soil, they also prevent soil erosion, but they prefer little or no foot traffic.

When, Where, and How to Plant
Plant from flats in spring after the last frost. They do best in partial sun in rich, well-drained soil, pH 6.5–7.0, spaced 12–18 in. apart. Vincas will also grow under trees because they can compete against surface tree roots.

Growing Tips
Soak deeply after planting. Water daily during the first week; thereafter, water every seven to ten days adjusting frequency and amount according to weather and growth conditions. The plants tolerate short periods of drought, high temperatures, and dry winds, but produce more flowers and develop more vigorously if adequate moisture is provided. Fertilize in late winter or early spring with a complete organic granular food.

Advice and Care
To revitalize vinca, cut with a rotary mower or prune in the early spring, before new growth emerges, or fall. This encourages dense growth and discourages the development of weeds. Except for aphids, slugs, and snails, few serious disease or insect problems affect this dense groundcover if it is planted in dappled shade. Aphids and other sucking insects are easily controlled by washing them off the foliage with a strong stream of water or applying Neem or horticultural canola oil. Control slugs and snails by handpicking and squishing, or by applying an iron phosphate molluscicide. If you live in a county that allows decollate snails, colonize these beneficials in your groundcover bed.

Companion Planting and Design
Vinca makes lovely green carpets sprinkled with splashes of lilac, blue, or white winking flowers alongside meandering paths, in woodlands, underneath shady trees, cascading over rocks, at the base of hedges, or around shrubs.

Try These
'Alba' has a growth habit similar to that of the species and has white blossoms. 'Bowles' has intense violet-blue blooms that are a bit larger than the species. It is a slower growing type but blooms longer, sporadically sending out flowers from summer into fall. It is good for container growing. 'Atropurpurea' has deep red wine blooms; 'Valley Glow' has moss green foliage with red stems holding small white flowers. A variegated type, 'Sterling Silver Silver' has blue blooms.

LAWNS
FOR CALIFORNIA

L ike our freeways, fast-food chains, shopping malls, and multiplex movie the-
aters, the lawn is an icon of American culture. A common image of a perfect
landscape is an impeccably manicured, velvety lawn, flecked with sunlight
amid the shadows of a couple of trees. Unfortunately, this image of perfection
too often comes at the cost of high maintenance: mowing, watering, aerating, fertilizing, weeding, broadcasting, and spraying for pests and diseases, which raises some
valid economic and environmental concerns.

Go for "Healthy and Attractive," Not "Perfect"

For a lower-maintenance and more environmentally friendly lawn, consider reducing
its size by incorporating more trees, shrubs, flowers, vines, and groundcovers into your
landscape. Also, instead of obsessing over idealized perfection, keep in mind that a
healthy and attractive lawn is achievable when mowed at the correct height, watered
properly, and fertilized correctly.

What Kind of Grass Should I Plant?

To determine the kind of grass you should plant, ask yourself (1) What is the
best match between the grass type and my location? and (2) What do I want
from my lawn? Stolons are specialized stems that grow along the ground; at the
point where leaf nodes touch the ground, new roots develop, creating a dense,
thick lawn. If you want rough-and-tumble areas for children, pets, or heavy foot
traffic, then a stoloniferous grass is a good choice. Bermuda, seashore paspalum,
and 'El Toro' zoysia are stoloniferous, warm-season grasses that grow actively
during the summer months, but go dormant when temperatures dip below
55 degrees Fahrenheit.

On the other hand, cool-season, clumping grasses like perennial rye and fescue
grow most actively during spring and fall, remain green in the winter, and may turn
brown during hot, dry summer weather. Unlike warm-weather species, cool-season
grasses are a much finer-textured turf. Unless they are sown thickly, some bare ground
may be exposed. Perennial rye does well in coastal fog belts and performs adequately
elsewhere, but Bermuda and zoysia grasses do better in the warm regions of California.
Fescue is appropriate for shaded areas, but Bermuda, seashore paspalum, and zoysia
are better selections for drought tolerance.

When trying to decide, don't forget to talk to neighbors whose lawns you admire,
and consult your local nursery and University of California Cooperative Extension
advisor. Every year there are new and improved grass varieties, including the UC Verde®

A well-kept lawn bordered by a flower bed makes an attractive and appealing yard.

buffalograss, that better tolerate heat and drought, require less mowing, and are more disease or insect resistant.

Installation and Care

Whether planting from seed, stolons, or sod, soil preparation is the same (except for plugs, such as UC Verde® buffalograss). Once the soil has been raked and cleared of debris, determine if it is sandy, silty, or clayey (read p. 21 for soil texture information). If you have clay soil, improve its texture to allow easy air and moisture movement by blending in about 20 to 30 percent humus mulch or compost, and mixing the organic material to a depth of 8 to 12 inches.

Once planted, firm the soil by pushing a roller over the surface—this enables seeds to germinate, or ensures that stolons or sod make close contact with the soil. Before rolling seeds, mulch the surface with ¼ inch of topdressing such as humus or topsoil; mulch with ½ inch before rolling stolons. Keep the surface well watered until the seeds, stolons, or sod are established. Do not fertilize until the lawn has been mowed twice. Feed with a granular or liquid lawn fertilizer according to the manufacturer's instructions.

The Rewards of a Well-Kept Lawn

Although lawns pose a number of challenges, with proper forethought and care the rewards will be well worth the effort. A well-kept lawn sustains the summer rites of barbecues, water fights, and lawn parties and remains the best possible surface for bare feet, frolicking children, and pets. Grass is the background beat to the grand rhythm of a complete landscape.

Bermudagrass

Cynodon dactylon

Maintenance Height ¾–1½ in.

Botanical Pronunciation
sin-OH-dahn DAK-tih-lawn

Zones 8–11

Bermudagrass has a reputation for being a troublesome invader of gardens, and to a certain extent it deserves its nickname "devilgrass." Its wiry stems can spread like weeds from one neighbor's yard into another neighbor's flower and vegetable beds. The shoots appear where they are not welcome unless you border your bedding plant areas, but when properly tended, Bermuda is an excellent turfgrass. Think about the sea of grass you admire during a Super Bowl game—it's more than likely the sod is a mixture of hybrid Bermudagrass for toughness, overseeded with rye for color. The grass by itself is gray-green, coarse-textured, and spreads by stolons (specialized above-the-ground stems), rhizomes (specialized underground stems), or seed, forming relatively dense turf.

When, Where, and How to Plant
Plant common Bermuda from seed in late spring or summer, hybrid Bermuda from sod or stolons from March to November. Bermudagrass grows best in full sun and loam soil with a pH of 7.0. Create a sandy loam down 8–12 in. by amending with organic material such as humus mulch or compost. When seeding (1 pound of seed covers approximately 1,000 sq. ft.), sow the seeds, topdress with ⅛ in. of loam soil or humus, and use a water roller to press seeds into the ground. Water immediately after installation and keep moist until germination. When stolonizing, distribute evenly across prepared soil, press into the earth with a water roller, topdress with ¼ in. of loam soil, and keep moist until stolons root. For sod, lay the sections on the prepared soil, press with a water roller, and thoroughly water.

Growing Tips
Once established, it is water thrifty but looks best when watered regularly. Fertilize every other month with a complete organic lawn food during the growth season after it comes out of dormancy and is uniformly green. Do not fertilize in fall or winter months.

Advice and Care
It grows best under extended periods of high summer temperatures and mild winters such as those in the low-elevation (below 3,000 ft.) areas from Mexico's border to the Southern California coast, the north end of Sacramento Valley, and in certain temperate zones surrounding San Francisco Bay. Bermuda lawns need frequent mowing at a maintenance height of ¾–1½ in. to maintain a neat, restrained, and attractive appearance. It has few serious disease or pest infestations, except sod webworm, the larvae of lawn moths that cause brown or bare patches. Introduce parasitic nematodes or spray with spinosad.

Landscape Use
For home landscapes, playing fields, and even animal fodder, Bermuda is ideal as a low-maintenance, warm-season turf. Confine with mow strips or edging to minimize encroachment.

Try These
Seeded types are 'Blackjack' and 'Yukon'. New hybrid 'GN-1' is wear resistant. 'Santa Ana', 'Tifdwarf II', 'Tifgreen 328', and 'Tifway 419' are available in stolons and sod.

Buffalograss

Bouteloua dactyloides

Maintenance Height
2½ in. (4–6 in. for meadow)

Botanical Pronunciation
BOO-the-loo-ah DAK-tih-loy-deez

Zones 5–11

When buffalo roamed North America's prairies, they grazed on tough, drought-resistant grasses. In 2003, the University of California developed a soft, green, fine-bladed buffalograss that is seedless, fast spreading, and very heat tolerant. True to its ancestral roots on the American prairie, buffalograss, with its deep root system (6–8 ft.), thrives on very little water. Once established, its dense and aggressive habit makes it difficult for weeds to invade the turf. It is the grass to use where there are hot, dry conditions, as well as along the California coast. Its low pollen rating of 1 (the American Lung Association recommends using plants that have a pollen rating of 6 or less) makes it a wise choice for a pollen-reduced landscape.

When, Where, and How to Plant
Make sure the area being planted is free of weeds and graded for proper drainage. Use a herbicide, then continue to water until weed and other seeds germinate; continue herbicide applications and watering until everything is eradicated. From March–August, plant from plugs grown in flats (one flat equals forty-one plants) so they are slightly below the soil level (not too deep or they will rot) and not above the soil level (or they will dry out). Space plugs on center between 8–18 in., depending on the desired rapidity of coverage (about two to four warm growing months). Eliminate air pockets by tamping soil around the sides and top of the plant. It does best with 7–8 hours of full sun.

Growing Tips
Water thoroughly after planting and continue regular watering (keep moist at all times, but not soggy)

until established and coverage is complete. Once established, water one to two times weekly in hot, dry areas and weekly or twice a month along the coast during summer. Reduce or withhold irrigation during winter dormancy. Apply slow-release or organic lawn fertilizer according to directions during the active growing season from March–October until full coverage. Thereafter fertilize once every three months during the growth cycle, but stop during winter.

Advice and Care
Weed by hand or use a pre-emergent herbicide, preferably organic. Mow at a height of 2½ in. when plants are 3½ in. high to encourage lateral spreading. Once coverage is complete, water as needed. Stop mowing during winter.

Landscape Use
Use wherever water savings and a sustainable landscape are desired. Its deep root system is ideal for slopes and erosion control or to create a short meadow, replace a water-thirsty lawn, or install a low-pollen lawn for people with allergies.

Try These
UC Verde® buffalograss is vegetatively reproduced (new plants are produced from a portion of an existing, parent plant), and developed specifically for California conditions. It's very disease and insect resistant, and once established thrives on ¼ in. of water per week, reducing water consumption up to 75 percent.

Fescue

Festuca arundinacea × hybrid

Maintenance Height 1½ to 4 in.

Botanical Pronunciation
FES-tuke-ah ah-RUN-dihn-ay-see-ay

Zones 5–11

For those who insist on a landscape with an evergreen blade-grass lawn, fescue fits the bill. It has the good looks of springtime bluegrass but stays green year-round. A bunch-type, cool-season grass, fescue traces its heritage to pasture grasses. It has the widest leaves of most turf species and a rough, somewhat clumping appearance. The surface of each leaf is coarse and ribbed, but underneath it is shiny and smooth. It is a popular grass in Southern and Northern California, but is not recommended for low-desert or high-altitude mountain regions. Somewhat drought-tolerant once established, it adapts moderately well to heat if there is adequate moisture, but it does not withstand temperature extremes. Consult your local garden center for cultivar blends appropriate for your area.

When, Where, and How to Plant

Fescue grows best in full sun or partial shade and well-drained, medium-textured soil with a pH of 5–7.2. To prepare for seeding or sodding, create a sandy loam down to a depth of 8–12 in. by amending with an organic material. Plant from sod anytime of the year during mild weather or from seed in the spring. If seeding, sow densely at 8–12 lbs. per 1,000 sq. ft., as it does not have runners. Sow the seeds, topdress with ⅛ in. of loam soil or humus, and use a water roller to press the seeds into the ground. Water immediately and keep moist until germination. For sod, lay the sections on the prepared soil, press with a water roller, and thoroughly water.

Growing Tips

Once established, whether from seed or sod, adjust watering frequency and amount according to climatic and growth conditions. Fescue needs more water than Bermuda or zoysia. Fertilize every other month during the cool season, fall through spring, with a complete organic lawn fertilizer.

Advice and Care

Mow with a rotary mower set 1½–2½ in. high during the cool season and 3–4 in. high during the warm season. Since fescue is a bunch-type grass, its open areas need to be reseeded. Once established, its vigorous growth discourages weeds. Brown patch (*Rhizoctonia* blight) is a fungus that can expand into a large circular or horseshoe shape; it affects cool-season turfs. Aerate and feed only with an organic fertilizer. If problem persists, apply a fungicide formulated for fescue lawns.

Landscape Use

In addition to home use, fescue is excellent for use in playgrounds, parks, racetracks, as erosion control on banks, and as farm fodder. Do not mix with other lawn seeds or the lawn will look like coarse weeds rather than grass.

Try These

'West Coaster' is dark green and drought, heat, and disease resistant. It thrives in part shade and is available by seed or sod. Sod types are the Medallion series, offered as 'Medallion Dwarf with Bonsai', that has shorter blades and slower growth.

Perennial Ryegrass

Lolium perenne

Maintenance Height 1½–4 in.

Botanical Pronunciation
LOE-lee-um PAIR-en-ee

Zones 9–11

Perennial ryegrass is inexpensive, easy to install, and quick to germinate from seed and to cover a bare expanse with a moderate amount of maintenance. It has a bright green color year-round and forms a soft, open sod, often with a clumping habit. Its blades are heavily veined on the upper surfaces and glossy underneath. Because of the veining and coarse texture it is difficult to mow, but improved varieties are finer textured, darker green, and more resistant to certain diseases. Lacking rhizomes or stolons, it spreads by tillering and does best in coastal fog belts, but grows adequately in other areas. It grows best during periods of cool temperatures and adapts well to sunny or partially shady conditions, but does not tolerate extended periods of heat.

When, Where, and How to Plant
Plant from seed anytime as long as the weather is mild. Perennial ryegrass grows best in full sun (although it withstands partial shade) and loam soil with a pH of 6.5–7.0. To prepare the soil for seeding or sodding, create a sandy loam down 8–12 in. by amending with organic material such as humus mulch or compost. Sow the seeds, topdress with ⅛ in. of loam soil or humus, and use a water roller to press the seeds into the ground. For sod installation, lay the sections on the prepared soil, press with a water roller, and water thoroughly. If seams separate, fill the gaps with horticultural sand and repress with a roller.

Growing Tips
Water immediately after installation and keep moist until seeds germinate. Once established, water twice a week, adjusting to climatic and growth conditions. Fertilize every other month during the cool season, from fall to spring, with a complete organic lawn food.

Advice and Care
Frequent mowing maintains a neat appearance. Mow with a rotary mower set 1½–2½ in. high during the cool season and 3–4 in. high during the warm season. Since perennial ryegrass seldom forms a tightly knit turf, reseed any open or worn areas. With its ability to sprout quickly and its vigorous growth, weeds are kept to a minimum. The most common diseases and pests are rust, controlled with a fungicide formulated for perennial ryegrass, and sod webworm, controlled with spinosad or parasitic nematodes.

Landscape Use
This cool-season grass is excellent in inexpensive seed mixtures and bluegrass mixes. It thrives in coastal fog belts, but adapts to other regions, except extended-heat climates.

Try These
Perennial ryegrass is most often used in new lawns, but improved varieties might be worth the extra money for ease of mowing and ability to withstand a wider range of conditions. Turf Builder™ perennial ryegrass has coated seeds to help protect it from drying out between waterings. 'Private' perennial grass is a new generation of perennial ryegrass that is heat and disease tolerant.

Seashore Paspalum

Paspalum vaginatum 'Adalayd'

Other Name Excaliber

Maintenance Height 1–3 in.

Botanical Pronunciation
PASS-pal-um VAJ-in-ah-tum

Zones 9–11

Our community is crisscrossed with many horse trails, and the sight of our equestrian friends sashaying by provides a tranquil respite from the hustle and bustle of life. Several stables are situated on dusty, highly alkaline river-bottom soils that require a turf rugged enough to retain its density after the wear and tear of galloping horses. The turf of choice is seashore paspalum, commonly known as Adalayd. This perennial, warm-season grass is a loose, medium-low, spreading turf with a somewhat coarse appearance. It has a color similar to that of bluegrass and is exceptionally tolerant of heavy foot, paw, and hoof traffic. Also adaptive to saline water conditions and alkaline soil, its deep roots make it an excellent choice for sandy areas.

When, Where, and How to Plant
Plant from stolons or sod in spring or summer. Seashore paspalum grass grows best in full sun, although it tolerates partial shade, and requires loam soil with a pH of 6.5–7.2. To prepare for stolonizing or sodding, create a sandy loam down 8–12 in. by amending with organic material such as humus mulch or compost. When stolonizing, distribute evenly across the prepared soil, press into the earth with a water roller, topdress with ¼ in. of loam soil, and keep moist until the stolons take root. For sod installation, lay the sections on the prepared soil, press with a water roller, and thoroughly water. It does not tolerate extended periods of subfreezing temperatures goes dormant if temperatures dip below 55 degrees Fahrenheit, and remains dormant for a longer time than Bermuda. But its tolerance of drought, high temperatures, soil and water salinity,

and resistance to foot traffic more than compensate for its small failings.

Growing Tips
Once established, adjust watering frequency and amount to climatic and growth conditions. Although drought resistant, 'Adalayd' looks best when watered about twice a week during the growth cycle. Fertilize lightly every other month, between May and October, with a complete organic lawn food.

Advice and Care
Mow with a front-throw reel mower set to about 1–2 in. In hot inland areas, mow the lawn at a height of 2–3 in. to avoid scalping and browning of stems and to conserve water. Seashore paspalum has a few drawbacks. Relatively disease resistant, it is occasionally susceptible to brown patch (controlled by a fungicide formulated for 'Adalayd') and for sod webworm (dethatch the lawn and spray with spinosad).

Landscape Use
Ideal for heavy foot traffic, its sea spray and alkaline soil tolerance and deep roots are good for sandy areas along the seashore, rugged coastal sites, dog runs, and pockets of light shade.

Try These
'Seaspray' paspalum is one of the few types offered as seed. It is slow to germinate, but maintains a consistent bright green color, creating a medium-textured lawn.

Zoysia Grass

Zoysia japonica 'El Toro'

Maintenance Height ½–1 in.

Botanical Pronunciation
ZOY-see-ah ja-PAWN-ih-kah

Zones 9–11

For gardeners who want a picture-perfect lawn and don't mind waiting a few seasons to get what they want, 'El Toro' zoysia grass is uniformly dense and erect, forming a verdant carpet. 'El Toro' spreads through rhizomes and stolons. It does well in much of Southern California and the San Joaquin Valley, where the days are warm and the nights remain mild. It needs less fertilizer, water, and mowing than cool-season turf. With stiff stems and fine, tight texture, this grass provides a rebounding resiliency to heavy foot traffic, has a low thatch, displays its spring green-up earlier, offers better color, and discourages weed invasions. During winter or whenever temperatures dip below 55 degrees Fahrenheit, zoysia goes dormant, turning a golden brown color until spring.

When, Where, and How to Plant
Plant from stolon, sod, or plugs in spring or summer. Zoysia grows best in full sun and loam soil with a pH of 6.5–7.0. To prepare the soil for stolonizing, sodding, or plugging, create a sandy loam down 8–12 in. by amending with organic material. When stolonizing, distribute the stolons evenly across the prepared soil, press them into the earth with a water roller, top-dress with ¼ in. of loam soil, and keep moist until they take root. For sod installation, lay the sections on the prepared soil, press with a water roller, and water thoroughly. Depending on how fast you want plugs to fill in, space them 4–6 in. on center, press in with a water roller, and water thoroughly.

Growing Tips
Water frequently until roots are established, then water once a week, adjusting watering frequency and amount according to climatic and growth conditions. Water the grass when blades begin to lose their bright green shine and start to turn a dull blue-gray. If water runs off, stop until the soil absorbs the excess moisture, then turn on the water again. Fertilize during the growing season with a complete organic lawn food.

Advice and Care
Zoysia needs frequent mowing to maintain a neat, attractive appearance and to control weeds until establishment. Mow with a rotary mower set ½–1 in. high. If you broadcast stolons at ¾ bushel per 50 sq. ft. in May, you can establish a zoysia lawn in three to six months. Control rust with a horticultural canola-based oil or a fungicide formulated for zoysia lawns. Billbugs, white grubs, sod webworms, and mole crickets can become pests, but lawn insecticides containing imidacloprid should remedy an infestation before it causes extensive damage.

Landscape Use
In addition to home landscapes, zoysia is ideal for golf courses, playgrounds, and parks.

Try These
Zoysia tenuifolia, commonly known as Korean grass, has a fibrous, shallow root system and is very slow growing—use it in a small areas such as a rock garden combined with ornamental shrubs, succulents, and palms.

PALMS
FOR CALIFORNIA

The lure of lush tropical landscapes in Hawaii, Bali, and other exotic locales is the stuff dreams are made of, and universally appealing for those of us who do not live in such places. This is because most the world's 2,800 palm species are found in tropical and subtropical regions, although their natural range is from as far north as Southern Europe to as far south as the North Island of New Zealand.

Princes in the Landscape

Palms are regarded as the "princes" of plants. Carl Linnaeus, noted Swedish botanist and founder of the modern binominal system of nomenclature, labeled them "Principes." Fortunately for California there are many areas that are ideal for the culture of the prince of plants. Rather than describe all palm species, this chapter will feature those that behave themselves in average home landscapes with temperate climates.

Distinctive Features of Palms

Palms are fibrous monocotyledons, members of the Palmae family of plants, which makes their appearance easily recognizable.

Superficially these plants may all seem to look alike, because many have clustering or clumping trunks with stalks of long evergreen fronds. On closer inspection you can see the differences. Palms can be categorized according to frond shape: the fan-frond, also called palmate (like the lady palm), and the feather-frond, or pinnate (like the pygmy date). Palmate fronds are round or semicircular in outline, while pinnate fronds are linear or oblong with segments arranged like the pattern of a feather. Although sagos are a unique group of plants that form seed-bearing cones rather than flowers, they also have evergreen, pinnate fronds.

Despite the fact that palms are usually used in garden designs for their form rather than color, there are many palms with bright fruits, such as the stranded clusters of ruby-red jewels on the fishtail palm and the brownish orange fruits of the Mediterranean fan palm.

Palms are monocots, which means they lack a main taproot. Instead, palms grow fibrous, adventitious roots from the trunk bases. They do not produce successive layers of growth in their trunks or stem; their trunks enlarge over time because their tissues expand, not because of new wood development. This is why injuries to the trunk should be avoided—such damage is permanent.

Care for Your Palms

Since palms are primarily surface feeders, they need regular supplies of moisture and soil nutrients, although some, like the Mediterranean fan palm, are drought resistant. All palms do well on organic palm food.

Palms lack a deep root system, allowing them to be moved relatively easily and transplanted successfully as long as a planting hole has been prepared in advance. Spring or summer months are the best time for transplanting since root growth is highest during those months.

Once a palm is established, use a pruning saw to carefully cut off dead or damaged leaf stalks; make sure the cuts are flush with the trunk. Mulching adds nutrients and improves the soil's porosity and water infiltrations. Lawns, groundcovers, and weeds should be kept away from palm trunks, because they compete for water and nutrients and increase the danger of damage from mowers and weed whackers.

Tropical Magic for the Landscape

Smaller palms such as the fishtail, the Mediterranean fan, and the pygmy date normally grow only 10–25 ft. tall; these are ideally suited for average-sized yards. Others, such as the lady palm, foxtail palm, and sago palm, are also excellent on the patio in containers or near the house. Palms have great value for use near swimming pools or other bodies of water, because they rarely drop fronds or other litter. Their graceful foliage is beautiful when silhouetted by back lighting. Palms play a variety of roles in the landscape that few other plants can duplicate. Whether indoors or out, sun or shade, in coastal or interior areas, there are species to fill many landscape situations. All palms cast a spell of tropical magic.

Sago palms form seed-bearing cones.

Fishtail Palm

Caryota mitis

Mature Height × Spread
10–20 ft. tall × clumping

Botanical Pronunciation
KARE-ee-oh-tah MY-tis

Zones 10–11

Multitrunked fishtail palms, with their thicket of sucker growths at their bases, have a lush, full appearance. Eight-ft.-long bipinnate fronds are further divided into distinctive wedge-shaped and feathered leaflets. The glossy dark green fronds provide a verdant canvas against which long strands of silvery green seeds hang in clusters of fifty or more beaded strings, like necklaces. Its seeds ripen into stunning ruby-red marbles throughout the year. Although they are monocarpic palms, meaning they die after fruiting, this takes quite a long time, about thirty years. Flowering panicles first appear near the top of the palm and open successively downward. When the last set of fruit matures, the entire stem dies, but not before being replaced by a new basal sucker.

When, Where, and How to Plant
Plant in spring from containers; plant singly or group in clusters of three to five. Fishtail palms require partial shade outdoors and medium to high light levels indoors. Plant in rich, well-drained soil with a pH of 6.0–6.5. Construct a watering basin twice the diameter of the original container and mulch with 2 in. of humus or compost, keeping away from the trunks. Fishtail palms need sheltered, humid environments and dislike drought, dust, or dry winds. They prefer warm weather with adequate moisture but are tolerant of cold temperatures down to 30 degrees Fahrenheit for short periods of time.

Growing Tips
Immediately after planting, soak deeply and thoroughly. Water three times the first week; thereafter adjust watering frequency and amount according to weather and growth conditions. Fertilize every other month during the growth cycle, spring through summer, with a complete organic palm food.

Advice and Care
Unless the fronds are thinned, the continual growth of suckers will cause the development of dense foliage from the tops to the bottoms of the clumps. Either form—thinned or left natural—is stunning, but the leaf outlines do not stand out unless some fronds are removed. Wear protective gloves and clothing when handling the fruit; the fibrous flesh contains caustic crystals of calcium oxalate that will irritate skin and mucous membranes. And never eat the fruit unless you have the cast-iron stomach of a Cassowary bird, one of the few creatures whose digestive systems are uniquely adapted to the caustic fruit. Fishtail palms attract few diseases or pests, except leaf spots caused by fungus and infestations of spider mites and scale. Apply a fungicide formulated for palms; for insect control, use horticultural canola or Neem oil or a systemic insecticide.

Companion Planting and Design
Distinctive, uneven leaves make a graceful focal plant outdoors or a dramatic container for tall, indoor spaces.

Try These
Other species such as *C. gigas* and *C. urens* grow from 40–80 ft. tall, making them impractical for most home gardens.

Foxtail Palm

Wodyetia bifurcata

Mature Height × Spread 15–30 ft × 15 ft.

Botanical Pronunciation
WODE-ee-she-uh BY-fur-kot-ah

Zones 9–11

As this story illustrates, there are many plants still waiting to be discovered throughout the world. An Aboriginal bushman named Wodyeti was the last of his tribe who had a vast knowledge of palms and their habitat in remote areas of Queensland, Australia. In 1978 he shared with botanists his discovery of a slender-trunked palm crowned with unusual bushy fronds; appropriately, they named it after him. Foxtail palm is the common name due to the resemblance of its spectacular fluffy fronds to the tail of a fox. As a solitary palm it is stunning, with a canopy of green as well as large, orange-red, oval-shaped (inedible) fruits that are the size of duck eggs. Once rare, foxtails are available at most California garden centers.

When, Where, and How to Plant

Although the foxtail palm will grow in partial shade, it prefers bright sunlight. Dig a hole the same depth as its original container and about twice its diameter. Amend the backfilled soil with humus or compost to create a sandy loam planting medium. Carefully remove the palm from its container without damaging its roots, and plant so that the base of the trunk is just above the soil surface. Tamp the surface to collapse air pockets, and water thoroughly. To keep indoors, plant in a commercial cactus mix, and place the pot in a brightly lit area.

Growing Tips

Once established, water regularly and deeply about every two weeks in the summer, adjusting for weather and growth conditions; decrease to once every four to six weeks during winter. Allow soil to dry out a bit before watering again. For indoor pots, water when the soil feels dry to the touch and never allow the pot to stand in water. Once or twice a year, fertilize with an organic or a controlled-release granular food for palms that is formulated with additional micronutrients such as magnesium and iron. Water the fertilizer in; do not dig into the soil, because this can damage surface roots. Apply a 2–3 in. layer of mulch extending out to the drip line, keeping it 2–4 in. away from the trunk, to hold moisture in the soil and protect the surface roots.

Advice and Care

Prune dead, brown fronds if desired for appearance, but do not cut the trunk. Nicks and cuts are permanent and cause insect or disease problems. For persistent mealybugs, aphids, or scale, wash off with a strong stream of water or spray with a canola-based horticultural oil. Root rot is often the result of soggy soil. Make sure the soil drains well and do not overwater.

Companion Planting and Design

Foxtail palms are handsome specimens in containers or planted in the ground as a focal point by swimming pools, mixed amid other evergreens, or located along a sidewalk or driveway.

Try These

There are no other species except *Wodyetia bifurcata*.

Lady Palm

Rhapis excelsa

Mature Height × Spread 5–8 ft. tall (clumping)

Botanical Pronunciation
RAP-is EX-sell-sah

Zones 9–11

Rhapis excelsa, commonly called lady palm, has a small stature, graceful appearance, and elegant silhouette that creates a soothing rainforest atmosphere. These are multistemmed dwarf fan palms that form dense thickets of light to rich green fronds from the base of each plant. With age, tan fibers weaving around the 5–8 ft. trunks become a dark charcoal color with beautiful texture. The stiff, glossy leaves are deeply divided and have five to eight widespread segments that resemble fingers on a hand. In summer, tiny spikes of creamy flowers and greenish yellow blossoms appear on separate male and female plants near the tops of their canes and among their lower leaves; when pollinated, they form clusters of small reddish berries, each berry containing a single seed.

When, Where, and How to Plant
Plant lady palms in spring or summer. Place them individually or in clusters of three, spaced 2–3 ft. apart. Although tolerant of short bouts of freezing temperatures and full sun, they prefer partial shade and temperate areas protected from prevailing winds and intense heat. Plant in well-drained loam soil with a pH of 6.5–7.0. Construct a watering basin twice the diameter of the combined rootballs (three times the diameter of the rootball if planted individually), and mulch with 2 in. of humus or compost. For additional information, see Planting Techniques, p. 20.

Growing Tips
Soak thoroughly after planting and three times the first week. Since lady palms are not drought tolerant, they require regular watering every seven to ten days, adjusting frequency and amount according to weather and growth conditions. Every other month during the growth cycle, fertilize with a complete organic granular palm food.

Advice and Care
Prune for shape and appearance by thinning out some of the crowded trunks. Remove dead or damaged fronds. Since seedling plants grow very slowly, division by clumps is the more popular method of propagation. Lady palm's slow growth is an advantage when container grown, because they can remain in the same pots for years without replanting. They attact few outdoor diseases or pests, but indoors they are susceptible to mealybugs and spider mites. Treat with Neem or canola-based horticultural oil, or a systemic insecticide formulated for palms.

Companion Planting and Design
Plant beneath the protective shade of taller trees. Clivia lilies, English ivy, and variegated cast-iron plant make excellent companion plants. The small stature and graceful appearance of lady palms make them ideal for foundation plantings, as focal points for small gardens, and in containers for patios or decks. For formal or exotic cutflower arrangements, use some of their stems as dramatic greenery accents. They can also be grown indoors if they get medium to bright light.

Try These
R. humilis, rattan palm, grows to 18 ft. × 12 ft., making a great houseplant.

Mediterranean Fan Palm

Chamaerops humilis

Mature Height × Spread 8–15 ft. (clumping)

Botanical Pronunciation
KAM-er-ops HUM-ih-lis

Zones 9–11

Mediterranean fan palm is a low-growing clustering palm with dark, shaggy fibers covering gracefully curved trunks. The stiff olive green or blue-gray fronds are deeply divided like the ribs of a fan, 18 in. long, segmented, and split at the top. They are dioecious, meaning there are male and female plants and both are needed to pollinate. The lightly perfumed male flowers are yellow and grow in thick, small panicles, while the female flowers are green, sparse, and stubby, and, when pollinated, produce shiny, brownish orange fruits that are treats for wildlife. Best suited to temperate regions, they are also one of the hardiest palms, enduring temperatures down to 15 degrees Fahrenheit, as well as drought, hot sun (if adequate moisture is provided), wind, and salt spray.

When, Where, and How to Plant

Plant from spring to fall from containers, spacing them 15–20 ft. apart. Mediterranean fan palms require rich, well-drained soil with a pH of 6.5–7.0. Build a watering basin three times the diameter of the rootball and mulch with 2 in. of humus or compost. For more information, see Planting Techniques, p. 20.

Growing Tips

Immediately after planting, soak deeply and thoroughly. Water three times the first week; thereafter water regularly and after one to two years, wait until slightly dried before watering again. Fertilize every other month, March through October, with a complete organic granular palm food.

Advice and Care

Remove the oldest fronds to expose the trunk structure and maintain a tidy appearance. Be cautious when handling Mediterranean fan palms, because they are armed with very sharp straight or hooked spines along their frond stalks. Propagate by seed or division. These slow-growing palms take many years to reach a respectable size. Few diseases or pests seriously affect Mediterranean fan palms, with the exceptions of leaf spots caused by fungus and infestations of spider mites and scale. Consult your local University of California Cooperative Extension advisor for recommendations of fungicides appropriate for your area. Control spider mites and mealybugs with a Neem or canola-based horticultural oil.

Companion Planting and Design

Plant these palms near pools, by the seashore, or in containers. Ideal companion plants are pink Indian hawthorn, golden mirror plant, and bougainvilleas.

Try These

C. h. argentea has silver-blue foliage with bright yellow blooms, maturing at 8–12 ft × 10–15 ft. It grows in zones 8–11 in full sun. *C. h.* 'Vulcano' is a compact form of the European fan palm, discovered in Sicily. It has short, stiff foliage with a compact growth to 6 ft. at maturity. Growing in zones 7–10, it likes full sun to part shade. *C. excelsa*, commonly known as hemp palm (syn. *Trachycarpus fortunei*), has a solitary, straight trunk, maturing at 10–15 ft. × 3–6 ft. with showy yellow flowers. The hemp palm grows well in zones 7–11 and will survive with protection in zones 5–6.

Pygmy Date Palm

Phoenix roebelenii

Mature Height × Spread
4–10 ft. tall × single trunked

Botanical Pronunciation
FEE-niks ROE-bel-in-ee

Zones 9–11

Along a bird sanctuary pool at the Tropical Rainforest Habitat in Australia is a diminutive stand of *P. roebelenii*, graceful solitary-trunked palms ranging in height from 6–10 ft. These are the smallest of the *Phoenix* palms, but we think they are the most elegant. With slender trunks and compactly mounded crowns of arching gossamer leaves, we wonder why this palm was burdened with the mundane name "pygmy date palm." The 4-ft. pastel green leaves are lightweight and soft and, accompanied by evenly spaced darker green leaflets that glisten in the sunshine. Small yellow flowers grow in clusters, followed by black fruits. Established pygmy date palms withstand short periods of drought, wind, and cold temperatures down to freezing, and tolerate heat with adequate moisture.

When, Where, and How to Plant
Plant in spring or summer from 5- or 15-gallon or specimen-sized containers; plant individually or in groups of three, spaced 2 ft. apart. Pygmy date palms look their best when in full sun or partial shade along coastal areas and complete shade in inland regions. They prefer rich, well-drained soil with a pH of 6.0–7.0. Build a watering basin twice the diameter of the combined rootballs if planting in a group, or three times the diameter of the rootball if planted individually. Mulch with 2 in. of humus or compost.

Growing Tips
Immediately after planting, soak deeply and thoroughly. Water three times the first week; thereafter water once every two weeks in summer, adjusting the frequency and amount according to weather and growth conditions and every four to six weeks in winter. Fertilize every other month from March to October with a complete organic granular palm food.

Advice and Care
Prune only to remove dead fronds. Pygmy date palms are dioecious and need both male and female plants for pollination and seed production. The small, black, egg-shaped fruits are edible, but not very palatable since they only have very thin layers of flesh. They contract few diseases, but they're susceptible to occasional infestations of spider mites and mealybugs. For insect control, use Neem oil or horticultural canola oil, following label instructions.

Companion Planting and Design
These palms are beautiful as night-lit silhouettes in smaller gardens, as foundation plantings, or beside a swimming pool. Ideal companions are sago palms, Japanese mock orange, and shore junipers. In our landscape designs, we use them in groupings of two or three as a focal silhouette. Since they mind their manners in small spaces, they make ideal container plants on a patio or deck, or along a walkway, where their lacy form and elegant detail can be fully appreciated. If you have a bright spot with sufficient humidity, they also grow indoors.

Try These
P. canariensis, Canary Island date palm, is slow growing to a giant 60 ft. tall with a 50-ft. crown, but can be kept manageable in a pot for years.

Sago Palm

Cycas revoluta

Mature Height × Spread 4–6 ft. tall (clumping)

Botanical Pronunciation
SY-kas reh-voe-LOO-tah

Zones 9–11

Decades ago our sago palms were tiny pups, growing from the bases of two stately sagos in the atrium garden of our parents' home. Now that the pups have matured into 4-ft. adults, we anxiously await to see which will become the male pollen-bearing "cone-heads" and which will become the female seed-bearing "dome-heads." Since they live for a hundred years or more, perhaps our grandchildren will want to inherit some of them, as a living tie to us and to my parents. Young sago palms are single-trunked. They branch into multiple trunks with age. Feathery pinnate fronds are bluish green when immature; once mature, they crown the fibrous brown trunk with 4-ft. rich, dark green fronds. A single plant may have over a hundred stiff, decorative leaves.

When, Where, and How to Plant
Plant anytime of the year in mild climate areas or in spring after the last frost from 1-, 5-, or 15-gallon or specimen-size containers and use them singly or in groups of three. Sago palms require a deep, sandy, well-draining soil with a pH of 6.5–7.0. Construct a watering basin three times the diameter of the original container and mulch with 2 in. of humus or compost. Refer to Planting Techniques on p. 20 for more information. It does well in full sun or partial shade. Sago palms tolerate high temperatures, drought, wind, and cold weather down to freezing.

Growing Tips
Immediately after planting, soak deeply and thoroughly, and water two to three times the first week. Once established, allow the soil to dry out slightly before watering again, about once every two weeks during the summer and less during wet or rainy weather. Fertilize every other month during the growth cycle from spring to summer with a complete granular organic palm food.

Advice and Care
Remove dead or damaged fronds as needed. Propagate from seed or detached offsets. When the female plant is pollinated, red egg-shaped seeds will mature in a nest of furry, brown, twisted fronds. When handling the seeds use protective gloves, because the seeds may irritate the skin. There are few diseases or pests, with the exceptions of iron chlorosis and infestations of mealybugs and brown soft scale. Apply chelated iron twice a year to correct iron deficiency. For insect control, use Neem or horticultural canola oil, adhering to label directions. Avoid overhead watering to prevent rot problems.

Companion Planting and Design
Prized by collectors and landscape contractors, sago palms' handsome but slow-growing habit makes them a valuable addition to Japanese-style landscapes, tropical gardens, courtyards, plazas, and containers for porch or patio. Their slow growth makes them a common specimen plant for bonsai plantings and for indoor pots. Ideal companion plants are rock cotoneaster, dwarf jade plant, and heavenly bamboo.

Try These
S. circinalis is known as the queen sago. It grows to 20 ft. tall with 8-ft.-long drooping fronds.

PERENNIALS

FOR CALIFORNIA

Perennials are flowering or foliage plants with life spans of more than two years; they are technically herbaceous, since they lack the woody stems and branches characteristic of shrubs and trees. Although some perennials will last only a few years, others survive for decades. Some have top growth that dies back every winter, but their roots live from year to year and send up new shoots each spring.

Lavender, geranium, erigeron daisy, and Marguerite daisy grace the front entrance of this home.

Perennials give color and texture to gardens in shady spots, slopes, and meadows, and take center stage in casual cottage landscapes. Their abundant foliage and flowers bursting forth from intimate or expansive spaces produce a glorious potpourri of scents, textures, and colors.

Good Marriages Between Plants

Before planting, determine if your perennial selections are compatible with one another and with the site, considering light, soil, and water needs. Study the bloom times of perennials in your neighborhood and select plants that flower together, as well as those that flower when nothing else is in bloom. Shasta daisies and delphiniums bloom from late spring through the end of summer, while daylilies blossom early, midseason, or late depending on the variety, and candytuft bloom throughout the year in warm-winter regions. Some, such as delphiniums, rebloom after their first flush of flowers are cut back and before they set seed. Clivia lilies and impatiens are perfect for shaded nooks and crannies under trees or shrubs, but if you need heat lovers and drought-tolerant types, gerbera daisies are a better choice.

Think about foliage as well as flowers, and mix bold-leaved, sun-loving ivy geraniums and heliotrope with finely textured Marguerite daisies or hellebores and leopard plants in shady nooks. When designing a perennial border, start with tall, long-lived specimens such as delphinium, foxglove, and daylilies, and stand them in the back. To support their taller neighbors and peek over their tinier friends, lily of the Nile and Shasta daisies are great fillers for the middle. Toward the front, plant ground huggers like candytuft, ivy geraniums, or impatiens. Near ponds, a tropical stand of thirsty canna lilies can effectively show off their lush, bold foliage and burgeoning flowers of eye-popping reds, oranges, yellows, and pinks.

In most mild-winter western regions, October is the best time to plant perennials or to divide or take cuttings from established ones. Planting or propagating in autumn gives perennials a head start over those that are planted in the spring.

Heirlooms and Cut Flowers

Part of the joy of gardening is being able to share your plants with others and, in turn, to receive plants from family and friends. Our Asakawa parents gave us cuttings from an ivy geranium variety called 'Rouletta', with magnificent semidouble white-and-magenta-striped clusters of blooms. We think of them every time we pass its trailing foliage and blossoms. Gifts of plants from people who mean so much give a whole new meaning to the word "heirloom."

A drift of daisies, lilies, or chrysanthemums is not only a feast for our eyes, but the petals are perfect cushions for fluttering butterflies, whirring hummingbirds, and buzzing bees. Nectar- and berry-rich perennials are important food sources for your garden wildlife. Whether the plants are flowering or fruiting, we enjoy cutting them to use in colorful mixed bunches. From the ornate to the minimal, from hot, intense splashes of yellows, reds, oranges, magentas, and rusts to cool whites, delicate lavenders, pinks, salmons, and creams, perennials make excellent cutflower arrangements suitable for any décor.

The Spice of Life

Perennials prove that "variety is the spice of life." They add color and texture for mass planting displays in meadow and woodland gardens, provide punctuation points for beds and borders, brighten pond and rock landscapes, nourish neighborhood wildlife, and beckon the outdoors in with fresh-flower arrangements. Whether you find them while treasure hunting at local nurseries or propagate them from seed, division, or cuttings, perennials serve as precious threads in your garden tapestry.

Blue Marguerite Daisy

Felicia amelloides

Bloom Period and Seasonal Color
Blue flowers bloom in spring, summer, and fall.

Mature Height × Spread 1½–3 ft. × 4–5 ft.

Botanical Pronunciation
feh-LEASH-ee-ah a-meh-LOI-deez

Zones 9–11

While on a winding bus trip toward the Cape of Good Hope in South Africa, we saw blue Marguerite daisies the color of the sky peeking over wind-eroded boulders perching on steep cliffs overlooking the converging Indian and Atlantic Oceans. These fast-growing perennials have elliptical-shaped, matte green foliage and single, blue-petaled, yellow-centered flowers balancing on extended wiry stems. Flowering is almost continuous, depending on the climate, but occurs most often during early summer through fall. These plants require warm weather and frost-free areas; once established, they are drought and wind tolerant. To enhance appearance and floral display, however, make sure an even amount of soil moisture is available. In mass plantings they are spectacular; they also make subtle container plants for patios and decks.

When, Where, and How to Plant
Plant in spring after the threat of frost has passed, from 4-in. pots or 1-gallon containers, spacing 3 ft. apart. *F. amelloides* prefers full sun and well-drained soil with a pH of 6.7–7.0. Construct a watering basin 3 ft. in diameter and mulch with 1 in. of organic material.

Growing Tips
Soak deeply after planting. Water three times the first week; thereafter adjust frequency and amount to climatic and growth conditions. Keep in mind that Marguerites prefer occasional deep watering to frequent shallow watering, and are drought tolerant once established. Fertilize in early spring with a complete organic granular food.

Advice and Care
Following their bloom cycle, prune for shape, to lace out dense growth, and to maximize the next flowering cycle. Pinch the plant back when it is only a few inches high by nipping off the tip of the main stem. Thereafter, pinch back the lateral growths a couple of times to develop a bushier, multibranched plant. The bushier the plant and the more abundant the lateral growth, the more profuse the production of flower buds. Also deadhead the flowers, because they don't fall off naturally. Control snails and slugs with iron phosphate or "pick-and-squish." Aphids can be controlled with horticultural canola or Neem oil.

Companion Planting and Design
Best used in informal gardens such as mixed borders, edges of lawns, or rock gardens. It is spectacular also in mass plantings as well as lovely companions to pink Indian hawthorn, English ivy, and prostrate natal plum.

Try These
Felicia amelloides 'Santa Anita' has flowers much larger than those of the species. *F. amelloides* 'Alba' has white flowers. 'Variegata' has cream/green variegated foliage, growing to 3 ft. × 3 ft., hardy to 20 degrees Fahrenheit. *F. bergeriana*, kingfisher daisy, is an annual that forms a dense, gray-green mat just 4 in. × 12 in. Grow from seed in spring for summer-long bright blue blooms. *F. fruticosa*, shrub aster, is evergreen to 4 ft. × 3 ft. with 1-in. lavender flowers.

Candytuft

Iberis sempervirens

Bloom Period and Seasonal Color
White flowers bloom in spring and summer.

Mature Height × Spread 6–18 in. × 10–12 in.

Botanical Pronunciation
EYE-ber-is SEM-per-vi-rens

Zones 5–11

We like to use candytuft as a rock garden accent because they create cushioned pockets of vegetation between the weathered stones. Candytuft is also effective when planted *en masse* as a foreground plant. During the warmth of spring and summer, these compact evergreens are smothered with large, abundant, four-petaled, white flowers arranged in multiple clusters of delicately scented blooms. In fact, that is the derivation for its common name, for their mounds of sweetly fragrant blossoms. *Iberis* is of Greek derivation, from Iberia, the ancient name for Spain, where several species grow wild. The white flowers contrast beautifully with the dark green foliage of most other plants. Used as cut flowers, they will last for several days as long as they are in a cool room.

When, Where, and How to Plant
Since growth is so slow, plant in the spring or summer from pony packs, color packs, or 4-in. or 1-gallon containers, spacing 8–12 in. apart. Plant in hot, sunny locations, preferably facing southward. They prefer well-drained soil with a pH of 6.6–7.1. Construct a watering basin 1 ft. in diameter and mulch with ½ in. of organic material such as compost or humus.

Growing Tips
Soak deeply after planting. Keep in mind that these plants don't appreciate too much moisture. During the first week, water every day; thereafter adjust watering frequency and amount according to weather and growth conditions. During the growing season, feed candytuft monthly with a water-soluble fertilizer such as liquid kelp or a slow-release fertilizer.

Advice and Care
Although candytuft isn't bothered by disease, pests, heat, and long periods of drought, it doesn't like too much shade, severe cold, or frigid winds. To promote a tidy, compact appearance, prune back the foliage by a third immediately after the flowers are spent. Be diligent about removing the dead flower heads and you will be rewarded with a continuous and abundant supply of blooms.

Companion Planting and Design
These low, semiwoody, densely spreading mounds are terrific as edgings for raised beds, borders, pathways, and terrace margins and as groundcover atop retaining walls, where they can meander shyly over the sides. We cut the flowers just as they are opening in the early morning and arrange them with bulb flowers such as grape hyacinth and tulips.

Try These
'Absolutely Amethyst' is a registered hybrid, touted as the first nonwhite candytuft available. It flowers about six weeks later than the species, is drought tolerant, and has gorgeous purple/amethyst blooms. Deer-resistant 'Masterpiece' has enormous clusters of 3-in. white flowers with pastel pink centers that bloom from spring to fall. 'Little Gem' is 4–6 in. tall; 'Snowflake' has larger blooms and clusters, putting on a big show in spring. *I. gibraltarica* is a perennial with light pink or purplish flowers.

Chrysanthemum

Chrysanthemum × grandiflorum

Bloom Period and Seasonal Color
Yellow, orange, white, purple, pink, red, green, bronze, and multicolored blooms in late summer to fall.

Mature Height × Spread 2–8 ft. × 2–8 ft.

Botanical Pronunciation
Krih-ZAN-thuh-mum ex gran-dih-FLORE-um

Zones 6–10

For more than two thousand years, chrysanthemums have been prized and cultivated throughout Asia. In Japan, only the emperor and his family are allowed to use the "Flower of Happiness" as their family crest. The early-flowering button and carpet mums sold at home centers today are but ephemeral reminders of the dazzling array of shapes and sizes grown and exhibited during Victorian times. Fortunately there is a resurgence of interest at flower shows for football mums, exotic spiders, striking Fujis, and flowering cascades with a rainbow of unusual and vibrant colors. In California, the natural bloom period is during the cooler season from late October to early November, long after the more pedestrian blossoms of button and carpet mum wannabes have wilted in late summer's heat.

When, Where, and How to Plant
Plant from containers in early spring, provide full sun, and well-draining, humus-amended soil. Where temperatures are hot, provide afternoon shade. Apply a 2–4-in. layer of humus mulch to protect roots from cold-hot temperature extremes, but keep the mulch away from the main stem to avoid insect or disease problems. For areas with extended hard frost, plant in containers to move to protected areas, or dig up the plants and put them in temporary containers until spring. Also select early-blooming varieties rather than mid-to-late selections. Provide sturdy stakes for support if needed.

Growing Tips
Water every two to seven days, adjusting for soil type, climate, and growth conditions. Feed every seven to fourteen days with an organic, water-soluble fertilizer such as liquid kelp until flower buds show color.

Advice and Care
On large flowering types, disbud by removing all lateral buds from each stem, leaving only the topmost center bud for the largest bloom and stake stems to support. After blooms are spent, cut down to about 8–10 in. Control aphids with a Neem or canola-based horticultural oil and use baits to get rid of ants. Early morning watering will allow the foliage to dry during the day, to avoid mildew and other diseases.

Companion Planting and Design
Hybrids of C. × grandiflorum are considered the most diverse and useful in a variety of settings. They are available in an array of flower forms, colors, and plant and flower sizes, as well as growth habits. Potted mums are sold throughout the year, but have been forced to bloom out of season. Once planted in the garden, this perennial will revert to its natural flowering cycle in the late summer-fall. The true "Queen of Fall Flowers," such as football mums, spiders, and Fujis are spectacular in flower beds or containers or flowing cascades in hanging baskets or tumbling over walls.

Try These
The giant-flowered 'Kokka Bunmi' with light lavender petals and purple reverse, the white spider 'Icicles', and cascading orange-red 'Firefall' are just a few selections.

Clivia Lily

Clivia miniata

Bloom Period and Seasonal Color
Red, orange, or yellow flowers bloom in spring.

Mature Height × Spread 2 ft. × clumping

Botanical Pronunciation
KLIV-ee-ah MIN-ee-ah-tah

Zones 10–11

A long the side of our home leading to the backyard is a meandering brick pathway where the bent overhead branches of a California pepper tree, jacaranda, and Victorian box provide protection from the intense brightness of the sun. Their cool shadows are a haven for our clivia lilies planted on a slope among trailing tendrils of English ivy. In the springtime, umbels of apricot-orange, creamy yellow, and fiery carmine funnel-shaped flowers shoot up from thick, straplike, dark green leaves. On stocky stems, these brilliant yellow-throated flower clusters emerge out of rhizomes. Because of the heavy, tangled surface roots, they dislike being disturbed. Blooming occurs over several weeks, after which clusters of large berrylike fruits form, ripen, and turn red or yellow.

When, Where, and How to Plant
Plant anytime during the year, in shaded or dappled-sun locations, from 1- or 5-gallon containers, spacing 2–3 ft. apart. Although you can plant by seed, it will be slow to flower, about three to five years. Clivias prefer well-drained soil with a slightly acidic pH of 6.6–7.0. Create a watering basin 2 ft. in diameter and mulch with 1 in. of organic material such as humus mulch or compost.

Growing Tips
Immediately after planting, soak deeply and thoroughly. During the first week, water two to three times to settle the soil against the roots, then adjust the frequency and amount according to weather and growth conditions. As a general rule, decrease watering in winter and increase in spring and summer. Because their leaves are so thick and waxy, persistent breezes and short periods of drought are not too troublesome. Fertilize in late winter or early spring with a complete organic granular food.

Advice and Care
Clivias grow well in frost-free, temperate climates. They tolerate heat if planted in the shade and if there is sufficient humidity and soil moisture. It does not like having its roots disturbed. Propagate them by division after the bloom cycle. Remove the outer, older, yellowing leaves periodically. Few diseases or pests affect these plants, except mealybugs, snails, and slugs. Control mealybugs with a canola-based horticultural oil or Neem oil. Get rid of snails and slugs with an iron phosphate mollulsicide.

Companion Planting and Design
Plant these shade lovers under trees or along dappled light borders. When few flowers are in bloom, their trumpet-shaped clusters of blossoms look glorious amid acanthus, ferns, and hellebore. You can also tie several together just beneath the flower or berry heads and place them firmly in a water-soaked oasis to create a topiary-tree arrangement with a domed pompon shape.

Try These
Clivia miniata 'Flame', commonly known as flame clivia lily, is one of the most brilliant red-orange varieties. Hybrids by Joe Solomone bear luscious yellow, cream, red, and other, pastel-colored flowers.

Daylily

Hemerocallis × hybrids

Bloom Period and Seasonal Color
Yellow, red, orange, pink, white, purple, brown, or bicolor flowers bloom in spring and summer.

Mature Height × Spread 2–3 ft. × clumping

Botanical Pronunciation
HEM-er-oh-kal-lis

Zones 5–11

The genus name *Hemerocallis* comes from the Greek words *hemera*, meaning "day," and *kalo*, meaning "beautiful." Both the Greek and common names tell you these lovely blooms are short-lived, but there are always more buds eagerly waiting to open in your garden. The hybrids tend to have a longer bloom life. From mounds of arching, narrow grasslike leaves emerge tall, flowering stalks whose color selections include astounding shades of cream, yellow, orange, red, pink, a deep maroon that is almost black, and many bicolored varieties. Daylilies are among the easiest evergreens to grow, requiring very little attention, and they offer gorgeous splashes of color throughout the spring and summer months. Providing there is adequate moisture, they do quite well even in hot and windy locations.

When, Where, and How to Plant
Plant in late winter or early spring from 1-gallon containers spaced 2–3 ft. apart. Although daylilies grow in full or partial sun, they prefer full sun in temperate areas. They flourish in deep, cool, fertile, moderately moist, loose-textured soil, pH 6.5–7.0. Construct a watering basin 1–2 ft. in diameter and mulch with 1 in. of organic material.

Growing Tips
Soak deeply after planting. Water three times the first week; once established, their thick roots store water, making them drought tolerant for short periods of time. Their foliage will yellow and wither during extended times of drought, but they should rebound once moisture is restored. Adjust watering according to weather and growth conditions.

They're hardy down to 10 degrees Fahrenheit. Fertilize in early summer with a complete organic granular food.

Advice and Care
For cut flowers, harvest them while they are still tightly budded but just beginning to show some color, and they will last for a week. Flowers, buds, young stalks, and roots are also edible if grown organically. Remove the stamens to avoid unsightly stains on your furniture or clothes. Slugs and snails sometimes graze on the tender shoots. If damage is extensive, go on a snail- and slug-stomping expedition, or use an iron phosphate molluscicide. For rust problems, spray with a horticultural grade canola oil or, if persistent, use a fungicide formulated for daylilies.

Companion Planting and Design
Use daylilies in planting beds or borders, along pathways, at the edges of lawns or woodlands, among shrubs, as mass plantings on steep slopes, or reflected in nearby water gardens. Some companions are spring bulbs such as ranunculus and freesias and annuals such as ageratum. Blue Marguerite and lily of the Nile make compatible companions.

Try These
Hemerocallis × hybrid 'Allegretto' has extra-large, 6-in. flowers that are orchid-colored, deepening to a rich wine hue in the flowers' throats. Dwarf varieties, staying under 2 ft., are 'Black Eyed Stella', yellow with red eye; and 'Pardon Me' in red. 'Lemon Vista' is yellow on 28-in. stems with a slight fragrance.

Delphinium

Delphinium elatum

Bloom Period and Seasonal Color
Blue, purple, pink lavender, magenta, red, and white flowers in summer to fall.

Mature Height × Spread 2–8 ft. × 2–4 ft.

Botanical Pronunciation
del-FIN-ee-um EE-lay-tum

Zones 5–11

When hearing the words "cottage garden," we immediately visualize a front yard carpeted with sun-drenched color dominated by towering, true-blue delphiniums reaching for the sky. If you live where the climate is cool and moist, such as the coastal areas of northwest California, and you equate landscape maintenance chores with pleasure, then delphiniums are meant to be part of your garden. Hybrids have pale green, 8-in., handlike leaves with flower spikes occupying the top halves of straight, stiff stems. Each bloom can be 4 in. across and forms tall, stately spires of dense florets. Delphiniums generally develop one main flower stem with small auxiliary stems that fill in the blank spaces, creating a massive summer show. After two or three years, replace with new plants.

When, Where, and How to Plant
Plant in spring from color packs or 1-gallon containers and space 2–3 ft. apart. They prefer full sun and well-drained fertile soil, pH 6.6–7.0. Build a watering basin 3–4 ft. in diameter and cover with 1–2 in. of organic material.

Growing Tips
Soak deeply after planting. Water three times the first week; thereafter adjust watering according to weather and growth conditions. Fertilize with water-soluble food, such as liquid kelp, every two to three weeks during spring and summer months.

Advice and Care
They do not like regions where the summers are hot and dry and the winters are cold. To promote better air circulation and to strengthen the plant, thin out all but three or four stalks. Deadhead spent flowers just above the foliage to promote continuous blooms. When stems die back, prune them off, allowing new foliage to grow from the base. Be aware that all parts of delphiniums are toxic, even seeds, so keep them away from young children or pets. Leaf miners, caterpillars, slugs, snails, and powdery mildew may attack. If damage is extensive, remove the infested leaves or stems and squish those slimy pests. For leaf miners, spray with spinosad, and for powdery mildew, spray with a canola-based horticultural oil.

Companion Planting and Design
Even though they require patient tending, delphiniums are must-haves for cottage gardens, for background ornamentals in flower beds or as mass plantings in a large setting such as a meadow. They combine well with foxglove, lily of the Nile, roses, ivy geranium, canna lily, and dahlia.

Try These
Delphinium elatum Pacific Giant series offers 'Blue Jay' with beautiful medium to dark blue flowers. 'Galahad' has clear white flowers with white centers; light blue blooms are available in 'Summer Skies'; 'Blue Bird' is medium blue. Shorter Pacific strains, growing to 2–2½ ft. include 'Blue Springs' and 'Magic Fountains'. Smallest yet is the strain 'Stand Up', growing to just 20 in. English delphinium mix is a typical cottage garden style growing from 6–8 ft. tall and coming in many colors.

Foxglove

Digitalis purpurea

Bloom Period and Seasonal Color
Purple, pink, white, rose, or yellow blooms in early spring to midsummer.

Mature Height × Spread 2–4 ft. × 2 ft.

Botanical Pronunciation
DIH-jih-ta-lis PUR-pew-ree-ah

Zones 6–11

Foxglove is known the world over as an effective heart medication—pardon the pun, but when planted on slopes in dappled shade, the 5-ft. flowering spikes in pastels of pink, peach, yellow, and cream will steal your heart. They also come in shades of purple and red, and are displayed as medium-height perennials in mixed or terraced garden. Foxglove grows on alpine slopes and meadows in their natural habitats, so they are perfect for partial-shade gardens in hot summer regions or full-sun where summers are cool. Their wrinkled leaves are rough-textured, covered with creamy hairs, and many more toward the bases of the plants. Trumpet-shaped flowers resembling gloves with the fingertips cut off face downward, clustered together along one side of stout spikes.

When, Where, and How to Plant
Plant in early spring from 4-in. pots or 1-gallon containers. They grow best in full sun or dappled shade in a well-drained, acidic soil, rich in organic material, pH 6.5–6.8. Build a watering basin 1–2 ft. in diameter, and mulch with 1 in. of organic material. Space plants 18 in. apart.

Growing Tips
Soak deeply after planting. Water three times during the first week; thereafter adjust frequency and amount according to climatic and growth conditions. They are thirsty plants and do not like drought conditions. Fertilize in early spring with a complete organic flower food.

Advice and Care
They withstand cold and some wind, but are not at their best in hot, dry weather. If you snip off spent flowers, the energy will go into the plants, which will become more vigorous, increasing their rosettes of foliage; there will be a second bloom, but the spikes will be shorter with fewer flowers. Since all parts of foxglove are toxic, do not use if you have children or pets who like to chew on plants. If you cut back any leaves damaged by snails and slugs, a flush of new, vital foliage will usually emerge. To control snails and slugs go on early-morning foot-stomping slime hunts or use a molluscicide.

Companion Planting and Design
Foxglove is another iconic cottage garden plant but is also spectacular in mass planting displays in meadow and woodland gardens, and they make colorful punctuation points as medium-height perennials in beds, borders, and containers. Mix with delphiniums, phlox, roses, impatiens, pink Indian hawthorn, and lily of the Nile.

Try These
Digitalis purpurea 'Excelsior' is an annual foxglove flowering in many mixed colors. It grows slightly shorter than the species. *D. purpurea* 'Campanulata' has upper flowers that unite to form large, cupped blooms with many segments. 'Camelot' reaches 4 ft. tall, blooming in the first year in rose, white, or cream, and lavender. Smaller 'Foxy' and 'Peloric' reach just 3 ft. 'Pam's Choice' grows to 4 ft. in zones 4–8. It has startling white blooms with maroon throats.

Gerbera Daisy

Gerbera hybrids

Other Name Transvaal Daisy

Bloom Period and Seasonal Color
Yellow, pink, red, or white flowers bloom
in summer.

Mature Height × Spread 8–12 in. × 12–16 in.

Botanical Pronunciation
GER-bure-ah

Zones 10–11

While selecting plants appropriate for cut flowers that are heat and drought tolerant and require little care, we immediately think of one of South Africa's plant gifts to the world: the gerber daisy, which was named for the German naturalist Traugott Gerber. It is one of the most decorative, symmetrically formed, daisylike flowers, known for varieties that offer hot, intense splashes of yellows, reds, oranges, magentas, or rusts, and some that have cool, delicate tints of pinks, salmons, creams, and greenish whites. In fact, they come in just about all the colors of the rainbow except blue and purple. From May to September, dull green crowns of large, jagged, coarse-textured leaves support their straight, bare, flowering stems. Plant in containers and move to protect against freezing temperatures.

When, Where, and How to Plant
Plant in spring from 4-in. pots or 1-gallon containers. These plants need full sun where summers are cool, or partial shade in hot areas, and loose, well-drained, loam soil, pH 6.7–7.1. To help prevent crown rot, plant the crown slightly higher than finished soil level. Space plants 12 in. apart. Build a watering basin 12 in. in diameter and cover with 1 in. of organic material keeping mulch away from the crown.

Growing Tips
Soak deeply after planting. Water three times the first week; thereafter adjust watering according to climatic and growth conditions. Fertilize in early spring with a complete organic, granular food.

Advice and Care
For aesthetic reasons, deadhead unsightly spent flowers, cutting them off at the base of their stalks. Wash off aphids with a strong stream of water and use bait to control ants. For snails and slugs, use an organic iron phosphate molluscicide.

Companion Planting and Design
The large, stiffly erect flowers on long stems make excellent cutflower arrangements suitable for any décor. As cut flowers, they can last up to three weeks if correctly treated. Re-cut their stems frequently because they are prone to blockage, and change the water daily, adding just a drop of bleach or some powdered flower preservative each time. Place them in a cool spot, away from direct sunlight. They are also terrific in rock or perennial gardens, or as border plants or groundcovers. Wallflowers, woolly yarrow, and blue Marguerite daisy are ideal companion plants.

Try These
Gerbera jamesonii 'Double Parade' has double flowers in many color variations. 'Crush' is a compact grower good for containers. It comes in shades of watermelon, rose, and vanilla and flowers a bit earlier, providing continuous blooms through summer. 'Aztec' has brilliant yellow-orange petals with dark centers. The large, florist-type flowers are excellent in containers, but to plant directly in the garden, select the *Gerbera* Everlast or Drakensberg series. They are available in red, orange, pink, white, and yellow 3-in. flowers supported by 12–14-in. wiry stems.

Heliotrope

Heliotropium arborescens

Bloom Period and Seasonal Color
Purple, white, and blue blooms from summer through fall.

Mature Height × Spread 1–4 ft. × 1–2 ft.

Botanical Pronunciation
HEEL-ee-oh-trope-ee ar-BORE-es-senz

Zones 10–11

From the Peruvian Andes, this beautiful plant is named for its tendency to grow toward the sun (*helios*). It grows as a shrub with deep, hunter green, prominently veined foliage adorned with large clusters of petite, perfume-saturated, often purple flowers that bloom from summer to autumn. Popular since the 1750s, its nickname is cherry pie because of the similarity in fragrance. Others liken it to the scent of vanilla. In Victorian England heliotropes appeared all over in gardens and herbaceous borders of parks. Despite the beauty and fragrance, deer are not fond of heliotrope and this would be an excellent plant to include in a deer-resistant garden. In mild climates it is a perennial, but where winter freeze is common, treat it as an annual.

When, Where, and How to Plant
For inland or warmer regions, plant in part shade; along the coast or cooler climates, full sun. Heliotrope needs well-draining, humus-amended soil. Can also be started from seed ten to twelve weeks before the last frost date. Plant in seed trays filled with a commercial seed-starting mix, keep evenly moist, supply bright, indirect light, and set outdoors after the last frost date. Since all plant parts are toxic, keep away from small children and pets.

Growing Tips
Water regularly every five to seven days particularly while a plant is immature and from summer to fall. Fertilize with a complete organic granular food from spring to summer.

Advice and Care
Pinch plants back shortly after planting or before their surge of growth in late spring to encourage blooming. Trim at the end of the bloom cycle for a more compact growth habit and deadhead regularly. Control whiteflies by washing off with a strong stream of water or spray with an organic pesticide such as spinosad. Because it has a residual of seven to ten days, reapply once or two times more if infestation persists. Spray in the late afternoon after the bees have returned to their hives. Once dry, it is no longer harmful to them. For rust problems, spray with a canola-based horticultural oil.

Companion Planting and Design
Heliotrope is a shrubby perennial that imbues its purple-flowered cherry or vanillalike fragrance to flower beds, window boxes, edgings, hanging baskets, or where it camouflages leggier shrubs and vines. It's very attractive when massed in groups of 3–5 plants and combined with candytuft, delphinium, and foxglove.

Try These
'Simply Scensational'™ has soft lavender blue blooms with white centers accented in yellow. The sweetly scented flowers perch on 24-in. stems. 'Black Beauty' has dark purple to black blooms on 3-ft. tall plants. 'Atlantis' is heat tolerant and has vanilla-scented blooms. 'Incense' is more compact at 14 in. × 14 in., bearing extremely fragrant purple flowers. For dwarf forms that grow under 12 in., 'Princess Marina' and 'White Lady' are wonderful in small spaces.

Impatiens

Impatiens walleriana

Bloom Period and Seasonal Color
Deep crimson, violet, pink, or speckled white blooms from spring to fall.

Mature Height × Spread 2 ft. × 3 ft.

Botanical Pronunciation
im-PASHE-enz WALL-ree-an-nah

Zones 11

Outside our dining room window are two hanging pots filled with impaties. Even though there is a hummingbird feeder with homemade nectar nearby, our "hummers" first dip their beaks into the throats of the impatiens. In addition to enjoying the sight of our resident hummers, we also appreciate the simple beauty of the impaties' vibrant colored flowers tumbling over the pots. Their violet-shaped, single and double flowers contrast nicely with their lance-shaped, fresh green leaves. The name impatiens refers to their impatience to germinate and grow: when their seed capsules are barely touched, they explode, dispersing their seeds over a wide area. Cuttings from the mother plant establish so easily that you can just stick them in the ground and most will root and grow.

When, Where, and How to Plant
Plant in spring from pony packs, color packs, 4-in. pots, or 1-gallon containers. Along coastal areas, they thrive in full sun, but as you move inland where it is hotter and drier, partial shade is best. Provide highly organic, well-drained soil, pH 6.5–7.0. Build a watering basin encompassing the planting area and mulch with 1 in. of organic material. Space plants 18 in. on center; or place single plants in 8-in. pots.

Growing Tips
Immediately after planting, soak deeply and thoroughly. Water three times the first week; thereafter water according to climatic and growth conditions. Since they come from tropical habitats, impatiens are not frost hardy, nor do they tolerate drought or dry, blustery winds—but they withstand heat if adequate moisture is provided. Fertilize lightly once a month during the spring and summer seasons with a water-soluble food such as liquid kelp or fish emulsion.

Advice and Care
For a more compact growth and abundant flower production, pinch back tip growth. Because established impatiens have large root systems, they can be dug up and moved easily. If transplanting, provide plenty of water until their roots have a chance to re-establish. They are relatively free from disease and infestations except snails and slugs. These are not life-threatening problems, but if damage is extensive, snip off the affected foliage, fertilize to encourage new growth and use an iron phosphate molluscicide. For spider mites, spray with an organic remedy such as a canola-based horticultural oil or a miticide.

Companion Planting and Design
Their bright colored flowers add to sunny or shaded color beds, borders, window boxes, or containers on patios. English ivy, camellias, and azaleas are wonderful companions.

Try These
Impatiens 'New Guinea Hybrid', with variegated foliage, has flowers fuller and more erect than those of the species. *I. balsamina* 'Rockapulco White' is clear white. Registered New Guinea impatiens 'Infinity' series offers vigorous plants growing to 1 ft., with large blooms carrying deliciously descriptive names: 'Blushing Lilac', 'Dark Salmon Glow', 'Lilac', 'Orange Frost', 'Pink Frost', 'Red', and 'Pink'.

Ivy Geranium

Pelargonium peltatum

Bloom Period and Seasonal Color
Red, pink, lavender, or white flowers bloom in summer.

Mature Height × Spread 8–12 in. × spreading

Botanical Pronunciation
PEH-lar-go-nee-um PEL-tot-um

Zones 10–11

Here's a perennial with an identity crisis. Is it a geranium or is it a pelargonium? Although it is commonly known as ivy geranium, it belongs to the genus *Pelargonium*, which only adds to the muddled confusion. The fact is, not all pelargoniums are ivy geraniums, but all ivy geraniums are pelargoniums. The main difference between geranium and pelargonium is in their flowers (symmetrical geranium flowers and asymmetrical pelargonium blossoms). We selected the ivy geranium not to befuddle you, but because it adds such vibrant colors to summer gardens, and in frost-free areas it flowers from March to November. The flowers range from lavender, pink, white, and red to veined purple, and have star-shaped, bright green leaves similar to ivy foliage but with dark circular zones.

When, Where, and How to Plant
Plant in spring after last frost from color packs, 4-in. pots, or 1-gallon containers. Full sun is best for optimum flowering and vigor, but they will grow in partial shade. The soil should be well drained and have a pH between 6.0 and 7.0. Space plants 18 in. on center. Construct a 12-in. watering basin and mulch with ½ in. of organic material. With sufficient humidity and moisture, ivy geraniums do well in most areas of California. They can withstand heat, gentle breezes, and even short periods of drought—but they are not frost tolerant.

Growing Tips
Soak deeply after planting. Water three times the first week; thereafter water every seven to ten days once established, adjusting to weather and growth conditions. Fertilize from spring to fall with a liquid food such as kelp once a month.

Advice and Care
Regularly deadhead spent blooms, including stalks, during the flowering cycle. Remove dead or yellowing foliage. To propagate by cuttings, take 5-in. stem sections, each including three nodes, in late summer. Make a slightly angled cut just under the bottom node and dip the end into rooting hormone. Cut off all leaves except the top one, and root in presoaked, medium-textured vermiculite. Place in a sheltered, shaded area. Do not water too much, and roots will form in about two weeks. Transplant into containers with potting soil when a sufficient root system has developed. Snails and slugs can be easily controlled with a molluscicide or by squishing underfoot.

Companion Planting and Design
Use ivy geranium cascading in color baskets, window boxes, terraces, balconies, or on trellises. Shasta daisy, lily of the Nile, and pink Indian hawthorn are ideal companion plants.

Try These
Pelargonium peltatum 'Galilee' is pretty with double, rose-pink flowers. 'La France' has semidouble, mauve-veined, white or purple flowers. 'Summer Showers', an ivy geranium that is available as seed, flowers in shades of red, pink, lavender, blush white, and burgundy about a hundred days after sowing. 'Summer Showers White Blush' has pale pink, lavender, and white blooms.

Lenten Rose

Helleborus hybrids

Bloom Period and Seasonal Color
Lavender, pink, white, purple, black, green blooms in winter to spring.

Mature Height × Spread 12 in. × 12–18 in.

Botanical Pronunciation
HEL-eh-bore-us

Zones 4–10

H *elleborus × hybridus*, also known as the Lenten rose, is a plant for all seasons. A reliable perennial, it performs very well in shade gardens with attractive, evergreen, leathery leaves and bears colorful white, pale pink, maroon to red, or deep purple flowers in late winter to early spring, when few other flowers are in bloom. The cup- or bell-shaped blossoms also come in a wide array of single and double forms, bicolored and freckled, as well as facing outward or downward. After flowering, its dark green foliage continues to make a bold statement in shaded nooks, and provides a fresh, contrasting backdrop for later-flowering spring bulbs and other perennials. Hellebores are not only beautiful to look at, but deer and rabbits leave them alone.

When, Where, and How to Plant
Plant hellebores in late winter or spring from containers. Provide humus-amended, excellent draining, slightly alkaline soil in partial shade. Unlike its Christmas rose cousin (*H. niger*), it tolerates warm winter climates, but shelter it from winter winds. From seed, plant in trays or peat pots filled with a commercial seed starting mix. Cover with a clear plastic top; keep the planting medium moist, but not soggy; and once the seeds germinate (30–180 days) with two to three sets of true leaves, transplant into a larger 3-in. pot. Plant seedlings outdoors during spring or summer.

Growing Tips
For the first growing season, water hellebores regularly to establish a deep, extensive root system.

Once plants are established, allow the soil to dry out slightly before watering. Feed with a complete organic granular fertilizer or cottonseed meal after the blooms are spent. Apply a 2–3-inch layer of mulch (away from crown) to keep roots cool in the summer and warm in the winter.

Advice and Care
Prune off old, brown foliage before blooming. Unlike many other perennials, the Lenten rose does not need to be divided every three to five years and can be left alone for up to twenty years. If it is necessary to divide, wear gloves to prevent any skin irritation. For powdery mildew, spray with a canola-based horticultural oil. To use as cut flowers in an arrangement, sear the cut stems over a flame for a few seconds, then soak in cold water. They are also exquisite floating in a bowl of water.

Companion Planting and Design
Plant hellebores under the canopy of trees, on slopes, in shady flower beds, or in containers. Perfect to naturalize in woodland, native, or shade gardens, and pathways. Combine with other spring-flowering bulbs, lacy ferns, and shade-loving impatiens.

Try These
'Ivory Prince' bears deep pink buds that open to white flowers in early spring. The flowers face upward and outward from the plant, unlike many other varieties that have nodding, downward flowers. 'Royal Heritage' blooms in late spring and 'Party Dress' bears stunning double flowers in a rainbow of colors.

Leopard Plant

Farfugium japonicum

Bloom Period and Seasonal Color
Green foliage with yellow or cream markings.

Mature Height × Spread
2 ft. × 2 ft. × spreading rhizomes

Botanical Pronunciation
FAR-foo-gee-um ja-PON-ih-kum

Zones 7–10

The leopard plant was formerly in the *Ligularia* genus, but is now classified as a *Farfugium*. Native to the rocky coastal cliffs in Japan, Korea, and Taiwan, *Farfugium japonicum* plants are bold-textured, evergreen perennials with large (4–10 in. across), leathery leaves that are round, kidney, or heart-shaped with ruffled or toothed margins. They stand on long stalks and grow in clumps that spread by rhizomes. From fall to winter, loose clusters of yellow, daisylike flowers emerge on fuzzy stems above the foliage. The Japanese prize this flowering perennial, calling it *metakaraku*, which means "sweet-smelling roots," and eagerly seek unique cultivars for their collections. They grow best in part shade and are hardy down to about 20 degrees Fahrenheit, but the foliage will die back until warmer weather arrives.

When, Where, and How to Plant
Plant in spring from containers and locate in partial shade. Does best in moist, well-drained, humus-amended, slightly acidic soil, but dislikes wet, soggy conditions. Provide a 1–2-inch layer of mulch in hot, dry regions or where prolonged freezes are common and remove the mulch in spring. Shelter from cold, drying winter winds.

Growing Tips
Water regularly every five to ten days depending on growth and weather conditions. Once established, extend watering intervals to every two to three weeks. It is also an irrigation indicator because when it dries out, it wilts. Feed with a balanced, organic granular fertilizer such as cottonseed meal before new growth begins in spring.

Advice and Care
Deadhead old flowers to encourage more blossoms. Divide clumps every five to seven years in the early spring or late summer. Dig up as much of the root system as possible and, using a sterile, sharp knife, cut the crowns into smaller sections to replant. Keep snails and slugs away with an organic bait such as iron phosphate or in Southern California, use decollate snails, but do not combine the bait with decollates. Both the foliage and flowers can also be used in stylized flower arrangements. Recipes for organically grown farfugium include boiling the stems, peeling the outer layers, and serving with soy sauce.

Companion Planting and Design
Prized for their bold and attractive foliage, leopard plants grow well in borders, containers, along edges of ponds or streams, or under the shaded canopies of trees. They are attractive when massed in a woodland or tropical setting, or in a shady mixed border. It is also dramatic enough as a single plant to serve as a focal point. Combine with primula, ferns, heuchera, and hosta. The variegated cultivars are often used to brighten shaded nooks.

Try These
'Argenteum' has smaller, deep green foliage with grayish green and white markings. 'Aureomaculatum' is commonly called the leopard plant because its leaves have yellow speckles, and 'Crispatum' has thick, ruffled foliage. 'Gigantea' (giant leopard plant) is true to its name with robust 5–18-inch-wide leaves standing on 3–4-foot stalks.

Lily of the Nile

Agapanthus africanus

Bloom Period and Seasonal Color
Blue or white flowers bloom in summer.

Mature Height × Spread 18 in. × clumping

Botanical Pronunciation
ag-ah-PANTH-us af-rih-KAWN-is

Zones 9–11

Lily of the Nile is one of our favorite perennials to use as a foreground plant in front of larger shrubs. With their dense, fountainlike clumps of foliage and showy blue umbrella-shaped clusters of flowers, lily of the Nile resembles a river of blue against a sea of green. Depending on climate and variety, they bloom in late spring through early summer, and their small, funnel-shaped flowers shoot up on leafless stalks at least 1–3 ft. high. In addition to blue, their flowers come in hues of violet-blue and white. Their beauty is accentuated by fleshy tubular roots that surround thick, dark green, ribbonlike leaves. Once established, they withstand strong winds, temperatures slightly below freezing, and even short periods of drought.

When, Where, and How to Plant
Plant in spring from 1-gallon containers. They prefer full-sun areas and well-drained soil, pH 6.5–7.0. Space plants 18 in. apart. Construct a watering basin 1 ft. in diameter; mulch with 1 in. of organic material such as compost or humus.

Growing Tips
Soak deeply after planting. Water three times the first week; thereafter water according to weather and growth conditions. They require minimal water in winter. In their native habitat, they grow near streams and ponds, so water much more frequently in early spring and summer. They prefer slightly moist soils on dry slopes near the coast. Fertilize in spring to summer every forty-five days with a complete organic granular food.

Advice and Care
Pruning is unnecessary, but remove spent flowers, including the dried stalks and dead leaves. Propagation by division is best after the flowering cycle is completed in late summer or early fall. Mature plants produce young side shoots that can be removed and repotted as long as there are sufficient root structures. In about six to eight months the roots will have established themselves enough to replant in the ground; they will bloom in about two or three years. Lilies of the Nile are not susceptible to pests except for snails and slugs; a molluscicide or handpicking and foot-smashing methods easily control these slimy creatures.

Companion Planting and Design
Lily of the Nile is ideal to use as a foreground plant in front of larger shrubs or in mass plantings near water features, or edging along a wall, fence, or driveway. They also combine beautifully in cutflower gardens or in containers on decks and patios. Cut flowers when one-third of the flowers on the cluster are open in the morning. Recut stem ends, regularly change the water, and add powdered flower preservative and they should last seven to fourteen days.

Try These
Agapanthus africanus 'Peter Pan', known as dwarf lily of the Nile, is more compact than the species, growing 8–12 in. tall with lavender-blue flowering stems. 'Albus' has clear white blooms and 'Queen Anne' has blue flowers.

Shasta Daisy

Leucanthemum × superbum

Bloom Period and Seasonal Color
White flowers bloom in summer.

Mature Height × Spread 2 ft. × clumping

Botanical Pronunciation
Loo-kan-theh-mum SOO-per-bum

Zones 5–11

No matter how many times Shasta daisies are used in landscapes, they never seem commonplace. The white, fringed flowers on 16-in. long stems add sparkle to any garden. A drift of Shasta daisies is not just a feast for the eyes—their flat petals are perfect cushions for resting swallowtails as they dip into the nectar. From mid-June to September, 3–4-in. blooms dance in the warm summer breezes out of rosettes of coarsely toothed, dark green, spoon-shaped, 10-in. leaves. During their blooming and growing season, they need warmth and adequate water, but tolerate some drought for short periods of time. Since the species was also found naturalized on Mount Shasta in Washington state, it is apparent that they survive freezing temperatures and blustery winds.

When, Where, and How to Plant
Plant in spring from 4-in. pots or 1-gallon containers. They can also be planted from seed. Follow the directions on the packet. Shastas thrive in full sun in rich, well-drained soil with a pH of 6.5–7.0. Space plants 12 in. apart. Build a watering basin 1 ft. in diameter and mulch with 1 in. of organic material such as compost or humus mulch.

Growing Tips
Immediately after planting, soak deeply and thoroughly. During the first week, water three times; thereafter, adjust watering frequency and amount according to weather and growth conditions. Fertilize lightly once a month with a water-soluble food suitable for bloom and foliage production.

Advice and Care
It is not necessary to prune, but deadhead regularly to encourage a longer flowering cycle. If you want to share your Shastas with your gardening friends, wait until the plants are about three years old and divide the clumps in the fall. Shastas may have occasional leafminer problems that can be controlled with spinosad every seven to ten days.

Companion Planting and Design
Shastas are great additions to informal borders in front of hedges or in cottage-style perennial gardens. Use them in colorful mixed bunches of flowers arranged loosely in a favorite vase, or arrange them in an elegant, all-white bouquet. Harvest when the flowers are only half-open and they will last as cut flowers for seven to ten days. Ideal plant companions are daylilies, anemones, phlox, and woolly yarrow.

Try These
'Esther Read' is used by the florist industry. 'Marconi' is a full-flowered, all-white variety. 'Aglaia' is a long-season bloomer from summer to fall; its tall, 24-in. stems are good for cutting. 'Real Dream' blooms late spring through summer and forms mounds 18 in. × 15 in. 'Snow Lady' is a compact grower 1 ft. tall and wide. 'Snowcap' is a dwarf, blooming late spring through summer on 6-in. tall plants spreading to just 12 in., making it a good choice for borders, containers, and rock gardens.

Wood Violet

Viola odorata

Bloom Period and Seasonal Color
Violet blooms in spring.

Mature Height × Spread 4–6 in. × 8–24 in.

Botanical Pronunciation
VIY-oh-lah oh-DORE-ah-tah

Zones 4–10

Technically, violas, pansies, and most violets are grouped under the genus *Viola*, but violas and pansies are commonly used as annuals in California, tossed aside when temperatures rise, while violas naturalize in wooded areas, in cottage or rock gardens. Whether used as a perennial or an annual, wood violets are the royalty of aromatic violets, with beautiful, heart-shaped, hunter green leaves bearing March blooms of deep violet, purplish blue, pink, or white perfumed flowers. They add color and delicate flavor to salads and cakes and, of course, are one of the most romantic of cut flowers, the poetic subject of songs and stories. Romantic as they may be, make sure they have not been sprayed with any pesticides or herbicides if you are using them as edibles.

When, Where, and How to Plant
Plant in spring or fall from 4-in. pots or 1-gallon containers, spacing 6–10 in. apart. Sow seeds in a commercial seed-starting mix, keep the medium moist but not soggy, and transplant into 3-in. pots after one or two sets of true leaves have emerged. Plant outdoors in the early spring or fall in mild winter regions. Wood violets prefer loam soil; if necessary, blend amendments such as humus mulch, compost, and preplant fertilizer to a depth of 12 in. Pick a partially shaded location where there is cool, well-draining soil with a pH of 6.8–7.2. Wood violets love cool climates and wither during drought, wind, and heat.

Growing Tips
Soak deeply and thoroughly after planting. During the first week, water daily, but once established, water every five to seven days depending on growth and weather conditions, and decrease frequency in winter. Feed monthly with a complete organic liquid fertilizer from spring to summer.

Advice and Care
Although wood violets are technically perennials, it may be best to treat them as annuals in areas prone to frost, because they tend to decline during freezing temperatures. For an improved spring floral display, cut runners and prune off errant or spindly growth in late autumn. If desired, divide clumps after flowering. To lengthen the bloom season, remove spent flowers. Protect from snails and slugs with an iron phosphate bait or handpick. In Southern California use decollate snails or bait, but not both.

Companion Planting and Design
Nestle wood violets under the dappled light of trees or peeking out of shaded rock gardens, border edges, or containers. Cut flowers just as they are beginning to open up. Cyclamen, 'Forest Pansy' redbud, and southern magnolia make lovely companion plants.

Try These
'Angel Tiger Eye' can be grown from seed and flowers eight weeks after sowing. Its blooms are gorgeous golden yellow with black veins. Also available from seed is the exceptionally fragrant 'Queen Charlotte' that is hardy to zone 6 with deep violet-blue blooms on 10-in. tall plants. 'Reine de Neiges' is pure white.

ROSES

FOR CALIFORNIA

In an area called the "Rose-Growing Capital of the World," millions of roses are raised commercially, eventually finding their way into gardens around the world. During winter the snow-capped Sierra Nevadas lie to the east of Visalia, where the ancient Kern River once flowed from these mountains into the San Joaquin Valley between Bakersfield and Oildale. Its flow transported rich soil down to the valley floor, creating an immense alluvial fan. Southward is the rain-shadow side of Southern California's transverse mountain ranges and westward is the eastern side of California's coastal range, effectively blocking the ocean breezes originating along the central coast and creating the perfect rose-growing environment.

Weather: Friend or Foe

When normal California weather prevails, spring and summer are the seasons in which roses need the most water, but two events create obstacles to producing perfect roses. The first occurs when Central and Southern California experience an El Niño phenomenon that produces exceptionally wet weather and warmer-than-average winters. Under these conditions, roses need to be forced into dormancy by pruning them in winter.

The second event happens in late summer or early fall, when high-pressure cells build up over the Nevada Mountains. The pressure differential with the air mass over California generates the "Foehn phenomenon," otherwise known as the Santa Ana winds in Southern California, the Diablo wind in the East Bay hills, and the chinooks in the Pacific Northwest. Prior to a predicted Foehn, provide additional irrigation and protection for plants, including roses.

Along the Pacific Coast, St. Patrick's Day is usually the last frost date, but the farther inland your garden is, the further into the year the last frost date moves. If an El Niño or La Niña event leads to increased rainfall, add organic amendments such as humus and compost and apply mycorrhizal fungi, saponin, and humic acid products to improve soil drainage.

How to Choose

Simplify the thousands of rose varieties available by doing some homework. Visit public rose gardens in your area such as Rose Hills in Whittier, Huntington Gardens in San Marino, and the Golden Gate Park Rose Garden in San Francisco. Don't forget to also contact the local Rose Society chapter and your neighborhood nursery for ideas.

Fragrance is another consideration, since the first thing one does when passing a rose is inhale its perfume. Refer to the James Alexander Gamble Fragrance Medal winners for fragrant varieties.

When a rose has won your heart and nose, purchase only Grade #1 plants because #1 canes are husky and vigorous, while other grades are less vigorous and smaller. With roses, you get what you pay for, and buying cheap is usually not economical in the long run.

The Roses in This Book

Although roses can be classified into many categories, this chapter includes climbing roses, floribundas, grandifloras, groundcovers, hybrid teas, and miniatures as the major classes (shrub roses are featured in the shrub chapter). While climbers with their large, arching stems provide spectacular vertical color for sturdy arches, fences, and walls, hybrid teas are erect growers with single, long-stemmed flowers used by florists. They can be combined with other perennials in border plantings.

Floribundas bloom in clusters and when the center bud is removed, the surrounding buds open simultaneously, creating an instant bouquet. Reflecting the parentage of floribundas and hybrid teas, grandifloras bear flowers on long stems that are borne in clusters. Miniatures refer to the bloom size, not the bush size, and range from 6 in. to 4 ft. tall. They provide a rose display in a tiny space, such as low borders, window boxes, and hanging baskets, or climbing on trellises.

The allure of a rose is irresistible and when its perfume matches its beauty, the blending of these two traits creates an alchemy that transports us to a world of magical wonder. Hopefully this chapter will transform "rosy" dreams into landscape reality.

Climbing roses provide spectacular vertical color.

HOW TO PLANT YOUR ROSES

Once you've selected a location based on sunlight, soil drainage, and spacing, follow the simple steps below and you'll have beautiful healthy, blooming roses in no time!

Step 1
After bringing your bareroot roses home, immediately soak roots in lukewarm water for 12 to 24 hours! Some gardeners add soil polymer powder, mud, or a little fertilizer.

Step 2
Dig a hole about 12 inches deep and 24 inches wide. Make sure it's large enough to give the plant's root system plenty of room to develop after planting. Loosen the soil at the bottom and sides with your shovel.

Step 3
Fill the hole with water. It should drain in one hour. If the water remains longer, dig deeper to improve the drainage—or add some amendments, such as compost or peat moss.

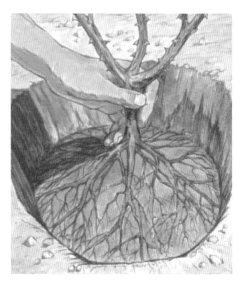

Step 4
Build a mound in the center of the hole to support roots. Set rose on top, making sure the crown (the point where canes join together at the shank) is at ground level, or a little lower in cold climates.

Step 5
Fill the hole with two-thirds of the remaining soil mixed with peat moss or compost. Tamp down gently with hands. Add water, let it soak in, then finish filling the hole with soil. Tamp down lightly and water well.

Step 6
Spread mulch, compost, or bark chips around to suppress weed growth and help retain moisture. Water three to four times a week until leaves begin to grow.

This information was provided courtesy of Jackson & Perkins.

Step 7
Your plants will leaf out faster if you mist the canes as often as possible while they're getting started. Roses need plenty of moisture both above and below the soil to develop fully.

Climbing

Rosa spp.

Bloom Period and Seasonal Color
Blends and white, lavender, pink, yellow, orange, red, striped, and bicolored flowers bloom in mid-spring.

Mature Height × Spread
(Variable) × 10–20 ft.

Botanical Pronunciation
ROSE-ah

Zones 5–11, depending on cultivar

When we moved into our current home we were so busy unpacking, organizing, cleaning, and painting that we barely noticed spring's cycle of renewal in our garden—until one day, as we were hurriedly eating our lunch, something quite beautiful caught our attention outside our dining room window. It was a perfect "stop and smell the roses" moment, for scrambling, spilling, and stretching 50 ft. over our fence down below were thousands of nosegay-sized clusters of pale yellow flowers. On closer inspection we realized that this was an old but still very vigorous banksia climbing rose, whose carefree looks and profuse blooms spread like butter over its dark green foliage. We took a deep breath, inhaled the delicate floral fragrance, and realized we were home at last.

When, Where, and How to Plant
Plant in late winter or early spring from bare rootstock, or anytime from 5-gallon containers. Some climbing roses tolerate partial shade, but most prefer full sun and sandy loam soil with a pH of 6.5–7.0. Space 15–20 ft. apart and plant with the bud union slightly above the surrounding soil.

Growing Tips
Soak deeply after planting. Water three times the first week, but once established, water every five to seven days during spring and summer. Decrease during autumn and withhold during winter unless drought prevails. Fertilize in late winter, early spring, and early summer with a complete granular organic rose food.

Advice and Care
Unlike vines, climbing roses do not attach themselves by way of tendrils or other growths, but instead have long canes that must be tied to a support. Climbers usually bloom on second-year or older growth, so it is only necessary to prune out dead or diseased wood on newly planted climbers. Once established, in late winter or early spring, while dormant, prune and leave four to eight structural canes, including some of the previous year's laterals. Generally speaking, climbing roses are less vulnerable to mildew than other types of roses, but rust and aphid infestations can occur during growth and bloom cycles; use a canola-based horticultural oil for these problems.

Companion Planting and Design
Ideal companion plants are clematis, Carolina jessamine, and California lilac.

Try These
The following are repeat bloomers. 'Altissimo' grows 15 ft. × 8 ft. with large crimson flowers and is stunning as an espalier, trellis, or pillar plant, as well as tumbling over a fence or wall. One of the best striped climbers, 'Fourth of July' has semi-double, 4-in. red-and-white flowers and an apple scent. Use on a pergola, arch, or trellis. 'Joseph's Coat' bears rainbow-colored flowers and its thorny habit is ideal for barriers and boundaries. 'Sally Holmes' has forty to fifty clusters of sweetly fragrant white blossoms tinged with a hint of apricot. It is best as a climber, but can be grown as a shrub.

Floribunda

Rosa spp.

Bloom Period and Seasonal Color
Blends and white, pink, lavender, yellow, orange, red, bicolored, and striped flowers bloom from summer to fall.

Mature Height × Spread 2–4 ft. × 3 ft.

Botanical Pronunciation
ROSE-ah

Zones 5–11

While it is true that floribundas lack the size, symmetrical beauty, and fragrance of their more popular counterparts, they flower from summer to fall, provide more color coverage on bushes, and are generally hardier, easier to maintain, lower growing, and less susceptible to wet-weather conditions. As the name implies, floribundas bloom abundantly and, in most cases, in clusters. Whether single- or multipetaled, flattened, cup-shaped, or high-centered, floribundas come in a wide array of colors, some with stripes, from the softest whites, creams, yellows, peaches, pinks, and mauves to brilliant golds, oranges, and reds. With a light and fruity fragrance, they are the roses of choice for formal or informal settings, or for any place that calls out for a large number of flowers.

When, Where, and How to Plant
Plant in late winter or early spring from bare rootstock, or anytime from 5-gallon containers. Floribundas prefer full sun and sandy loam soil with a pH of 6.5–7.0. Space 4–6 ft. apart. Construct a watering basin 4 ft. in diameter and mulch with 1 in. of humus or compost.

Growing Tips
Soak deeply after planting. Water three times the first few weeks; thereafter adjust frequency and amount according to climatic and growth conditions. Decrease water in fall and winter. Fertilize in late winter, early spring, and early summer with a complete organic granular rose food.

Advice and Care
Do not prune a newly planted floribunda, just remove any dead wood. Once established after twelve months, prune lightly for shape and remove one-third of its total height. For prolific blooms, disbud the plant, which means to take out the center flower bud shortly after the side buds emerge so that the plant's energy is directed toward the side buds. As the plant goes dormant, remove any remaining leaves and clear the ground of all leaves and weeds. Generally speaking, they are less vulnerable to mildew than other types of roses, but rust, scale, and aphid infestations can occur during growth and bloom cycles; use a canola-based horticultural oil for these problems.

Companion Planting and Design
The taller varieties make ideal hedges, while the dwarf varieties are perfect for the fronts of borders, as container plants, or in mass plantings. Ideal companion plants are Japanese mock orange, hybrid tea roses, and foxglove.

Try These
'Enchanted Evening' is one of the best mauve-lavender floribundas, with large clusters of citrus-scented flowers; it is resistant to blackspot, mildew, and rust. 'Hot Cocoa' has unique chocolate-colored blooms, with tints of purple and cinnamon-orange and a moderate old rose fragrance. 'Julia Child' was personally selected by America's favorite chef, and bears butter-gold blooms with a strong spicy licorice scent. Disease-resistant 'Trumpeter' has scarlet-orange blooms and flowers from early spring to winter as long as the weather is mild.

Grandiflora

Rosa spp.

Bloom Period and Seasonal Color
Blends and white, pink, lavender, yellow, orange, red, bicolored, and striped flowers bloom from summer to fall.

Mature Height × Spread 6–8 ft. × 4–6 ft.

Botanical Pronunciation
ROSE-ah

Zones 7–11

Once upon a time, a young human princess was about to be crowned while at the same time, two rose parents ('Charlotte Armstrong' from the hybrid tea family and 'Floradora' from the floribunda family) gave birth to a new class of rose, the grandiflora. Hybrid grandiflora 'Queen Elizabeth' and her royal followers derive their form and long cutting stems from the hybrid teas, and inherit their hardiness and near-continuous, abundant clustered blooms from the floribundas. Our grandiflora stands 7 ft. tall on thornless stems, adorned with massive clusters of fragrant, 4-in., clear pink blossoms whose ruffled edges are tinged with a darker pink. Without a doubt, 'Queen Elizabeth' deserves to be the reigning monarch of grandifloras. Grandifloras blend well with other perennials and shrubs.

When, Where, and How to Plant
Plant in late winter or early spring from bare rootstock, or anytime from 5-gallon containers. Grandifloras prefer full sun and sandy loam soil with a pH of 6.5–7.0. Space 8–12 ft. apart. Construct a watering basin 4–6 ft. in diameter and mulch with 2 in. of humus or compost.

Growing Tips
Most grandifloras withstand short periods of cold temperatures, blustery winds, and high temperatures if adequate moisture is provided, but they do not tolerate drought. Soak deeply after planting. Water three times the first week; thereafter, adjust frequency and amount to climatic and growth conditions. Fertilize in late winter, early spring, and early summer with a complete organic granular rose food.

Advice and Care
Do not prune a newly planted grandiflora, just remove any dead wood. Once established, prune in late winter or early spring before new growth. Remove dead or weak wood and prune back to an outward-facing bud, about one-third of its original height. Clear the ground of all leaves and weeds. They are disease resistant, but powdery mildew, blackspot, rust, and aphid infestations can occur during growth and bloom cycles. To control powdery mildew, wash off the foliage in the early morning. Use a canola-based horticultural oil for blackspot, rust, and aphids.

Companion Planting and Design
Ideal companion plants are hybrid teas, floribundas, and climbing roses. Since grandifloras are the largest of the bush roses, it is best to use them as single specimen shrubs, grouped in a hedge, or as background roses behind lower-growing plants. They also make ideal specimen plants in large containers.

Try These
'Cherry Parfait' grows to 5 ft. × 5 ft. with white edged in red blooms. 'Crimson Bouquet' has deep, rich red blooms and is hardy to zone 6. Since it is not as tall as other grandifloras, it is ideal for hedges or combined with other perennials or shrubs in the landscape. 'Fame', one of the longest-lasting cut roses, has deep pink blooms on a 4-ft. tall shrub.

Groundcover

Rosa hybrid

Bloom Period and Seasonal Color
Rainbow of colors from spring to first frost.

Mature Height × Spread 1½ -3 ft. × 2–6 ft.

Botanical Pronunciation
ROSE-ah

Zones 5 and up

Although certain climbing roses have been anchored and trained to cover expansive areas, recent groundcover roses have been developed to grow horizontally in low, dense habits without any training fuss and carpeting bare ground easily. Vigorous and undemanding, they combine the beauty of "the Queen of Roses," with a spreading and spilling habit. Its easy-care nature, disease-resistant foliage, and nonstop blooming throughout the growing season make groundcover roses useful for mass planting, in hanging baskets or window boxes, mixed with perennials or shrubs, lining a path or covering a slope. Most cultivars stay knee-high or lower (1–3 ft. × 2–6 ft.) and can remain so without too much help, but if necessary, cut back by two-thirds while still dormant in spring.

When, Where, and How to Plant
Plant from bare rootstock in late winter or early spring or almost anytime from containers. Provide full sun in humus or compost amended soil. Plant slightly above the graft or the same soil level as its original container, space 2–3 ft. apart, and make sure the soil drains well.

Growing Tips
Thoroughly soak after planting. Water three times weekly the first few weeks and every five to seven days once established, depending on growth and climate conditions. Fertilize with a complete organic granular rose food spring to summer. Apply a layer of mulch or a pre-emergent herbicide in early spring and fall to control weeds.

Advice and Care
Prune out dead wood and vertical-growing stems. It has excellent disease resistance, but protect from snail and slug damage with an iron phosphate bait. Discourage browsing deer and rabbits with olfactory repellents or motion-activated lights or sprinklers. For gophers and moles use manual traps. Rose midges (larvae of small flies) and thrips (yellow or brown insects) cause deformed leaves and buds. Spray with spinosad every seven to ten days until the problem is remedied. For spider mites spray with a canola-based horticultural oil or a miticide.

Companion Planting and Design
Groundcover roses are ideal for difficult slopes, rocky areas, and steep banks, as well as cascading over hanging baskets or mixed containers. Use to cover bare spaces between perennials and shrubs or between taller roses. They're also perfect bordering paths and driveways.

Try These
'Snow Cone' bears white, dogwood-like flowers growing 2 ft. tall and as wide. The 'Drift' series of roses offer a wide array of colors growing 18 in. × 24 in. and are perfect for small garden spaces. 'Happy Chappy' is a multicolored plant with bright orange, pink, and yellow flowers from spring until winter's first frost. At 2 ft. × 3 ft., it gives quick, wide-spreading coverage. 'Baby Blanket' grows a vigorous 3 ft. × 6 ft., and is ideal for challenging slopes and cascading over baskets or mixed containers. 'Flower Carpet' also comes in assorted colors and is a great spreader.

Hybrid Tea

Rosa spp.

Bloom Period and Seasonal Color
Blends and white, pink, lavender, yellow, green, orange, red, bicolored, and striped flowers bloom from spring through fall.

Mature Height × Spread 4–6 ft. × 3–5 ft.

Botanical Pronunciation
ROSE-ah

Zones 5–11

The hybrid tea is the aristocrat of all roses, the long-stemmed beauty of choice for Mother's Day, Valentine's Day, May Day, weddings, graduations, coronations, and ovations. With the exception of black and true blue, there are varieties in every color of the rainbow, including white, pink, red, lavender, yellow, orange—even green—as well as bicolors and blends. Many are fragrant and, depending on the region, bloom from spring through fall. Despite the fact that they are the most selected rose plant in gardens, there are a few caveats to keep in mind: hybrid teas have an upright, rigid growth habit, bloom less frequently than floribundas, are less adaptable to wet weather, and are less tolerant of adverse climatic and soil conditions.

When, Where, and How to Plant
Plant in late winter or early spring from bare root-stock, or anytime from 5-gallon containers. Most hybrid teas prefer full sun and sandy loam soil with a pH of 6.5–7.0. Space 4–6 ft. apart. Construct a watering basin 4 ft. in diameter and mulch with 1 in. of humus or compost.

Growing Tips
Soak deeply after planting. Water three times the first week; thereafter water every five to seven days, adjusting frequency and amount according to climatic and growth conditions. Hybrid teas do not tolerate drought conditions. Fertilize in late winter, early spring, and early summer with a complete organic granular rose food.

Advice and Care
Do not prune a newly planted hybrid tea, just remove any dead wood. Once established after twelve months, prune in January or February when the plants are dormant to remove old, woody canes that have "dog legs" (where one stem grows out of another); leave the vigorous newer canes that are green and growing straight out of the plant's base. Mildew, blackspot, rust, and chlorosis are typical for hybrid teas. For mildew, blackspot, and rust, use a canola-based horticultural oil, or a systemic fungicide formulated for roses. Chelated iron is an effective corrective for iron deficiencies. Insect infestations of aphids, thrips, scale, and caterpillars can occur during growth and bloom cycles from April to November. Handpick and squish caterpillars or use B.t., wash off aphids with a stream of water in the early morning, and try introducing beneficial insects such as ladybugs and praying mantis to control sucking insects. For thrips, spray with spinosad.

Companion Planting and Design
Ideal companion plants are other hybrid teas, clematis, 'Edward Goucher' abelia, and rock rose.

Try These
'Double Delight' has spicy scented blooms that are white with creamy yellow edged in strawberry red. 'Mister Lincoln', with deep red blooms, is the most popular hybrid tea and has strong melon scent. For a stunning white, floriferous, vigorous, disease-resistant, and very fragrant hybrid tea, 'Sugar Moon' is a great choice.

Miniature

Rosa spp.

Bloom Period and Seasonal Color
Blends and white, pink, lavender, yellow, orange, red, bicolored, and striped flowers bloom midsummer to first frost.

Mature Height × Spread
6 in. to 3 ft. × 6 in. to 1 ft.

Botanical Pronunciation
ROSE-ah

Zones 5–11

In Victorian times the miniature rose was a popular potted plant, but it was thought to have disappeared by the end of the nineteenth century. Then in 1918, Major Roulet saw a tiny rose growing on a window ledge in Switzerland, and he named this tenacious survivor *Rosa rouletii*. This double-flowered, deep rose-pink elfin specimen became the founder of the modern miniature rose class. They are the smallest of roses in flower size, some no bigger than the head of a hatpin, while others are larger, and they come in an ever-widening range of colors with many blends and striped patterns. In form they are just as varied, from simple five-petal flowers to the full, high-centered types that resemble scaled-down versions of hybrid teas.

When, Where, and How to Plant
Plant in spring or early summer from 4–6-in. pots; grow as a container specimen or space 6–12 in. apart. Most miniatures prefer full sun for at least six hours a day and sandy loam soil with a pH of 6.5–7.0. If planted in the ground, construct a watering basin 1 ft. in diameter and mulch with 1 in. of humus or compost.

Growing Tips
While most miniatures are winter hardy and tolerate short periods of wind and high temperatures if adequately watered, they do not like drought conditions. Soak deeply after planting. Water daily during the first week. Regular watering is most important, especially in dry weather, because miniatures do not have the root systems of larger varieties. Fertilize every week from spring to late summer with a complete water-soluble rose food at half-strength, or use a slow-release food.

Advice and Care
They go dormant in winter, leaf out in March, bloom in midsummer, and continue to flower until the first frost. Do not prune a newly planted miniature rose, just remove any dead wood. Once established after twelve months, prune in January to train and remove old leaves and dead wood, and trim for shape. Clear the ground of all leaves and weeds. As flowers fade, snip stems back to an outside bud. Generally speaking, they are susceptible during growth and bloom cycles to mildew, blackspot, rust, and insect infestations of aphids and thrips. For blackspot, mildew, and rust, use canola-based horticultural oil. To control rose slugs and thrips, spray with spinosad.

Companion Planting and Design
Use to brighten the front of mixed borders or containers or to accent a rock garden. Mix with Transvaal daisies, candytuft, and alyssum.

Try These
'Sun Sprinkles' has small, but many-petaled, yellow blooms that have a light, spicy scent. 'Tropical Twist' has apricot pink-coral blooms, maturing into a compact 2 ft. tall and wide bush. 'Coffee Bean' is genetically linked to 'Hot Cocoa' in miniature form, with smoky red-orange flowers and a light tea fragrance.

SHRUBS

FOR CALIFORNIA

While at New Zealand's Taranaki Rhododendron Festival, we visited several private gardens, including one owned by a sprightly eighty-five-year-old. Visiting her garden was like entering a painting filled with a variety of textures and a rainbow of colors, all accomplished by massive plantings of azaleas and rhododendrons interspersed with areas of lush lawns, brilliant pink and red camellias, lemon-scented mock oranges, and assorted pine trees, as well as alabaster gardenias and canary yellow hibiscus. With a gifted painter's eye, she used her shrubs as more than mere multitrunked woody plants plopped in a landscape between trees, flowers, and lawns. Instead they were grouped in borders and hedges, interplanted in flower beds, highlighted as specimens, and clustered in foundation plantings—proving that shrubs can be the base coat, top coat, or colorful trim for any garden.

First Do Your Homework

Before purchasing and planting a shrub, carefully consider local climatic conditions, site locations, and the shrub's particular needs and habits. A little homework beforehand will save time, money, and effort afterward as you maintain the plant's health or minimize pruning to keep it within bounds. A little 1-gallon yew pine or Hollywood twisted juniper will grow much taller, just as a young child grows until reaching full adulthood. If such a shrub is planted as a foundation shrub in front of an average-sized home, in a few years it might be much too tall, obscuring the house or blocking window views. For foundation plantings and borders, it is wiser to plant low- to medium-height evergreen or deciduous shrubs.

A Multitude of Choices

Whether the landscape calls for evergreen or deciduous, berry or flower bearing, screening or showcasing, there are shrubs for every purpose. For showy spring flowers and deep green foliage in shaded areas, few plants can compete with azaleas, camellias, and hydrangeas. Others are known less for their flowers but have variegated foliage, including golden mirror plants, which look as if a painter took a paintbrush and stippled the leaves with gold. Some, like heavenly bamboo, laurustinus, and many southern highbush blueberries, provide blazing autumn color and bright berries. If fluttery visitations from ruby-tinged hummingbirds, plump bees, and boldly patterned monarch and swallowtail butterflies are important to you, find sunny areas for the Japanese mock orange, mystery gardenia, lilacs, and shrub roses—their delicate fragrant flowers and sweet nectar are perfect metaphors for the sweetness of life. For those who think good hedges make good neighbors, Italian cypress, yew pines, and laurustinus are ideal choices. Hollywood twisted junipers are excellent accent plants in areas that allow for their mature dimensions, often grouped or planted in pairs on opposite sides of driveways and walkways in formal landscapes.

A Multitude of Uses

Instead of planting in linear, single-file formations, add depth by planting taller shrubs toward the back and low-spreading or ground-covering varieties in the front. Cluster identical shrubs for focal points, or combine with trees to create a shade garden or wooded landscape. Evergreen shrubs that prefer pruning are great when planted for formal hedges or verdant

Shrub roses are ideal as foundation plants.

walls. Use taller evergreen shrubs as a backdrop for the seasonal changes of shorter deciduous shrubs, annuals, and bulbs. Avoid combining drought-tolerant shrubs with thirsty ones, or shade-lovers with sun-seekers. While upright and pyramidal shapes draw the eyes skyward and lend themselves to the more formal landscape, the weeping, mounding, or spreading shapes anchor our vision to ground level and reflect a more relaxed plan.

To soften or camouflage, to brighten or shade, to flower or green—whatever the purpose, there are shrubs for every need. They make graceful bridges between tall trees and smaller perennials, lawns, groundcovers, and annuals, and also shine as gregarious floral showpieces, or hide in the muted shade of more forceful plants. Even in winter, many deciduous shrubs have colorful bark patterns or interesting branch structures. Use them as a gifted artist would use a rainbow palette of texture and color.

Azalea

Rhododendron indica

Bloom Period and Seasonal Color
Red, white, pink, orange, and variegated flowers bloom in spring.

Mature Height × Spread 4–6 ft. × 4–6 ft.

Botanical Pronunciation
RO-doe-den-dron IN-dih-cuh

Zones 9–11

People are often confused about whether a plant should be called a rhododendron or an azalea. All azaleas are rhododendrons, but not all rhododendrons are azaleas. In other words, azaleas, whether evergreen or deciduous, are one of the three main categories of rhododendrons (the others being *Vireya* and true *Rhododendron*). Azaleas are one of the most popular shade plants used in landscapes. In spring, single or double funnel-like flowers cluster on almost every branch tip in just about every color except bright blue. Once their flowers are spent, their elliptical-shaped, dense, hunter green foliage dominates, with delicate hairlike filaments covering the surface. Their profuse blooms and domelike form lend themselves to formal and informal landscapes. Just remember, azaleas are rhododendrons, and they require the same care.

When, Where, and How to Plant
Plant in the spring from 1- or 5-gallon containers. There are sun-tolerant azaleas, but all varieties do much better in partial shade, and all need porous, organically rich soil that permits air and moisture movement. A soil pH of 5.5–6.5 is a basic requirement for growth. Mix equal parts peat and sandy loam soil. Plant the rootball 2 in. above the soil surface to account for settling. If you have dense, clay soils, plant azaleas in containers, raised beds, or mounded areas.

Growing Tips
Moisture should always be available in the root zone, but don't keep the soil soggy. Adjust the amount and frequency of watering according to growth and climatic conditions. Fertilize after blooms are spent with an organic, acid food or cottonseed meal. Since azalea foliage tends to become chlorotic because of a lack of iron, periodically apply chelated iron to the foliage or the soil in amounts specified by the manufacturer.

Advice and Care
If any flower petals remain after the bloom cycle, deadhead them—do not allow them to go to seed. The fine-textured foliage hair traps dust that should be washed off periodically. Monitor azaleas for spider mites and thrips. Control mites with a miticide or a canola-based horticultural oil and use spinosad for thrips.

Companion Planting and Design
One of the most popular shade plants used in formal and informal landscapes as shrub, topiaries, or in containers, they combine well with camellias and hydrangeas.

Try These
R. indica 'Rosea' is a southern Indian azalea with semidouble rose-red flowers that open from roselike buds; it grows 4–6 ft. tall and 4–6 ft. wide. A midseason bloomer is 'California Snow', whose large, pure-white blooms are true double flowers. *R. indica* 'Chimes' is one of the most radiant semidouble-blossomed varieties of the Belgian Indian group, with dark red blooms occurring midseason. Brooks hybrids were developed to be more heat tolerant. Compact in form with large flowers, 'Madonna' has white blooms, 'My Valentine' comes in rose, and 'Red Wing' is deep red.

Camellia

Camellia spp.

Bloom Period and Seasonal Color
Red, white, pink, yellow, or variegated flowers bloom in late winter and early spring.

Mature Height × Spread 6–15 ft. × 4–8 ft.

Botanical Pronunciation
kah-MEE-lee-ah

Zones 8–11

Camellia has glossy bright green leaves and symmetrical, 4-in. flowers, either single or double in form, blanketing these multibranched evergreen shrubs. For short periods of time they can tolerate temperatures as low as 10 degrees Fahrenheit; if it is hot and dry, their foliage will scorch. Be on the lookout for camellia blight, a fungus with an interesting cycle. During winter and spring rains, moisture splashes the soil and moves the fungus from the soil to the branches and foliage, then to the buds and opening flower petals. When and if the buds open, the petals decay and are brown and mushy. If infected buds, flowers, and leaves are left on the ground, the cycle will continue and destroy your plant's flower production.

When, Where, and How to Plant
Plant 4–8 ft. apart from 1- or 5-gallon containers in late winter or early spring. Refer to p. 20 for more information. Choose a shaded area with sun exposure until ten in the morning. Camellias need acidic soil, pH 6.0–6.5.

Growing Tips
It is most important to avoid overwatering—once established, keep the soil a bit on the dry side. If planted in loam soil, water thoroughly about once a week or as weather and growing conditions dictate. As the bloom season ends and the new growth begins, fertilize with cottonwood meal or a specially formulated food designed for camellia. If it is a granular fertilizer, make sure you distribute it evenly in the watering basin, and soak-in thoroughly.

Advice and Care
Unless the plants are overgrown, you do not normally need to hard-prune the canopies. It is a good idea to clear away and dispose of any spent flowers and fallen leaves to help control camellia blight. If you prefer a more aggressive approach, use a fungicide to control the blight, but be aware that this will not eliminate the fungus; it will only serve as a control. Bud drop is another malady, caused by unfavorable temperatures, moisture stress, malnutrition, frost, bud mite, or root rot. Monitor these conditions to minimize the bud drop symptom.

Companion Planting and Design
Since the roots are not invasive, this is an ideal shrub to grow in shaded plant groupings about 3 ft. from the foundation of a home. Plant with other shade-lovers such as azaleas, Japanese maples, and hydrangeas.

Try These
C. *japonica* 'Kramer's Supreme' grows 6–10 ft. bearing very large peony-form flowers in a deep red color. It also has a slight fragrance and blooms midseason. C. *japonica* 'Debutante' has abundant, large, light pink, peony-form flowers and is an early bloomer. The hybrid 'High Fragrance' has very fragrant small, ivory-pink, peony-form blooms on a 3–4-ft. bush. C. *sasanqua* 'Shishigashira' is more sun tolerant, with semidouble red flowers on a low-growing shrub.

Golden Mirror Plant

Coprosma repens 'Aurea'

Bloom Period and Seasonal Color
Flowers are insignificant.

Mature Height × Spread 3–4 ft. × 4–6 ft.

Botanical Pronunciation
Ko-PRAHZ-mah REP-enz AR-ree-ah

Zones 9–11

Golden mirror plants are so named because their spatula-shaped leaves have shiny, waxy surfaces. They are low-growing, spreading shrubs with variegated green-and-gold foliage. Many varieties produce small, colorful clusters of seeds in hues of yellow-orange to red that are eaten and dispersed by visiting birds. In their natural habitat they grow along the seacoast and can tolerate strong winds but not extended periods of freezing temperatures or drought conditions. As long as there is adequate humidity and moisture, *Coprosma repens* can withstand heat. Although their flowers are insignificant, their variegated foliage adds color and texture to the landscape. Golden mirror plants are dioecious—the male and female flowers are on separate plants. Plant male (with stamens) and female (with pistils) plants close together for seed development.

When, Where, and How to Plant
Plant golden mirror plants from 1- or 5-gallon containers in the fall, late winter, or early spring. Avoid planting in the summer months because they dislike hot, dry conditions. Since they are found along the coast, they tolerate pH soil readings as high as 7.2 and do best in full-sun or partial-shade locations. Space 6–8 ft. apart in well-drained, slightly acidic soils. Refer to p. 20 for more information. Mulch the surface of the ground beyond the canopy of the plant with 2–3 in. of humus mulch or compost.

Growing Tips
Water regularly to encourage the development of deep roots, especially during heat waves. If fertilizing is necessary, apply a complete organic or slow-release food in early spring.

Advice and Care
To maintain their shape, prune back only the errant branches. Deadheading is unnecessary. Propagate in spring from semihardwood cuttings. They are resistant to diseases and pests.

Companion Planting and Design
Close to the ocean, use them as low-maintenance plants—once they are established, they require little care. Plant several different varieties together in your landscape for interesting contrast. Also use them in mass plantings such as hedges and windbreaks to provide a milder microclimate for other plants such as ivy geraniums, lily of the Nile, and impatiens.

Try These
C. *repens* 'Golden Splash' has uniformly golden-yellow foliage while C. *r.* 'Marble Queen' has light green-and-white foliage and grows 2–3 ft. tall. 'Tequila Sunrise' foliage is green and gold edged in red-orange, growing 2 ft. tall and 2–3 ft. wide. C. *r.* 'Pink Splendor' has deep green foliage with yellow margins that later turn pink. C. *r.* 'Argentea' has green leaves flecked with silvery white. C. × *kirkii* 'Gold King' is a low-growing prostrate form that is good for bank cover. Growing 8–12 in. and spreading 2–3 ft., it has petite, deep green leaves accented with golden splotches. Prune to encourage dense growth. C. × *kirkii* 'Variegata' is good for baskets since it only grows to 6 in. tall, but spreads to 5 ft.

Heavenly Bamboo

Nandina domestica

Bloom Period and Seasonal Color
White flowers bloom in spring, berries in fall.

Mature Height × Spread 4–6 ft. (clumping)

Botanical Pronunciation
nan-DEEN-ah DOE-mes-tih-kah

Zones 7–11

Heavenly bamboo is popular in temple gardens because its appearance is similar to that of bamboo, yet it has a hardier nature and colorful leaves. Compound, lacy foliage is multicolored, in hues of red, orange, yellow, and green, and held on upright, canelike stems. During the summer, white sprays of flowers are pollinated by honeybees, butterflies, and wind but the resulting bright red berries that form in the fall are the more spectacular feature of these plants, and provide food for your resident and migratory birds. The plants are dioecious, meaning male and female flowers are borne on separate plants. Both are needed for cross-pollination for the development of berries. Once established, heavenly bamboo tolerates drought, cold, and heat, but prefers protection from the wind.

When, Where, and How to Plant

Plant heavenly bamboo anytime from 1- or 5-gallon containers where winters are mild. Partial shade is preferred, although they will grow in full sun. Heavenly bamboo plants tolerate pH ranges from 6.5–7.0. They prefer loam soil but will adapt to denser soil. Make the watering basin twice the plant's diameter, create a berm 4–6 in. in height, and mulch the basin's surface with 2 in. of compost or humus mulch. For accent groupings in your landscape, plant them 4 ft. on center. Refer to p. 20 for more information.

Growing Tips

Thoroughly water after planting; thereafter irrigate about twice a week until established. Never allow the root zone to completely dry out, because the foliage will wilt and the plant might not recover. Fertilize twice a year, in early spring and late summer, with a complete organic granular food.

Advice and Care

If you do not want berries to develop, deadhead the spent flowers—otherwise, leave the blossoms alone. Once the berries have dropped off, you can remove the flower stems (pedicels) if their appearance is an annoyance. If you want to emphasize the vertical beauty of their stems, remove the lower leaves from the bottom two-thirds of the plant. Very few diseases or pests affect heavenly bamboo, which is also known to be deer resistant. Wash periodically to clean out accumulated debris.

Companion Planting and Design

You can plant heavenly bamboo *en masse* to serve as foundation plantings. They also grow well with prostrate Natal plum, shore junipers, and pink Indian hawthorn. Heavenly bamboo's autumn-colored leaves and red berries are wonderful seasonal additions to your cutflower arrangements.

Try These

New varieties are developed with enhanced spring and fall foliage colors. *N. domestica* 'Gulf Stream' grows to 4 ft. with bronze new growth and red fall color. Dwarf variety 'Fire Power' grows just 2 ft. tall and wide. 'Harbor Dwarf' grows to 3 ft., and 'Sienna Sunrise' grows 3–4 ft. with fiery red new foliage. Taller types, growing to 6–8 ft., are 'Moyers Red', 'Plum Passion', and 'Royal Princess'.

Hollywood Twisted Juniper

Juniperus chinensis 'Torulosa'

Bloom Period and Seasonal Color
There are no flowers; the Hollywood twisted juniper is coniferous.

Mature Height × Spread 8–15 ft. × 6–10 ft.

Botanical Pronunciation
JUNE-ih-per-is CHIH-nen-sis TOR-yew-lose-ah

Zones 5–11

*J*uniperus chinensis 'Torulosa' is a dense, tall, erect, and twisted freeform shrub. Imported from China and Japan, it has adapted easily to mild Mediterranean climates such as that found in Southern California. We suspect that its common name, Hollywood twisted juniper, comes from the fact that it was planted so extensively along the streets and in the gardens of Tinsel Town. It has finely textured, matte green foliage that emits a pungent smell when crushed. In summer, it forms clusters of small bluish cones that look like berries. Once established, it is extremely tolerant to wind and drought conditions, as well as temperatures down to -10 degrees Fahrenheit. If sufficient moisture is provided, it also withstands the extreme temperatures of the desert.

When, Where, and How to Plant
Choose from a variety of container sizes, even 24–36-in. boxed specimens. Spring or fall, plant these shrubs in full sun or semishade in a well-drained, slightly acidic soil with a pH of 6.5–7.0, and space at least 8–10 ft. on center. Create a watering basin twice the diameter of the plant's canopy; water thoroughly to collapse air pockets in the root zone. Mulch this surface with 2 in. of compost or humus mulch. Refer to p. 20 for more information.

Growing Tips
Water one to two times per week until established; thereafter, water deeply every seven to fourteen days, adjusting for climatic conditions and growth. Fertilize in fall and spring with a complete organic granular food.

Advice and Care
There is no need to prune, unless it is grown as a topiary or espalier. If you want to control their height, width, and twisted form, train these plants into topiaries or espaliers by selectively pruning for shape in late winter or early spring. Select the main vertical trunks that define the plant's form and identify the lateral branches where the growth of new foliage occurs. Next, take a picture or make a sketch of your plant, and using a pen, draw in the desired shape or design that you want. As time goes on, prune accordingly until your creative idea becomes a reality. Few if any pests bother this plant, but spray with water periodically to clean out accumulated debris.

Companion Planting and Design
Use Hollywood twisted juniper as an accent plant in large spaces. It is often planted in pairs on opposite sides of driveways and walkways in formal landscapes. Plant along coastal areas where constant prevailing winds sculpt their shapes into dramatic twisted forms. For companion plants, try pink Indian hawthorn, bird of paradise, and Japanese mock orange.

Try These
'Torulosa Variegata' has splashes of yellow variegations in the foliage. 'Gold Lace' has green foliage with gold tips, spreading to 6 ft. 'Gold Star' is compact with blue-green inner foliage and gold outer foliage.

Hydrangea

Hydrangea macrophylla

Bloom Period and Seasonal Color
Pink, blue, red, lavender, greenish white, or white flowers bloom in spring.

Mature Height × Spread 4–6 ft. × 6–8 ft.

Botanical Pronunciation
HI-dran-gee-ah MAK-ro-fi-lah

Zones 6–11

Many believe the name hydrangea, with its origin in the word *hydra*, means that the plant requires massive amounts of water. Actually, the name was given because the seed capsules look like water pitchers. Hydrangeas are large, mound-shaped shrubs with long 6–8-in., dark green leaves that have coarsely serrated margins. They are used as accent plants in shady environments and are also available in flower shops as blooming potted plants. Their spectacular round clusters of blossoms can reach diameters of 10 in. Although their natural color is light pink, hydrangeas have variable colors that depend on their genetic history, soil chemistry, and location. Hybrids come in shades of red, pink, lavender, purple, blue, white, and whitish green, and bloom throughout the spring months.

When, Where, and How to Plant
In the spring, after the last frost, select 1- or 5-gallon hydrangeas. Plant in partially shaded sites, although they will tolerate full sun as long as it is cool and humid. They prefer an acidic soil, pH 6.5–7.0. To ensure vigorous plants and good percolation, use a highly organic soil mixture of equal parts loam and planting mix. After you have a watering basin that is 4–6 ft. in diameter and 4–6 in. high, spread a blanket of humus mulch or compost that is 2–3 in. deep over the basin's surface. Plant 6 ft. on center. See p. 20 for additional information.

Growing Tips
Successful cultivation requires an abundant supply of moisture, in an area protected from the wind and freezing temperatures. It is imperative that you water deeply, thoroughly, and regularly, keeping in mind the important variables of temperature, season, and wind activity. Fertilize with an acidic formulated food or cottonseed meal, once in early spring after the last frost and once in early summer.

Advice and Care
In early summer, after blooming, prune back about 20 percent. Cut out dead wood, dried inflorescences, and errant, crossing branches to ensure sufficient air circulation and that light is able to reach the centers of the plants. If you want a profusion of smaller blossoms, remove the terminal buds in early spring. This stimulates the development of multiple flowers on the lower portion of the stems. To keep flowers blue, apply aluminum sulfate to the soil; to keep them pink or red, add lime. Control aphid infestations by washing the critters off with a strong stream of water or use a canola-based horticultural oil.

Companion Planting and Design
Hydrangeas are perfect as foundation plants combined with mystery gardenias, camellias, and saucer magnolias.

Try These
'Endless Summer' (blue mophead), 'Blushing Bride' (white mophead that ages to pink), and 'Twist-n-Shout' (pink or blue lacecap) bloom on old and new wood. 'Shooting Star' or 'Hanabi' is another lacecap with pure-white, double, star-shaped flowers that eventually turn a pale green.

Japanese Mock Orange

Pittosporum tobira

Bloom Period and Seasonal Color
Aromatic white, citrus-scented flowers bloom in spring.

Mature Height × Spread 6–8 ft. × 6 ft.

Botanical Pronunciation
PITT-oh-spore-um TOE-by-rah

Zones 9–11

Japanese mock orange, considered a large shrub or small tree, is a vigorous grower with shiny green leaves. As a tree it can reach a height of 12–15 ft., but if grown as a shrub, it can be limited to 6–8 ft. Even though it does not produce oranges, it bears wonderfully aromatic citrus-scented clusters of creamy white spring flowers. Once established, Japanese mock orange tolerates drought, wind, and even heat if enough moisture is available, but it dislikes extended periods of freezing temperatures. We grouped a dwarf St. Mary's magnolia tree, mystery gardenias, and variegated Japanese mock orange in an enclosed patio. On warm spring and summer evenings, it was delightful to enjoy their fragrances wafting on the nightly breeze.

When, Where, and How to Plant
Plant Japanese mock orange from 1- or 5-gallon containers in spring or fall. Place in full sun or partial shade and provide a porous soil that permits good percolation. Soil pH needs to be slightly acidic to neutral, 6.5–7.0. Build a watering basin 6 ft. in diameter with an edge 4–6 in. high. Mulch the basin's surface with 2 in. of humus mulch or compost as needed. Space 6 ft. on center if using as a hedge, 10 ft. if using as a single focal plant. Refer to p. 20 for more information.

Growing Tips
In loam soils, soak deeply every seven to ten days, adjusting watering frequency according to climatic and growing conditions. Fertilize with a complete organic granular food in early spring.

Advice and Care
Prune for shape or cut back errant growth in late winter or early spring. Deadheading the flowers is unnecessary unless you wish to eliminate seed development. Control aphid infestations by washing off with a strong stream of water or applying a canola-based horticultural oil.

Companion Planting and Design
With blossoms resembling clusters of creamy white stars against a backdrop of green or variegated foliage, it makes an excellent hedge plant or an ideal choice for a scented garden. For companion plantings we recommend magnolia trees, mystery gardenias, lily of the Nile, and bird of paradise. Both the green and variegated varieties of Japanese mock orange make wonderful fillers for fresh flower arrangements.

Try These
P. tobira 'Wheeleri', commonly called Wheeler's Dwarf, is a very dense plant with a mounded 2–3-ft. tall form. There is no need for pruning if spaced 8–10 ft. on center; it is available as solid green or variegated in 'Turners Variegated Dwarf'. 'Cream de Mint' has mint green leaves with cream edging and grows 2½ ft. tall. *P. undulatum* is a Victorian box from Australia. It matures slowly to 30 ft. or more, making a dense green screen when planted 10–15 ft. apart. It also has creamy, fragrant white flowers in spring.

Laurustinus

Viburnum tinus

Bloom Period and Seasonal Color
Pink buds and white flowers are present throughout the year.

Mature Height × Spread 5–10 ft. × 6 ft.

Botanical Pronunciation
VI-burn-um TY-nus

Zones 8–11

Laurustinus is a medium to large evergreen shrub with a dense branching structure that characteristically grows from its base upward, creating a mass of foliage and flowers. The leathery leaves are dark green above and lighter in color underneath. It blooms periodically throughout the year, but is most abundant in the late winter to early spring. The buds are initially pale pink, and then as they open, they transform into clusters of delicately fragrant white flowers. Indigo berries appear simultaneously with the flowers, creating a lovely contrast of fruits and blossoms on a single plant. Since the flowering cycle is fairly continuous throughout the year, the simultaneous appearance of buds, blooms, and berries is one of the unique features of laurustinus.

When, Where, and How to Plant
Plant in early spring or early fall from 1- or 5-gallon containers. This popular plant grows in just about any location, sun or shade, but full sun is preferable for flower and berry production. Avoid planting in areas where there are extended periods of freezing temperatures or frigid winds. Make sure the soil is porous, loam, and well draining with 20–30 percent organic material. Soil pH needs to be slightly acidic or neutral, 6.5–7.0. Build a watering basin large enough to encourage lateral root growth. Space 6–8 ft. on center if you want a hedge whose mature height is 6–10 ft. Create a long watering basin 2 ft. from the hedge line and build two parallel berms, 6 in. high. Mulch the surface of the basin with 2 in. of compost or humus mulch.

Growing Tips
Laurustinus is not drought tolerant, but it can withstand heat if you provide adequate moisture. After planting, water thoroughly and deeply to collapse air pockets in the root zone. Subsequently, water every seven to ten days, adjusting for growth and weather conditions. Feed in spring and fall with a complete organic granular fertilizer or cottonseed meal.

Advice and Care
Prune for shape and size after spring bloom; deadhead only to prevent seed production. Laurustinus is a dense grower. Frequent pruning is unnecessary, but to encourage continued growth, lace the plant about once a year in fall, cutting out the dead wood, pruning off any errant growth, and opening the canopy. Control mildew and aphids by washing off with a strong stream of water or applying a canola-based horticultural oil.

Companion Planting and Design
It makes a fine hedge, foundation planting, or even an individual focal plant. Red clusterberry cotoneaster, saucer magnolia, and glossy abelia make ideal companion plants.

Try These
There is a variegated form, 'Variegatum', that has white and pale yellow marbled foliage. 'Spring Bouquet' has smaller leaves and is more compact, growing to 4–6 ft. tall and wide.

Lilac

Syringa vulgaris hybrids

Bloom Period and Seasonal Color
Lavender, blue, pink, white, and purple flowers in spring.

Mature Height × Spread 10–20 ft. × 6–15 ft.

Botanical Pronunciation
sih-RINJ-ah VULE-gah-rus

Zones 3–10

The fragrance of lilacs announces the arrival of spring with a captivating flourish. In the past, lilacs used to come in just two colors—purple and white—but current hybridizers offer a potpourri of colors ranging from lilac, white, blue, purple, magenta, violet, pink, and bicolors, as well as different growth habits, bloom sizes, shapes, and flowering times. All lilacs (approximately 20 species) belong to the genus *Syringa*, but the most popular is *Syringa vulgaris*, described by Walt Whitman as having "heart-shaped leaves of rich green . . . with the perfume strong I love." Until recently, most lilacs were cold-climate plants thriving best in USDA zones 3–7, but fortunately for Californians, Descanso lilacs—hybrids with heat tolerance and excellent bloom production where winters are mild—are now available.

When, Where, and How to Plant
Plant in winter to early spring from bare rootstock or spring to fall from containers. When planting, take care to situate it so that the graft is slightly above the level of the soil. Provide well-draining, slightly alkaline soil, and plant in full sun. It is not necessary to add soil amendments unless the soil is very clayey or sandy. Refer to p. 20 for more planting information. They also need space to encourage good air circulation; avoid planting in or near lawns because of different watering needs.

Growing Tips
Once established, water every seven to ten days to keep the soil moist but not soggy and decrease or withhold near the end of September to encourage dormancy in Southern California. Where winter temperatures are colder, dormancy will occur naturally. Resume watering around February if there is little rainfall, just when the buds begin to swell. Feed with an organic granular fertilizer just before buds form, usually in late winter.

Advice and Care
For the most flowers, prune lilacs for shape after their blooms are spent. Deadhead old blooms to encourage reblooming. Spray with a canola-based horticultural oil for downy mildew, scale, and aphids.

Companion Planting and Design
Group lilacs to form visual screens, but space them to ensure good air circulation. Tall shrub lilacs provide shade for patios, and particularly fragrant and colorful cultivars can be spotlighted as specimen plants. They are also wonderful as foundation plants in a cottage garden. Add spring-blooming bulbs around the base of lilacs or under plant with blooming perennials such as hellebores or wood violets.

Try These
The hybrid 'Bloomerang' does well in zones 3–7, grows 4–5 ft. tall and as wide, and bears violet-blue flowers in spring and again throughout the summer where temperatures remain cool. French hybrids such as the purplish red and white-edged 'Sensation', or the lilac 'Mr. Lincoln', need winter chill. Descanso hybrids such as 'Lavender Lady', 'Angel White', the blue-flowered 'Blue Skies', and 'Blue Boy' are developed for mild-winter regions. These low-chill selections grow from 8–10 ft. tall and as wide.

Mystery Gardenia

Gardenia jasminoides 'Mystery'

Bloom Period and Seasonal Color
White flowers bloom in summer.

Mature Height × Spread 4 ft. × 4 ft.

Botanical Pronunciation
gar-DEEN-ee-ah JAZ-min-oy-deez

Zones 9–11

The genus *Gardenia* was assigned by botanist John Ellis (1711–1776) in honor of American naturalist Dr. Alexander Garden (1730–1791), and has been a longtime favorite among florists. Its waxy flowers make wonderful corsages and bouquets, as well as simple but elegant floating arrangements in brandy snifters. Gardenias are small shrubs with lustrous dark green leaves and branches that spread out and up unevenly. Their dramatic, creamy white, 3-in., double-flowered blossoms are like camellias, and intoxicate passersby with their unforgettable perfumed scent. The bloom period is from late spring to the end of summer, provided there are adequate daylight hours and warm temperatures. The flowers of 'Mystery' bloom in succession over a long blooming season, so you will rarely see a plant full of gardenias at any one time.

When, Where, and How to Plant
Plant in spring or early summer from 1- or 5-gallon containers. Select a sunny or morning sun location that is sheltered from prevailing winds—such as the east side of a house or patio. An acidic soil pH of 6.0–6.5 is preferred. It should be rich in organic material such as compost, humus mulch, or planting mix. Make sure its porosity allows for good percolation. Space 4 ft. on center. Refer to p. 20 for more planting techniques.

Growing Tips
Monitor the soil moisture content. Mystery gardenias do not like to have their roots standing in water. Fertilize mid-spring with an acidic food or cottonseed meal. During the summer months, if you find an abundance of yellow leaves toward the lower areas of your plants, it may be due to nitrogen deficiency. Apply a liquid kelp foliar feed as a corrective measure. Although they are susceptible to iron chlorosis, you can correct this problem by applying chelated iron in a water-soluble form directly to the foliage or soil.

Advice and Care
Since gardenias are native to southern China, where it is temperate and humid, they do not tolerate dry, windy, or extended cold-weather conditions. Prune to maintain shape or remove dead wood. As a precaution against the vectoring of diseases from plant to plant, and to encourage continued bloom, it is a good idea to deadhead the spent flowers. Control leafminers with spinosad and aphids with a canola-based horticultural oil or by washing off with a strong stream of water.

Companion Planting and Design
These subtropical shrubs are ideal as small patio trees, espaliers, or container plants. Yesterday-today-and-tomorrow, hibiscus, and impatiens are ideal companion plants.

Try These
G. jasminoides 'Radicans', known as the miniature gardenia, has a spreading growth pattern, growing to 12 in. high and 2 ft. wide, with rich, green petite foliage and prolific small, white, and fragrant flowers in summer; it's used as groundcover in warmer areas. 'Veitchii', considered reliable and ever-blooming, is compact: 3–4½ ft. × 6 ft.

Pink Indian Hawthorn

Rhaphiolepis indica 'Enchantress'

Bloom Period and Seasonal Color
Rose-pink flowers bloom mid-spring to early summer.

Mature Height × Spread 2–4 ft. × 3 ft.

Botanical Pronunciation
RAF-ee-oh-lep-is IN-dee-kah

Zones 8–11

*R*haphiolepis indica 'Enchantress' has a form that is known as "roundy-moundy" in the nursery trade. This term is given to plants that do not require shearing to maintain their shape because they grow so evenly and densely. Commonly called pink Indian hawthorn, it is an evergreen shrub with glossy, green, leathery leaves and serrated margins. From mid-spring to early summer, the entire plant bursts forth with massive clusters of rose-pink flowers that make it look like a beautiful spring bouquet. In the community where we live, these plants abound *en masse* because of their easy maintenance and profuse flush of spring blossoms. After the flowers are spent, blue-black berries develop and remain throughout the fall season, providing a feast for the birds.

When, Where, and How to Plant
Plant in spring or fall from 1- or 5-gallon containers. For optimum growth and bloom production, select a site in full sun, although these plants tolerate locations in partial shade. Make sure the soil texture for the backfill is loam with about 20–30 percent organic material such as compost or humus mulch, and that the soil is slightly acidic, with a pH of 6.5–7.0. After planting, build a watering basin 4–5 ft. in diameter and 4–6 in. in height; mulch the basin surface with 2 in. of compost or humus mulch. For mass plantings, space 3 or 4 ft. on center in either a triangular or square pattern. See p. 20 for more planting techniques.

Growing Tips
Water deeply and thoroughly immediately after planting; thereafter water as needed depending on climatic and soil moisture conditions. If you have any doubts about the moisture content, put a spade in the soil about 6 in. deep and push it back to expose the soil profile; if it is wet, wait two or three days before deep soaking. Fertilize early spring and early fall with cottonseed meal or slow-release food.

Advice and Care
Deadhead only if you do not want the berries. It is wise to lace out the maturing plant. Prune back any errant growth to maintain the naturally symmetrical shape. Control aphids by washing off with a strong stream of water or applying a canola-based horticultural oil. Control snails with a molluscicide such as iron phosphate.

Companion Planting and Design
Pink Indian hawthorn makes ideal border plants or large groupings on banks combined with other landscape plants. Because of its compact nature, it is also a popular plant with bonsai enthusiasts. Golden mirror plant, heavenly bamboo, and rock rose make good companions.

Try These
R. indica 'Ballerina' is small, growing to just 2 ft. × 4 ft. with deep pink flowers. *Rhaphiolepis umbellata* is from Japan and commonly known as yeddo (syn: *R. ovata*) hawthorn. It has fragrant white flowers with bright pink-red stamens.

Sasanqua Camellia

Camellia sasanqua

Bloom Period and Seasonal Color
Red, white, pink, or variegated flowers bloom in late winter or early spring.

Mature Height × Spread 3 ft. × 4 ft.

Botanical Pronunciation
kah-MEE-lee-ah sah-SAN-kwah

Zones 7–11

Sasanquas are considered among the hardiest of the camellia species. They bloom from fall to early spring and can withstand temperatures as low as 0 degrees Fahrenheit. Among the most sun tolerant of the camellias, they flower best in winter sun; survive hot, dry climates; and also thrive in light shade. Even though their flowers are smaller (usually 3 in. diameter), many are fragrant and they are more prolific bloomers than *C. japonica* or *C. reticulata*, making a floriferous show for months. Colors range from white to pink to light red to variegated; flowers are single, semidouble, or double. Other than feeding, watering, and deadheading, sasanqua camellias require very little care. Their roots are not invasive so they make ideal choices for group plantings.

When, Where, and How to Plant

Plant from 1- or 5-gallon containers in late winter or early spring. A semishady location is not critical, but the foliage might scorch if there is too much sunlight or low-humidity conditions. Plant in acidic to neutral soil, pH 6.5–7.0. Space 4–6 ft. apart. See p. 20 for planting information. For containers, fill with a commercial azalea-camellia planting mix.

Growing Tips

Avoid overwatering and allow to dry out slightly before watering again. If in loam soil, water thoroughly about once a week or as weather dictates. Fertilize as the bloom season ends and the new growth begins (usually in spring) with a specially formulated food for camellias. If using a granular fertilizer, distribute it evenly in the watering basin, and soak in thoroughly.

Advice and Care

Unless the plants are overgrown, it is unnecessary to hard-prune the canopies. Inspect foliage and branches for brown soft scale and mite infestations. If left untreated, these parasites will proliferate, hinder normal foliage and stem development, and desiccate the plant. Use a suffocant like horticultural oil to control, following manufacturer's directions.

Companion Planting and Design

Sasanquas are perfect for those who love camellias but need a more sun-tolerant species for their landscape. They grow in the ground or in containers, as patio trees, in hanging baskets, or as low, spreading shrubs. Espalier them against a wall or fence for a dramatic display—the glossy, dark green foliage contrasts beautifully with the profuse display of flowers. Plant with other shade-tolerant plants like azaleas, vinca minor, and hydrangeas.

Try These

C. sasanqua 'Apple Blossom' is white with cerise-red edges, and crowned with golden stamens. It blooms midseason, grows upright, and is excellent for an espalier. 'Shishigashira' is low growing and spreading, with semidouble, bright red flowers. It is ideal for hanging baskets or for groundcover. 'Setsigekka' has large white semidouble blooms on a bushy shrub. 'Bonanza' is low growing and spreading, with scarlet red blooms. 'Yuletide' blooms in late fall to early winter with single, red flowers that welcome the holiday season.

Shrub Rose

Rosa hybrids

Bloom Period and Seasonal Color
Most colors except blue in spring to fall.

Mature Height × Spread 1½ × 2–6 ft.

Botanical Pronunciation
ROSE-ah

Zones 4–11

Shrub roses, often known as landscape roses, have been bred to be hardy, repeat blooming, colorful, and often fragrant. Easy growing, disease resistant, summer- and winter-hardy, they are perfect for areas where disease and weather conditions make other types of roses more of a growing challenge. Some shrub roses stand tall, with rambunctious, ever-extending canes, while others remain demure and compact. Dr. Griffith Buck developed hardier varieties for landscaping that needed little or no maintenance, and many of David Austin's hybrids combine hardiness and vigor with the beauty of old-fashioned roses. Their flowers and hips are rich in vitamin C and used in cooking, medication, and flower arrangements. Birds enjoy the hips during winter months. Use shrub roses for screens, hedges, and mass plantings.

When, Where, and How to Plant
Plant in winter or spring from bare rootstock or spring to summer from containers. Provide full sun and sandy loam, slightly acidic soil. See p. 20 for more rose planting and pruning information. Space 4–6 ft. apart or closer for hedges.

Growing Tips
Soak thoroughly after planting. Water about three times during the first few weeks and once established, water every five to seven days. Fertilize spring to summer with a complete organic food recommended for roses or use a slow-release food formulated for roses.

Advice and Care
Wait for twelve months before pruning shrub roses. Trim off dead, interfering, or damaged stems and branches. Deadheading will stop bloom and rose hip production. Shrub roses are known for disease resistance, but if mildew, rust, or aphid infestations become persistent and a strong stream of water does not control them, spray with a canola-based horticultural oil or a systemic insecticide/fungicide formulated for roses. To keep ants from farming aphids, set out ant baits.

Companion Planting and Design
Plant shrub roses in casual gardens or mix with other perennials and shrubs. For spring to fall color, plant in containers or as an edging for lawns or carefree borders, and alongside ponds, patios, pathways, and embankments. Group in threes or fives along fences or mix in with perennial beds. Many set beautiful hips in autumn for fall and winter, and if grown organically, can be used in cooking.

Try These
'The Imposter' bears single-flowered, pink with deeper pink splattered blossoms resembling clematis. It continues to bloom in a variety of climates including triple-digit temperatures, but will stop blooming if deadheaded. 'The Charlatan' resembles Higo camellias, with golden stamens on red filaments against a bed of soft pink petals. It can be grown as a shrub or a climber in warmer areas. The 'Knock Out' line of roses is known for its extreme hardiness and easy care, as well as disease resistance. For a mounding shrub, select 'Carefree Spirit', which bears huge clusters of cherry red, five-petaled flowers. 'Bonica' offers semidouble, peachy pink blossoms on arching canes with a fresh apple fragrance.

Southern Highbush Blueberry

Vaccinium corymbosum hybrids

Bloom Period and Seasonal Color
Pink or white flowers in spring and fruits in late spring to summer, depending on variety.

Mature Height × Spread 3–6 ft. × 3 ft.

Botanical Pronunciation
VAK-sin-ee-um KORE-im-bose-um

Zones 3–11

I n the past, the flower garden and the orchard and veggie areas were kept apart, but edibles can be just as ornamental, with vibrant foliage, spectacular flowers, and brightly colored fruit. Blueberries are among the edibles that should be included with other more traditional ornamental shrubs, because they make tall, handsome shrubs for hedges or borders, or in containers. Their leaves start out reddish bronze in the spring, then gradually transform into dark green hues. Fragrant white or pink bell-shaped blooms are followed by clusters of green berries that transform into plump, deep blue mouth poppers. The foliage later dons autumnal colors of scarlet reds and sunset yellows before dropping and signaling the start of winter dormancy, and southern highbush cultivars do not require winter chill to produce fruit.

When, Where, and How to Plant
Blueberries do best in full sun, in rich, amended, well-draining, and acidic soils. Southern highbush selections thrive in mild coastal and warm inland regions. Plant from early fall to early spring from containers or bare root, spacing 4–6 ft. apart. Set plants at the depth of their original containers or slightly above. They can also be planted in 15-gallon containers or half wine barrels. Fill with an organic commercial acid potting soil. Although most southern highbush are self-fruitful, plant several cultivars for an extended season (there are early-, mid-, and late-season varieties) and more bountiful harvest.

Growing Tips
Water thoroughly after planting and keep soil moist, but not soggy. Once established, water weekly or more during hot summer months. To meet their acidic needs, apply a 2–3-in. layer of mulch and fertilize with cottonseed meal or a fertilizer formulated for edibles that need acidic conditions in spring and late summer.

Advice and Care
Little pruning is required until the third year. During winter, before buds form, remove any damaged or dead wood and prune out branches that are over three years old (their productivity declines) to encourage new growth at the base. Prune lightly again after harvesting for shape. Remove all fruit buds during the first growing season to divert the plant's energy into plant development. Discourage birds, browsing deer, and other hungry critters by planting in wire cages and covering with bird-netting. Water-activated motion sensors are also effective.

Companion Planting and Design
Blueberries are great in borders or containers, or as a hedge. For a really colorful combination, plant with 'Raspberry Shortcake', a delightful, compact raspberry that is thornless.

Try These
'Misty' and 'O'Neal' are perfect for an early harvest. For mid- to late harvest, plant 'Cape Fear', 'South Moon', and 'Reveille'. For showy pink blossoms and fruit, select the evergreen 'Sunshine Blue'. Midsummer-bearing 'Peach Sorbet' has leaves ranging from peach, pink, and orange to emerald green, with a midsummer crop and foliage that remains evergreen, turning to an eggplant purple in most climates. 'Jelly Bean' is another midsummer berry perfect for zones 4–8.

Tiny Tower Italian Cypress

Cupressus sempervirens 'Tiny Tower'

Bloom Period and Seasonal Color
Evergreen foliage.

Mature Height × Spread 8 ft. × 2 ft.

Botanical Pronunciation
kew-PRES-sus sem-per-VIRE-enz

Zones 7–10

Is there a compact Italian cypress that retains its diminutive size for years and years? The answer is a resounding yes! The Tiny Tower Italian cypress possesses dense, blue-green foliage on a stiff, columnar form that is slow growing, standing 8 ft. tall and 2 ft. wide. Although it needs no shearing, it can be clipped into interesting topiary shapes. Its architectural form makes for a striking accent whether in the heat of summer or under winter snow. It is a perfect fit in containers and in small city gardens. If left alone, it will take years to reach a more statuesque height of up to 25–30 ft. and a width of 3 ft., but it can be clipped or contained to maintain a shorter stature.

When, Where, and How to Plant
Plant from containers in spring or fall spacing 3 ft. apart. Provide full sun in well-draining, amended, slightly acidic soil. See p. 20 for more planting information. In containers, fill with a commercial cactus mix and add 10–20 percent of humus, compost, or worm castings.

Growing Tips
To establish a deep, extensive root system, water newly planted cypress regularly every five to seven days during the first growing season, adjusting for soil and weather conditions. Once established, reduce watering to every fourteen to twenty-one days. Feed with a complete granular fertilizer before new growth begins in spring.

Advice and Care
This cypress is deer resistant and has few disease or insect problems. Regularly wash off accumulated debris in the interior from spring to fall to control spider mite and aphid infestations. Spider mites are arachnids that suck nutrients from the host plant and are detectable by their whitish webs. If mites persist, use a commercial miticide, not an insecticide. For aphid control, select an insecticide containing imidacloprid. Usually root rot is the result of poorly draining soil or from overwatering mature cypress. Once mature, they are drought tolerant.

Companion Planting and Design
It's perfect to plant along driveways or grouped together as focal points in formal gardens. Pairs of 'Tiny Tower' are also used as welcoming topiaries by front doors, backdrops in small spaces, or as a centerpiece in specialty gardens such as kitchen herb gardens. Plant with aromatic perennials such as French or Spanish lavender and groundcovers or upright forms of rosemary. For more formal gardens, combine with shrub and groundcover roses and clematis.

Try These
'Swane's Golden' is a very narrow Italian cypress with new growth that is a bright yellow and has a lovely evergreen scent. It is slow growing, eventually reaching a height of 15–20 ft. and a width of 2–3 ft. It is ideal in containers, as a windbreak, or where there is seaside exposure. 'Glauca' comes to mind as the classic Mediterranean cypress with blue-green foliage towering at 60–80 ft. tall and 4–6 ft. wide. It's an ideal columnar specimen for large landscape areas, privacy screens, and areas exposed to seaside conditions.

Yew Pine

Podocarpus macrophyllus

Bloom Period and Seasonal Color
Evergreen foliage.

Botanical Pronunciation
PODE-oh-karp-us MAK-roe-fy-lus

Zones 8–11

The yew pine is a columnar conifer, a densely foliated evergreen used in formal landscapes. Yew pines are used effectively as hedge plants. Although its form resembles the *Taxus* Eastern yew (hence the common name, yew pine), it is a *Podocarpus*, not a *Taxus*. The yew pine is a good substitute for the Eastern yew in western gardens. Its leaves are dark green, shiny, and finely textured. Since it is a conifer, there are no blossoms. Once established, yew pines tolerate wind, cold temperatures down to freezing, drought, and heat for short periods of time. Male yew pines bear catkins that shed pollen on the seeds of the female plants, forming small yellow cones.

When, Where, and How to Plant
Plant in fall or spring from 1-, 5-, or 15-gallon containers. If you want a more mature size, 24–30-in. boxed specimens are available. *P. macrophyllus* grows in sun or shade and prefers porous, well-drained loam soil with a neutral pH of 7.0. Space approximately 4 ft. apart if you want a cluster of three or four, but for a screening hedge, plant 3 ft. on center. Create a watering basin; mulch the basin with 2 in. of compost or humus mulch. Refer to p. 20 for additional planting information.

Growing Tips
Once established, water every two weeks, adjusting for weather and growth conditions. Fertilize twice a year, early spring and early fall, with a complete organic granular food.

Advice and Care
It is unnecessary to prune yew pines, but they can be topped to control the height for a hedge. Just be aware that their diameter and density will increase. Few diseases or pests attack this plant. Washing with a strong stream of water can control aphid or scale infestations, or apply a canola-based horticultural oil.

Companion Planting and Design
Plant them between windows where tall, narrow plants offset and complement the architectural lines of the structure. It is an excellent choice for a foundation planting, visual screen, or boundary definition, where symmetry plays an important part in the landscape design. Hollywood twisted junipers, silverberry, and lavender starflower go well with the yew pine in formal landscapes.

Try These
P. macrophyllus 'Maki', a dwarf yew pine, grows slowly to 4–6 ft. × 2 ft. It prefers sun or partial shade and is popular with bonsai enthusiasts. *P. henkelii*, Henkel's yellowwood, grows 8–10 ft. tall and is columnar like *P. macrophyllus*, except branches and foliage droop. *P. gracilior*, the fern pine, grows to 60 ft. × 20 ft., is reliable, and is pest- and carefree. Its habit varies with the means of propagation. From seed, they tend to be upright. If cutting grown, the fern pine develops finer, softer foliage with more pliable stems, making them good for espaliers.

TREES
FOR CALIFORNIA

Planting trees is a way of leaving a botanical footprint long after we are gone. We recently planted a crape myrtle tree—since they live for several hundred years, ours will probably remain to serve the next generation long after we are gone, and may still be flourishing centuries from now.

Lovely Plants of Inestimable Value

Trees are among the loveliest of living things—but they are not here as mere cosmetics, just to make our parks, streets, and gardens look nice. They help produce the air we breathe, trap and hold pollutants, offset the buildup of carbon dioxide, control and stabilize the world's climate, and feed and shelter much of the world's wildlife. An acre of trees supplies enough oxygen each day for eighteen people. Trees reduce water loss caused by surface runoff, soil erosion by wind and water, and the amount of harmful substances that wash into waterways. In addition to their economic value as lumber and sources of fuel, they screen unsightly views, soften harsh outlines of buildings, absorb and block noise, and define space.

And don't forget trees that bear edible fruit. Particularly if space is limited or for a more blended design, consider growing fruit trees not only for their crops, but for their ornamental value as well. Exquisite pink-and-white clouds of perfumed sweet cherry trees fall in a spring blizzard of floral snowflakes to make way for summer-warmed cherries and baubles of orange persimmons and red pomegranates hang in suspension, awaiting harvest in the fall while the allure of winter's light outlining their bare branches is like Vivaldi's symphonic ode to nature, *The Four Seasons*. Rather than sequestering fruiting trees in a separate orchard, try incorporating them with the rest of the plants; they can transform a bland landscape into a Garden of Eden.

As gardeners and tree lovers, we believe gardens should contain at least one tree, preferably more. For small areas, plant dwarf varieties or espalier to make a decorative screen, or to camouflage a sterile wall. If planted along the eastern and western walls of a house, they provide shade from the hot morning and afternoon sun. In winter, tall, thick trees can deflect blustery winds over and around your home.

Planning Ahead

To ensure that your trees will live long and well, give them a helping hand by planning ahead. Since trees come in a variety of shapes and sizes, from a few feet tall to towering giants, choose carefully so as not to underwhelm or overwhelm the location you have in mind. Whatever function you want the tree to fulfill—shade, privacy, shelter from wind—select the one most suitable and take into careful consideration the ultimate size, both height and width.

Don't plant trees too close to one another because they will compete for space, light, food, and water, and may become deformed or stunted. Avoid planting trees directly in front of windows and doors or close to paths, driveways, electrical wires, drainage pipes, and gas lines. Careful placement is important, because once trees are established they are difficult and often expensive to move.

Trees offer sheltering shade for both people and plants.

Be a considerate neighbor and think about whether or not your tree will cast unwelcome shade on the property of others, block their view, or produce bothersome flowers or fruits that may drop messily in their yard. Stepping in their shoes beforehand prevents feuds later.

Trees of Life

Trees have tenaciously survived and adapted to many modern-day environmental stresses. They continue to inspire us, touch our spirits, and connect us to our past, present, and future. The phrase "tree of life" is no exaggeration, for without them, there would be no miracle of life. Although this chapter includes only a minuscule sampling of the thousands of trees available, perhaps our recommendations will inspire you to expand your repertoire of landscape sentinels.

Bailey's Acacia

Acacia baileyana

Bloom Period and Seasonal Color
Spring blooms in yellow.

Mature Height × Spread 20–30 ft. × 25–40 ft.

Botanical Pronunciation
ah-KAY-shee-ah BAY-lee-ah-nah

Zones 9–11

---

cacia baileyana is a round-headed tree with a wide canopy composed of pendulous branches. Its silvery, blue-green, feathery, fine-textured leaves contrast beautifully with the fragrant clusters of small canary yellow flowers that burst forth in early spring. Although among the hardiest of acacias, it does not tolerate blustery winds or sustained below-freezing temperatures. In its native habitat, acacia grow under the canopies of eucalyptus, protected from winds. From temperate climates, they need adequate soil moisture to withstand extended periods of drought or heat. Once their flowers are spent, seedpods emerge, providing summer morsels for birds. Acacia's longevity is only about twenty to thirty years, but its beauty in the garden more than compensates for its short life.

When, Where, and How to Plant
The best times to plant acacias are in fall or early spring from 5- to 15-gallon containers. Bailey's acacias prefer a wind-protected, full-sun location in soils with a neutral pH of 7.0. Since the root systems tend to be shallow and lateral, they benefit from the good percolation of loam soils, which encourages the development of deeper root systems. Immediately after planting, build a watering basin 6–8 ft. in diameter by creating a berm 6 in. high, then mulching its surface with 2–3 in. of compost or humus mulch. If you are planting in groups, space them 15–20 ft. on center. Refer to p. 20 for more planting information.

Growing Tips
Water once a week until established, thereafter every two weeks or longer as dictated by weather and growth rate. To maximize bloom and leaf growth, fertilize in early spring with a complete organic granular or slow-release food.

Advice and Care
It is unnecessary to deadhead the flowers, but to encourage new growth, prune away dead and diseased wood. Few pests or diseases will affect it but root rot may result from poor-draining soil.

Companion Planting and Design
Use it as a single tree for a focal point or on a bank with several trees. It also grows well with bottlebrush, silverberry, or Japanese mock orange.

Try These
A. b. 'Purpurea' has new outer growth that is deep burgundy, offering a lush contrast to blue-gray under foliage. It grows about 20–30 ft., but it is not as wide as Bailey's acacia. On banks, it provides a colorful accent. *A. cultriformis*, knifeleaf acacia, has silver-gray leaves serrated on the edges, resembling knives. It is a smaller tree growing to just 15 ft. tall and wide, with classic acacia scented blooms in early spring. *A. redolens* grows shorter and wider making it another good choice for banks as a groundcover or to cover expansive areas with poor soil. It grows 1–6 ft. × 15 ft. with a thick blanket of yellow blooms in spring.

California Sycamore

Platanus racemosa

Bloom Period and Seasonal Color
Spring blooms in red hues.

Mature Height × Spread 60 ft. to 80 ft. × 60 ft.

Botanical Pronunciation
PLA-tin-us RACE-mose-ah

Zones 9–11

Sycamores are large and robust trees. Admired for their graceful, twisted branches; their thin, mottled trunks; and their broad, light green, maple-like leaves covered underneath with fine, rust-colored hairs. Tiny clusters of reddish blossoms appear from April to May, followed by spherical, brown, spiky seedheads that hang down in clusters throughout winter. In the cooler autumn months, most of their leaves turn yellow and fall to the ground, and their bark characteristically flakes off, revealing an attractive patchwork of grays, whites, and light browns. Once established, this native tolerates short periods of drought and enjoys heat and wind if there is sufficient moisture, but does not survive long, freezing winters.

When, Where, and How to Plant
The best planting time is fall, second best is early spring. Plant from 5- or 15-gallon containers or a 30–36 in. specimen box. Select a full-sun site with well-drained soil, pH 7.0. Space grouped trees 30–40 ft. on center; site a single tree at least 30 ft. from any structure or paved area. Never plant over leach lines or under power lines. Build a 10–15 ft. watering basin and cover with 2–3 in. of organic material. See p. 20 for additional planting information.

Growing Tips
Irrigate every five to seven days until established; thereafter water every seven to fourteen days, depending on weather and growth conditions. Withhold water during winter dormancy. Fertilize in late winter with a complete organic granular food.

Advice and Care
Prune out dead wood while they're in winter dormancy. Some people develop allergic reactions when handling the leaves, particularly the woolly undersides; wear gloves when handling and avoid contact with them during windy days. These trees are susceptible to sycamore blight, a fungal disease that attacks the ends of new growth in the spring, but should not cause permanent harm. This disease is a kind of blessing in disguise because in burning back the ends of the branches, wood growth becomes gnarled and irregular, creating artistically dramatic silhouettes.

Companion Planting and Design
Feature them as ornamental focal specimens, to highlight their crooked but picturesque branching structures. They are one of the best shade trees for drier soils and milder climates. They can even be planted in lawns if there is excellent soil drainage. Cluster them in groups of three or more as they are in nature, and combine them with shade-tolerant native or drought-resistant plants such as glossy abelias, California lilacs, and silverberry.

Try These
Platanus acerifolia 'Bloodgood' (also known as Bloodgood London plane tree) has a broad, pyramidal form and withstands urban pollution; it is resistant to sycamore blight. *P. acerifolia* 'Columbia' is resistant to blight and to mildew. Where windy conditions prevail, avoid London plane trees. They are also not recommended to plant near those suffering from asthma.

Cherry

Prunus spp.

Bloom Period and Seasonal Color
Spring fragrant blooms in white to rose-pink.

Mature Height × Spread
Flowering: 12–15 ft. × 12–15 ft.
Sweet: 15–20 ft. × 12–15 ft. (pruned)

Botanical Pronunciation
PROO-nus

Zones 4–10 depending on variety

Sweet cherry (*Prunus avium*) trees are the largest of fruit trees, and are just as lovely as their cousins, the flowering cherries. In spring, their reddish brown bark and stout, rising branches form graceful pyramidal crowns, draped in fragrant white or pink blossoms in spring followed by rough, lance-shaped leaves. Plump heart-shaped cherries festoon the trees in late spring or early summer. Their sweet flesh ranges in color from purple-black, cerise, and yellow to white, and some taste as powerful as a superb red wine without the fermentation. Since there are high-chill and low-chill cultivars, select the best ones for your area. Flowering cherry tree cultivars also have varied chill hours as well as standard upright, weeping, spreading, and columnar habits.

When, Where, and How to Plant
Plant while still dormant, from January to March, from bare rootstock or in spring from 5- to 15-gallon containers, spacing 25–30 ft. apart. Sweet cherries need full sun and well-drained loam soil with a pH of 5.5–6.5. Flowering cherry can take part shade in inland locales. To avoid crown root rot and fungal disease, plant so that the graft is slightly above the surrounding soil. Construct a watering basin 12 ft. in diameter and cover with 2 in. of organic material such as compost or humus mulch. See Planting Techniques, p. 20.

Growing Tips
Water every five to seven days initially, thereafter water every seven to fourteen days and reduce or stop irrigation during fall and winter, supplementing if rainfall is insufficient. Once established, fertilize in late winter or early spring with cottonseed meal.

Advice and Care
At planting, prune sweet cherry to about 24–30 in. An additional summer pruning after harvest is recommended besides winter pruning to control size and to allow for easier harvesting. For flowering cherry cultivars, prune to remove any damaged, interfering, or errant branches while dormant. The trees are relatively free from disease and pests, but root rot may occur in poorly draining soil. Net sweet cherries before harvesting if they need protection from birds. Set manual traps or an olfactory repellent for gophers.

Companion Planting and Design
Flowering cherry trees are must-haves for Japanese-style gardens or as focal shade trees, but fruiting cherry trees are also very ornamental.

Try These
Among the many flowering cherry trees, 'Kwanzan' bears spectacular rose-pink double flowers, while 'Snow Fountain' bears weeping, white double blossoms. For mild-winter regions, select 'Pink Cloud', with profuse deep pink flowers on a 20-ft.-tall tree. Sweet cherry 'Black Tartarian' has medium, round fruit with purplish black skin, dark red flesh, and semisweet, juicy, delicious flavor, but needs 900 hours of winter chill. It ripens in early June; pollinators are 'Bing', 'Royal Ann', or 'Stella'. For mild-winter regions, select 'Minnie Royal' and 'Royal Lee' and plant in the same hole for delicious, dark red, medium-sized cherries.

Crape Myrtle

Lagerstroemia indica

Bloom Period and Seasonal Color
Lavender, pink, and white blooms in late summer with golden yellow fall foliage.

Mature Height × Spread 15–20 ft. × 20 ft.

Botanical Pronunciation
LAH-ger-strome-ee-ah IN-dih-kah

Zones 7–11

*L*agerstroemia indica is a striking tree with large trusses of frilly magenta flower panicles in late summer. It's commonly known as crape myrtle because of the similarity of its crinkly textured flowers to crepe fabric. Its foliage is transformed from deep green to golden yellow in the fall. In winter, when barren of leaves, its deciduous bark reveals a smooth beige surface with maroon streaks. Since crape myrtle lives for several hundred years, ours will probably be in the front yard long after we are gone, and there is comfort in knowing we have planted something with such longevity. Once established, it does very well in heat, wind, freezing temperatures, and even drought conditions—although it will thrive better, of course, if adequate moisture is available.

When, Where, and How to Plant
Plant in late winter or early spring, from 5- or 15-gallon or specimen-sized containers. For optimum bloom production, plant in full sun, though it will survive partial shade. Porous, well-drained soil is essential. Slightly alkaline soils, pH 7.2, are fine, but slightly acidic soils, pH 6.7, are better. If planting in a group, space 15 ft. to 20 ft. on center; space a single specimen at least 15 ft. from a structure or paved area. Create a 10–12 ft. watering basin, and blanket with 2–3 in. of organic material. Also refer to p. 20 for additional planting information.

Growing Tips
Water deeply every five to seven days to encourage deep root development until established, then water every ten to fourteen days, adjusting for weather and growth conditions. Withhold water during winter dormancy. Fertilize in late winter with a complete granular organic food.

Advice and Care
Prune for shape in late winter. To encourage two bloom cycles, prune twice a year, once in late winter and once after the first blooms are spent. Crape myrtles in California are susceptible to mildew, but new mildew-resistant varieties have been hybridized. In spring, sucking insects such as aphids tend to proliferate on tender emerging buds. Wash off with a strong stream of water in the early morning; if they persist, use a canola-based horticultural oil.

Companion Planting and Design
Crape myrtle is lovely with butterfly bush, pride of Madeira, and shore juniper.

Try These
Hybrids such as 'Zuni' (9 ft.), bearing dark lavender floral trusses, and 'Glendora White' (9 ft.), with snowy white flowers in dense, showy clusters, are also more resistant to mildew. Other mildew-resistant hybrids include the 20-ft.-tall 'Arapaho', with cranberry red blooms, and 'Muskogee' (25 ft.), bearing lavender flowers and red foliage in autumn. *L. indica* 'Catawba' is a small tree, growing to just 6–10 ft. It has brilliant fall foliage in orange-red and purple blooms. The Petite series offers small 5-ft. tree-types, while 'Pink Velour' grows to 10 ft., 'Red Rocket' to 20 ft., and 'Watermelon Red' to 25 ft.

European White Birch

Betula pendula

Bloom Period and Seasonal Color
Insignificant flowers with yellow fall color.

Mature Height × Spread 20–30 ft. × 15–20 ft.

Botanical Pronunciation
beh-TOO-lah PEN-doo-lah

Zones 5–11

Birches are graceful, open-branched, and pyramidal, and their smaller branches are pendulous, with bright green, wedge-shaped leaves that shimmer in the slightest breeze. The bark is tough and water resistant, and peels off in curling patches. Although fast growing, their mature height is relatively modest, and their roots are not as aggressive as other trees. Catkins, food for birds and deer, develop from insignificant flowers and fall to the ground when ripe. *B. pendula* endures temperatures as low as -40 degrees Fahrenheit and as high as 100 degrees Fahrenheit, as long as there is adequate moisture. Their open canopies enable them to survive strong winds, but they cannot thrive in drought conditions.

When, Where, and How to Plant
Purchase bare rootstock or stock that is balled and burlapped in winter, or plant from containers in spring. Plant in a sunny location in well-drained soil with a pH of 6.5–7.0. Space 10–12 ft. apart and plant far enough from structures so that canopies will attain optimum growth. To encourage vigorous lateral growth of the root systems, build watering basins 4 ft. beyond their drip lines; mulch the surface of the basins with 2–3 in. of organic material. See Planting Techniques, p. 20.

Growing Tips
Birches are riparian trees (meaning they grow along riverbanks) and need deep watering every seven to ten days once established. Withhold water when dormant in winter. Fertilize with an organic granular food or cottonseed meal in late winter or early spring and again in fall.

Advice and Care
Prune for shape during winter dormancy if necessary. When stressed from lack of moisture, birches become susceptible to birch borers. Watch for entrance holes where the borers tunnel into the tree and sawdust-like debris called frass accumulates. Use a systemic pesticide containing imidacloprid and follow manufacturer's directions.

Companion Planting and Design
Deciduous birches are graceful and pyramidal in shape and their dormant bare branches create an elegant silhouette in the winter landscape. Select a tree with multiple trunks, because its silhouette will create a visually interesting focal point for the garden. Plant with saucer magnolias, silverberry, and cotoneasters.

Try These
B. pendula 'Crimson Frost' has burgundy foliage and is somewhat resistant to borers. 'Trosts Dwarf' is good for bonsai and rock gardens at just 3 ft. × 3 ft. *B. pendula* 'Laciniata' has deeply cut leaves and a open habit with weeping branches. *B.pendula* 'Youngii', Young's weeping birch, is dome shaped with weeping willowlike branches and stands 15 ft. *B. nigra* 'Heritage' is a giant at 50–90 ft. and 40–60 ft. wide, with stunning dark red bark that becomes tinged with black as it matures. It is resistant to excessive heat, cold, moisture, and bronze birch borers, but a smaller birch borer–resistant cultivar at 15 ft. is *B. nigra* 'Summer Cascade'.

Ginkgo

Ginkgo biloba

Bloom Period and Seasonal Color
Bright yellow fall foliage.

Mature Height × Spread
35–50 ft. × 30–40 ft.

Botanical Pronunciation gink-GO bih-LOBE-ah

Zones 5–11

Ginkgo biloba trees were saved from extinction by Chinese monks, who planted them on their temple grounds. Their slender trunks are covered with reddish bark and their graceful, fan-shaped, double-lobed leaves turn from glossy green in spring to golden yellow in fall. The male ginkgo is more upright while the female is lower growing with a spreading habit. Ginkgo trees, being deciduous, are cold hardy and they also love summer heat and tolerate wet or dry conditions. Its nuts are used in Asian cuisine and its extract contains medicinal properties. For their beauty, multiple uses, and adaptability to many adverse environmental conditions, ginkgo trees are the perfect choice for just about any setting.

When, Where, and How to Plant
Plant in early spring from 5- or 15-gallon or specimen-sized containers. Ginkgos prefer full sun and porous loam soil with a 7.0 pH. Place ginkgos in a spot sheltered from winds. Space grouped ginkgos 20–30 ft. apart; site a single plant at least 30 ft. from the nearest structure or paved area. Do not bury the graft. Construct a watering basin 10–12 ft. in diameter and expand this basin to correspond with the tree's growth. Mulch the surface with 2–3 in. of organic material. See p. 20 for planting information.

Growing Tips
Water deeply every seven to ten days until established; thereafter water once a month, adjusting for growth and weather conditions. Fertilize in late winter and in early fall with a complete organic granular food.

Advice and Care
Prune only if shaping is necessary, in late winter while the tree is still dormant. A twenty-year-old female tree planted closely to a male will produce offensive, odiferous fruit that resembles a fleshy brownish orange plum. It is best to avoid planting female trees if possible. Unfortunately, even if you peeked at the undersides of their leaves, it would be difficult to tell the sex of the tree until it matures! Seriously, most grafted gingkos marketed at garden centers are male. It's pest, disease, salt, *and* smog resistant.

Companion Planting and Design
Known for its graceful, fan-shaped leaves, ginkgos, also called maiden hair tree, are lovely in cutflower arrangements and exquisite in the summer and fall garden. Use them as a focal garden tree, street tree, contemplative gardens, or bonsai specimen. Heavenly bamboo, saucer magnolia, and pride of Madeira are just a few suggestions for companion plants.

Try These
Varieties are created by grafting or by cuttings and are male plants. *G. biloba* 'Autumn Gold' is quite symmetrical and upright, growing to 45 ft. × 35 ft., with lovely deep green, fanlike leaves that turn bright gold in fall. 'Princeton Sentry' is narrow at maturity, growing to 50 ft. tall, but less than half as wide at 15–20 ft. 'Jade Butterfly' is more petite, growing just 12–15 ft.

Golden Rain Tree

Koelreuteria paniculata

Bloom Period and Seasonal Color
Summer blooms in bright yellow with golden fall foliage.

Mature Height × Spread 20–40 ft. × 30 ft.

Botanical Pronunciation
KOLE-roo-tih-ree-ah pah-NIK-ew-lot-ah

Zones 6–11

Standing among eucalyptus and acacia trees in our neighborhood is a golden rain tree that is visually prominent in summer because of its long clusters of small, bright yellow flowers. These fragrant flowers give way to papery lantern-shaped masses of lime green seedpods that eventually turn a brownish buff color and persist throughout the winter. A medium-sized tree with an open-branched, flat-top form, it is covered with compound 18 in. leaves that are green in spring and summer, turning an autumn gold in the fall. Golden rain tree is one of the few species that have yellow blossoms, and it blooms later than most other trees. Despite its delicate beauty, it is quite hardy and adaptable, able to withstand drought, heat, wind, air pollution, and freezing temperatures.

When, Where, and How to Plant
Plant in fall or spring from 5- or 15-gallon or specimen-sized containers. Although it grows best in full sun, it will do well in partial shade. This adaptive tree tolerates alkaline or acidic soils with a pH ranging from 6.5–7.2 and survives in clay, loam, or sandy soils. If planting a single tree, space 30–40 ft. on center; if planting a group, space 20–30 ft. Create a watering basin 10 ft. in diameter, and blanket with 2–3 in. of organic material such as humus mulch or compost. Refer to p. 20 for planting information.

Growing Tips
Immediately after planting, irrigate deeply and thoroughly; although drought tolerant, it does best when watered every seven to ten days, depending on climatic and growth conditions. Fertilize in late winter with a complete organic granular food.

Advice and Care
Prune only for shape or to remove dead wood. The seedpods are very attractive and add to the fall and winter enjoyment of the tree. It's not suitable for seaside conditions. Red-shouldered bugs and other sucking insects may attack the foliage and developing pods. Rake up the pods and spray the tree with a canola-based horticultural oil or a systemic insecticide with imidacloprid.

Companion Planting and Design
Golden rain tree is an excellent ornamental lawn tree, lending itself as a focal point in a tropical landscape, or as a backdrop for a low growing, sweeping foreground planting. It also does well when planted with other taller trees such as the tulip tree, ginkgo, and camphor.

Try These
K. paniculata 'Fastigiata' is narrow, growing to 25 ft. tall, but only 4–6 ft. wide. Its tight compact growth habit makes it a good choice for small planting areas. It does not produce as many blooms as the species, but is more cold tolerant. *K. bipinnata*, Chinese flame tree, has finer, bipinnate leaflets that give a textured, fernlike appearance, growing 20–40 ft. tall and as wide; its seed capsules turn orange, red, or salmon.

Grecian Laurel

Laurus nobilis

Other Name Sweet bay

Bloom Period and Seasonal Color
Yellow blooms in spring.

Mature Height × Spread 20–30 ft. × 25 ft.

Botanical Pronunciation
LAH-rus NOE-bil-is

Zones 9–11

aurus nobilis is a slow-growing tree with upright branches and a conical, slender form when young. With age it becomes a broad pyramid with leathery dark green leaves that are strongly aromatic when crushed. In spring it is laden with clusters of small lemon yellow flowers. Once pollinated, these flowers become olive-like fruit, green at first and eventually turning black in the fall. Butterflies and bees are attracted to the nectar in its flowers, and cooks enjoy using its dried bay leaves for stews, soups, and sauces. Valued for its handsome form as well as its adaptability to different soil types, wind and sun exposure, heat, and even freezing conditions for short periods of time, Grecian laurel is a perfect choice for containers, kitchen gardens, and most landscapes.

When, Where, and How to Plant
Plant in fall or spring from 5- or 15-gallon containers. Locate in full sun or partial shade, preferably in loamy, well-draining soil with a neutral pH of 7.0. If planting in a group, space 10–15 ft. on center; site a single tree at least 15 ft. from structures or paved surfaces. Build a watering basin 10 ft. in diameter and mulch the surface with 2–3 in. of organic material. Consult Planting Techniques on p. 20 for more information.

Growing Tips
Water about twice a week, increasing watering frequency in the summer, until the tree is well established, then water every ten to thirteen days, depending on climatic and growth conditions. Fertilize in late winter with a complete organic granular food.

Advice and Care
Prune for shape or to control size in spring. This tree can also be trained as a topiary in a container or in the ground, or pruned as a hedge or shrub. If foliage is damaged by brown soft scale or transient chewing insects use a canola-based horticultural oil for scale and spinosad for chewing insects. Although organic, spinosad has a residual of seven to ten days. Spray in the late afternoon after bees have returned to their hives. Bay laurel is also a deer-resistant plant.

Companion Planting and Design
The dense form of the sweet bay makes it an excellent visual screen or a container specimen for a patio. Its handsome shape and adaptability to a variety of soil types makes it a perfect companion to English ivy, glossy abelias, and prostrate Natal plum, as well as aromatic plants such as rosemary.

Try These
L. nobilis 'Saratoga' is a compact variety and makes an excellent patio tree, growing 20–30 ft. × 15–25 ft. and winter hardy to 20 degrees, with fragrant yellow blooms from late winter to spring. *L. n.* 'Aurea' has leaves tinged in yellow. *L. n.* 'Emerald Wave'® has wavy, emerald green, aromatic leaves on a rounded, tight form, slow-growing 12–15 ft. It is hardy in zones 8–11.

Hong Kong Orchid Tree

Bauhinia × blakeana

Bloom Period and Seasonal Color
Late winter through mid-spring blooms in wine red, purple, or pink with white streaks.

Mature Height × Spread 20–30 ft. × 25 ft.

Botanical Pronunciation
BOW-hin-ee-ah BLAKE-ee-ah-nah

Zones 9–11

The Hong Kong orchid tree is one of the most beautiful of all the bauhinias, and unlike the others, it does not bear messy seedpods, because it is sterile. The spreading branches form an umbrella-shaped crown with bright green butterflylike leaves. From late winter through mid-spring, spectacularly colorful flowers with white-streaked petals adorn the canopy. If the tree is in a frost zone, the orchid-shaped flowers emerge before the flush of foliar growth; if in a temperate zone, the flowers will bloom against the backdrop of the foliage. In their native habitat, Hong Kong orchid trees withstand short periods of frost and thrive in heat with sufficient humidity and soil moisture. Their long bloom period and abundant large, fragrant flowers attract butterflies, birds, and bees.

When, Where, and How to Plant
Plant in fall or spring from containers that are 5- or 15-gallons or larger. To maximize bloom production, choose a site in full sun with a neutral to slightly acidic soil, pH 6.5–7.0. Like most trees, this hybrid prefers well-drained soil. If planting several on a slope or in a group, space 15 ft. on center and the canopies will eventually grow together. Plant a single ornamental at least 20 ft. from a structure or paved area. Make sure the watering basin is 20 percent larger in diameter than the tree's canopy, and mulch the surface just after planting with 2–3 in. of compost or humus mulch. See Planting Techniques, p. 20.

Growing Tips
Water thoroughly after planting. Once established, water every seven to ten days, adjusting to climatic conditions and growth cycles. Fertilize with a complete organic granular food in spring and fall.

Advice and Care
Periodic pruning of errant growth maintains the tree's shape. Deadheading is unnecessary because pods do not form on this species. To achieve a classic tree shape, prune vigorously in December; remove branches below 4–5 ft. to expose the trunk and any crossing branches that rub against each other or grow toward the center of the tree. Borers may attack if tree is stressed due to drought. To control, use a systemic containing imidacloprid.

Companion Planting and Design
The orchid tree is grown in landscapes for its lavish display, often when many other trees are seasonally barren. Many municipalities use these hybrids as street or parkway trees. They are excellent trees on windy slopes because their open canopies allow the wind to pass through without damaging their branching structures. Plant *en masse* as a visual screen, or plant a single tree as a focal point amid other tropical plants like angel's trumpet, plumeria, and hibiscus.

Try These
B. galpinii (*B. punctata*) is an evergreen shrub that sprawls to 15 ft. wide, making a good slope or bank cover. It blooms from spring to fall in red to orange flowers that blanket the plant.

Incense Cedar

Calocedrus decurrens

Bloom Period and Seasonal Color
Evergreen.

Mature Height × Spread 60–70 ft. × 20–30 ft.

Botanical Pronunciation
kal-oh-SEED-rus deh-KUR-renz

Zones 8–10

alocedrus means "beautiful cedar," and with its dense coniferous branches covered with small bright green scale leaves and its majestic height, this evergreen is aptly named. It has a shapely pyramidal form, is neatly symmetrical, and bears small cylindrical cones. As a young tree, its foliage grows densely down to the ground; as it ages, its lower branches drop away, revealing a straight trunk that is maroon in color. Commonly known as incense cedar, the tree is found on mountain slopes at 4,000- to 8,000 ft. elevations from Baja, California, to Oregon. Incense cedar does not do well in hot, dry, windy climates unless it has proper root development and soil moisture, but it survives in temperatures as low as -10 degrees Fahrenheit.

When, Where, and How to Plant
The best time to plant is in fall or spring from a 1-, 5-, or 15-gallon container. Incense cedars do best in full sun in a slightly acidic soil, 6.5–7.0, with a porous texture. Since they will eventually grow to be very tall trees, plant 30–50 ft. on center and at least 35 ft. from any structures or paved areas. Create an 8–10 ft. watering basin, but as the tree grows, expand the watering basin to encourage maximum lateral root development. Apply a 2–3-in. layer of mulch. Also see p. 20.

Growing Tips
Water deeply every seven to ten days for the first two years; thereafter water every ten to fourteen days, adjusting for weather and growth conditions. It can withstand extended periods of drought if it is watered generously for one or two years when young, facilitating the development of an extensive root system. Fertilize in late winter or early spring with a complete organic granular food.

Advice and Care
Prune only if the canopy needs lacing to allow sunlight to reach interior growth. To maintain, wash out all the debris inside its canopy with a strong stream of water twice a year. Trees under duress from drought or poor-draining soil are susceptible to bark beetles. Add more organic amendments such as humic acid and soil penetrant containing saponin to the soil, water regularly, and if the infestation persists, apply a systemic insecticide with imidacloprid once a year until the problem is remedied.

Companion Planting and Design
Incense cedars are ideal trees for group plantings, high visual screens, and single tall accents, or windbreaks in large landscapes. They blend well with other coniferous plants like pines, junipers, and cedars and their fragrant branches are used in holiday décor.

Try These
Although there is primarily one incense cedar available at retail garden centers, there are many other interesting cedar species and cultivars such as *C. deodora* 'Feelin' Blue', a dwarf hybrid (2–4 ft. × 6 ft.) with a spreading habit and bluish green needles, and its dwarf cousin 'Feelin' Sunny', with golden yellow foliage.

Jacaranda

Jacaranda mimosifolia

Other Name Brazilian rosewood

Bloom Period and Seasonal Color
Spring blooms in lavender or white.

Mature Height × Spread 25–40 ft. × 30–40 ft.

Botanical Pronunciation
HAK-ar-an-dah mih-MOSE-ih-fole-ee-ah

Zones 10–11

During a springtime visit to Pretoria, South Africa, the city seemed to be covered with a haze of mauve-blue trumpet flowers: thousands of jacaranda trees were in full bloom, a breathtaking sight! The tree's spreading branches create an umbrella-shaped, rounded crown with an open form. After the flowers are spent in late spring, large, fernlike, compound, pale green leaves appear, along with small, woody, pancake-shaped seedpods that will ripen and split open the following year. Since they are native to dry habitats, jacarandas tolerate drought and heat, but these brittle trees do not hold up well against strong winds, nor do they withstand freezing temperatures. If there is a cold snap in late winter, the leaves may turn yellow and drop off.

When, Where, and How to Plant
Plant in spring from a 5- or 15-gallon or specimen-sized container. Plant in full sun, in well-drained soil with a pH of 7.0. Space 20–30 ft. on center. Build a watering basin 10 ft. in diameter and mulch the surface with 2–3 in. of organic material such as humus or compost. Consult the Planting Techniques section, p. 20, for more information.

Growing Tips
Water once a week until established; thereafter, water every ten to twenty days and withhold water when dormant in winter. Fertilize in late winter or early spring with a complete organic granular food.

Advice and Care
It is only necessary to prune for shape or to remove dead branches. Do not plant a jacaranda in your lawn, because it does not like too much water. In fact, its flowering is more profuse during a dry year. Avoid locating a tree too close to any paved areas or structures because its shallow rooting nature will cause problems as it matures. If you see a black sooty mold or sticky honeydew, aphids are the cause. Wash them off with a strong stream of water; if they persist, use a canola-based horticultural oil, and use baits to get rid of the ants that are "farming" the aphids.

Companion Planting and Design
Its gorgeous haze of mauve-purple trumpet flowers and fernlike leaves provide spring and summer beauty to a water-thrifty garden. Combine with other waterwise plants such as butterfly bush, echium, and cotoneaster. Do not plant in lawns, becaue it prefers to remain on the dry side. Use jacarandas as medium-sized shade trees as well as color accents.

Try These
J. mimosifolia 'Alba' has white trumpet-shaped flowers. Its common name is white jacaranda. It has fewer blooms, but lusher, denser foliage. *J. jasminoides* is the only other known species. It is native to the Amazon River Basin area, and found in the high desert locales. Smaller growing (just 6–12 ft. × 4–8 ft.), it has a long bloom period, bearing lilac-blue flowers from spring to early summer.

Japanese Maple

Acer palmatum

Bloom Period and Seasonal Color
Purple, bronze, red, and yellow fall foliage.

Mature Height × Spread 15–30 ft. × 15–20 ft.

Botanical Pronunciation
A-sir PALM-aye-tum

Zones 6–11

Japanese maples are very desirable because of their delicate, open canopies; slender, artistically branched limbs; and rounded crowns. Their shiny light green leaves are sharply toothed and palmate shaped, and in fall they are transformed into a blaze of purple, bronze, red, or yellow. Once the nondescript flowers are spent they produce boomerang-shaped seeds called keys. Each key is composed of a pair of winged seeds known as samaras that are dispersed over long distances by the wind. The willowy branches and fine foliage are prized additions to cutflower arrangements, particularly in stylized arrangements such as Ikebana. For best development, do not locate the trees in areas where they are exposed to extended periods of heat, drought, and wind. Because they are deciduous, they withstand subfreezing temperatures.

When, Where, and How to Plant
Fall or spring are the best planting seasons, but bare-root maples or ones that are balled-and-burlapped can be planted in January or February. These plants prefer partial shade and a slightly acidic, pH 6.5–7.0 loam soil that's porous enough for water to percolate easily through the root zones. If drainage is a problem, plant in a raised bed or container. Select a site protected from the wind, and use 5-gallon plants spaced 10–12 ft. apart. Build a watering basin that is 20 percent beyond the drip lines, and mulch the basin's surface with 2–3 in. of organic material. For more information, refer to the Planting Techniques, p. 20.

Growing Tips
Water every five to seven days once established and withhold water during winter. Fertilize in early spring as needed, with a camellia/azalea food or cottonseed meal.

Advice and Care
Prune for shape in late winter or early spring when the trees are still dormant. Control chewing insects with spinosad applied every seven to ten days until the infestation is over.

Companion Planting and Design
Japanese maples can be trained as large shrubs, small trees, or even bonsai. Combine them with other plants that do well in dappled sunlight, such as camellias, azaleas, and rhododendrons, or plant in containers. For a single Japanese maple as a focal point in your landscape, select a multiple-trunked specimen in a 24–30 in. box, for immediate visual impact.

Try These
A. palmatum 'Atropurpureum' is popular for its reddish foliage and grows 15–25 ft. For cool summer areas, 'Butterfly' is small, growing to just 10 ft. × 5 ft. with light green leaves lined in pink margins, magenta in the fall. 'Sango Kaku', coral bark maple, has winter bark showing in coral red. 'Dissectum', laceleaf Japanese maple, has the finest-textured foliage of the maples. It requires a humid, temperate environment and grows to 10–20 ft. Besides 'Atropurpureum', 'Emperor 1', with dark red foliage that turns bright scarlet in fall, adapts well to warm Southern California climates.

Magnolia

Magnolia spp.

Bloom Period and Seasonal Color
Fragrant creamy white, lavender blooms
in spring.

Mature Height × Spread 20–60 ft. × 15–50 ft.

Botanical Pronunciation MAG-no-lee-ah

Zones 5–11

Fossilized records of magnolias, dating back over five million years, are a testament to their long genetic history. The southern magnolia, *M. grandiflora*, is a favorite flowering evergreen tree because of its ability to survive many climatic conditions. Its dense, rounded canopy is covered with lacquered 10-in. leaves and enormous plate-sized, citrus-scented, creamy white, summer-blooming flowers. Once the flowers are spent, bright red seeds develop on cone-shaped heads, decorating the tree from summer to early fall. Saucer magolia, *Magnolia × soulangeana*, is grown as a small deciduous tree or large shrub with multiple trunks, fresh green foliage, and raspberry-pineapplelike fragrant pink, purple, or white tulip-shaped blooms. Established magnolias love heat and humidity, and their dense branches and leathery foliage allows them to withstand high winds.

When, Where, and How to Plant
The best time to plant is fall or early spring from 5- or 15-gallon containers. Plant in full sun in soil with a pH range of 6.5–7.2, adequate moisture, and good drainage. Space individual southern magnolia trees at least 40 ft. apart; space groupings at least 30 ft. apart so their canopies will touch each other. Saucer magnolias are smaller growing, so space 6–12 ft. on center. Initially, your watering basin needs to be at least 10–15 ft. in diameter and covered and maintained with 2–3 in. of rich organic material such as humus mulch or compost. For more information, consult the Planting Techniques, p. 20.

Growing Tips
For southern and saucer magnolias, water every five to seven days until established; thereafter, water every seven to ten days, adjusting for weather and growing conditions. Reduce frequency or withhold water for saucer magnolias when dormant fall-winter. Fertilize in late winter with cottonseed meal. Magnolias are sensitive to salt buildup; apply products containing humic acid and saponin.

Advice and Care
Prune minimally to remove dead wood. For scale infestations, spray with a canola-based horticultural oil or use a systemic insecticide with imidacloprid.

Companion Planting and Design
Southern magnolia is a stately focal point in lawns or an attractive shade tree. Saucer magnolia is also spectacular as a focal point, planted near an entryway or in large containers. Combine with azaleas or hellebores.

Try These
M. grandiflora 'St. Mary', matures at 20 ft. wide and is good when a smaller tree is desired, as well as moderate grower, compact, and narrow formed 'Little Gem', but 'Majestic Beauty' lives up to its name at 35–40 ft. Saucer magnolia can be grown as a small tree or large shrub, and has named varieties such as 'Black Tulip', with large deep wine-red blooms, growing to 30 ft. × 15 ft. 'Lilliputian' is smaller, maturing at 18 ft. × 10–15 ft. with pink blooms late in the season. 'Alba Superba' has pure-white flowers on an upright form.

New Zealand Christmas Tree

Metrosideros excelsa

Bloom Period and Seasonal Color
Bright-red stamens in late spring-summer.

Mature Height × Spread 20–30 ft. × 25 ft.

Botanical Pronunciation
MET-roe-sih-dare-ose ex-CELL-sah

Zones 10–11

This medium-sized tree with multiple trunks and a root system that can cling precariously to craggy cliff faces is adaptable to sandy soils, salt spray, and prevailing ocean winds. The New Zealand Christmas tree, named by the Maoris because of its blooms at Christmas, is a slow-growing evergreen shade tree, densely covered with elliptic leaves that are dark green on top and silvery beneath. Erect and vase-shaped, its flowers resemble brilliant red pincushions, but are actually crimson-colored clusters of stamens that hang like rounded bottlebrush ornaments. Once established, the tree tolerates drought, withstands heat, and is an excellent choice for temperate coastal regions, but not for areas where extended periods of frost or dry winds are common.

When, Where, and How to Plant
Plant in spring from a 5- or 15-gallon container. It thrives in a full-sun location in a slightly acidic soil, pH 6.7–7.0, that has good percolation. If planting a group, space the trees 15–20 ft. on center; plant a single tree at least 20 ft. from a structure or paved area. Make a watering basin 10–12 ft. in diameter and cover with 2–3 in. of rich organic material like humus mulch or compost. See the Planting Techniques section for more information, p. 20.

Growing Tips
Water once a week until established; thereafter water every fourteen days or longer, depending on weather and growth conditions. Fertilize in early spring with a complete organic granular food or cottonseed meal.

Advice and Care
Deadheading is unnecessary, but prune in winter about every three to four years for shape and to open up the dense canopy. The invasive eugenia psyllid and the eucalyptus longhorned borer can be problems. To fight these infestations, apply a systemic with imidacloprid once a year and spray trees with water to clean out accumulated debris.

Companion Planting and Design
Although *M. excelsa* is most commonly grown as a tree, it can be trained into a solid hedge or visual screen as an alternative to myoporum (*Myoporum laetum*) or Japanese mock orange (*Pittosporum tobira*). Rock cotoneaster, glossy abelia, and golden mirror plant are equally hardy companions for this tree. It is also a valuable nectar source for hummingbirds as well as a colorful accent in tropical landscapes, along with bougainvillea and mandevillas.

Try These
M. excelsa 'Aurea' has yellow blooms and 'Gala' has gold-tipped dark red stamens with yellow hues in the center of its foliage. The 5–6-ft.-tall *M. e.* 'Variegata' has green-and-gold-variegated edged leaves, providing a stunning backdrop for its crimson flowers. It is wind and salt tolerant, growing in zones 10–11. Native to Hawaii, *M. collina* 'Springfire' grows 8–12 ft. × 4–6 ft, with red-orange blooms and grayish green foliage.

Olive Tree

Olea europaea

Bloom Period and Seasonal Color
Off-white flowers in spring followed by black olives in summer.

Mature Height × Spread 15–25 ft. × 20 ft.

Botanical Pronunciation
oh-LEE-ah YUR-oh-pah

Zones 9–11

An olive tree, with its picturesque open branches, upright habit, and narrow gray-green leaves with a touch of silver on the undersides, evokes memories of the old, gnarled, vase-shaped common olive tree in Grandmother Asakawa's backyard. Although she harvested and cured the olives, the oil pressed from an olive tree's fruits has been the primary reason for its worldwide popularity. It takes about ten years before the tiny off-white flowers produce fruits, or drupes, but it compensates for this slow start by living for 1,500 years or more. From the Mediterranean, it loves temperate areas with cool winters and long, hot summers for olives to ripen properly. Once established, an olive tree prefers dry soils and tolerates short periods of drought and Santa Ana winds.

When, Where, and How to Plant
Plant in fall or spring from 5-gallon, 15-gallon, or specimen-sized containers. Specimen trees in California can be successfully moved and transplanted at just about any age or size. Plant in full sun in a loam soil with a pH of 6.6–7.0. Site a single tree 20–30 ft. from structures or paved areas; space grouped trees 15–20 ft. apart. Cover a 10–12 ft. watering basin with 2–3 in. of organic material. See Planting Techniques, p. 20, for more information.

Growing Tips
Irrigate thoroughly after planting. Water once a week until established; thereafter water every two weeks or longer, depending on growth and weather conditions. Fertilize in late winter with a complete organic granular food.

Advice and Care
Prune for shape and to remove dead wood after harvesting the olives. In order for olives to be edible, they must be cured or processed to neutralize their natural bitterness. For those who consider the drupes a messy nuisance, spray the tree's flowers with a plant growth regulator such as Florel™ or Olive Stop™. It may require several applications. As new growth emerges in spring, aphids, olive scale, and black scale infestation can be remedied with an application of a canola-based horticultural oil. If the foliage begins to fade, yellow, brown, and wilt, the problem might be verticillium wilt, a soil-dwelling fungus. Take a sample to your county agricultural department or to the University of California Cooperative Extension for verification and control recommendation. Do *not* use a chemical fungicide or insecticide if harvesting olives.

Companion Planting and Design
Perfect for Mediterranean and water-wise landscapes, combine olive trees with 'Edward Goucher' abelia, bottlebrush, and rock rose as companions.

Try These
O. europaea 'Monher' is a fruitless olive tree, also known as Majestic Beauty olive. 'Swan Hill' bears no fruit and little or no pollen. Fruiting type 'Arbequina' is a Spanish variety good for home gardens, cold tolerant to 10 degrees Fahrenheit. Many of the commercial fruiting types are available to the homeowner as large specimen trees.

Peppermint Tree

Agonis flexuosa

Bloom Period and Seasonal Color
Small white flowers winter to summer.

Mature Height × Spread 15–25 ft. × 15 ft.

Botanical Pronunciation
ah-GAWN-is FLEX-soo-oh-sah

Zones 10–11

There are several interpretations regarding the derivation of the genus *Agonis*. It could be from the Greek word, *agonos*, meaning "without angles," referring to its soft, drooping branches, or *agon*, which means "a cluster," accurately describing the arrangement of its fruit. Whatever the derivation, this Australian native, commonly known as peppermint tree, is an ideal evergreen for California gardens. It is a small, slow-growing, thick-trunked tree with a fibrous, blackish bark and narrow, matte green leaves that cascade in a weeping habit. From afar it resembles a weeping willow and when its leaves are crushed or torn, the aroma of peppermint fills the air. Drought and heat resistant once established, the peppermint tree is as beautiful as a larger weeping willow, but remains much smaller.

When, Where, and How to Plant
Plant in spring or fall from containers and keep it 15–20 ft. away from structures or paved areas. Provide full sun and well-draining, humus-amended soil. It is tolerant of windy coastal conditions as long as temperatures do not dip below 28 degrees Fahrenheit. Refer to p. 20 for more planting information.

Growing Tips
Water once a week until established; thereafter water every ten to fourteen days or longer. In extreme heat, it may need additional watering, especially during the first growing season, to establish a deep, extensive root system. Once established, it is moderately drought tolerant, but will do best with deep, regular irrigation. Fertilize with an organic, granular food or a slow-release food formulated for trees in the late winter or early spring.

Advice and Care
Prune out any dead or interfering wood before spring growth; otherwise prune only to maintain its weeping habit. It has few disease or insect problems; if spraying with water does not control spider mite damage, use a canola-based horticultural oil or a systemic miticide. Poor drainage can lead to phytophthora or root rot. Improve drainage with a product containing saponin, or by adding more humus or compost to the soil.

Companion Planting and Design
Use this spreading, medium-sized tree with its weeping willowlike foliage as a specimen tree in a lawn, in a patio container, as an espalier, or plant it as an informal hedge. After flowering, small, woody, brown fruits appear in clusters. Suitable companions include salvias or other plants that are native to Australia.

Try These
Purple peppermint 'After Dark' bears brilliant scarlet new growth that transforms into dramatic deep burgundy leaves as it ages. Although slower growing with narrower leaves, this cultivar bears the same white flowers with burgundy centers in clusters from spring to summer. 'Nana' is a dwarf form, 3–4 ft. × 6–8 ft., and can be grown as a shrub with green leaves and red new growth. 'Jedda's Dream' is another shrub form, but it reaches 6–8 ft. × 4–6 ft. with reddish purple foliage. All possess the distinctive peppermint fragrance.

Persian Silk Tree

Albizia julibrissin

Bloom Period and Seasonal Color
Pink flowers in summer with green pods in fall.

Mature Height × Spread 30 ft. × 30 ft.

Botanical Pronunciation
al-BEEZ-ee-ah JOO-lee-brih-sun

Zones 6–11

Albizia julibrissin, one of the prettiest Persian silk trees, grows at a moderate pace and has a flat-topped crown with spreading branches. The feathery light green foliage creates an attractive background for profuse clusters of pink pompon flowers that blanket the canopy during summer. Like other Leguminosae plants, long, green, pealike seedpods emerge from the spent flowers and turn a deep brown in the fall, eventually splitting and providing food for visiting birds. While many cattle farmers use the leaves and seedpods for feed, those who do not own cattle can recycle the greenery and pods by composting and using the decomposed material to enrich garden soils. Since these trees are deciduous, they tolerate winter temperatures as low as -10 degrees Fahrenheit.

When, Where, and How to Plant
Spring is the best season to plant, from 15-gallon containers. Plant in full sun in loamy soil with a pH of 6.5–7.0. Be sure to plant in a site that is protected from wind. Space 20 ft. apart if planting in a group. Site a single tree at least 15–20 ft. from structures or paved areas, and never plant above leach lines. To encourage lateral root development, mulch the watering basin surface with 2–3 in. of compost or humus mulch and maintain the surface year-round. Refer to Planting Techniques on p. 20.

Growing Tips
Water every five to seven days until established; thereafter water every seven to ten days from spring through fall because their delicate foliage cannot withstand extended periods of drought, wind, or heat without adequate irrigation. Withhold water when the trees are dormant in the winter, but supplement during extended drought. For optimum bloom display, feed an organic granular food or cottonseed meal.

Advice and Care
Prune for form during winter dormancy. Except for possible aphid infestations in the spring, few insect or disease problems affect Persian silk trees. Spray aphids off with a strong stream of water or use a canola-based horticultural oil. If aphid or other sucking insect infestation is severe, use a systemic formulated with imidacloprid.

Companion Planting and Design
Persian silk trees make beautiful accents in tropical gardens. Their spreading canopies provide shade for other tropical plants, such as pink powder puff, hibiscus, and gardenias.

Try These
A. julibrissin 'Rosea' has very deep pink puffball flowers and matures slightly smaller than Persian silk tree. It is considered a hardier type. 'Alba' has clusters of white pompon flowers. 'Summer Chocolate' has burgundy foliage with pink, scented blooms. It is fast growing with a wide canopy on a smaller tree, maturing at 20 ft. × 15 ft. 'Boubri Ombrella'™ has hot cherry pink fragrant flowers on young trees in early summer. It is multitrunked, growing 30 ft. tall and wide with dark green foliage, and thrives in zones 6–9.

Persimmon

Diospyros kaki

Bloom Period and Seasonal Color
White blooms in spring with gold, orange-red fall foliage.

Mature Height × Spread 15–20 ft. × 15–20 ft.

Botanical Pronunciation
DEE-oh-spy-rus KAH-kie

Zones 8–10

Persimmons are lovely trees with full, spreading branches that provide perfect shade. Their large, 4–6-in., glossy green leaves turn into hues of rich gold and orange-red in fall, matching the brilliant orange fruits that hang like glowing lanterns from their gray branches. In winter, leaves drop, and in the warmth of spring they blossom under the shelter of new foliage. After waxy, white flower petals float away, tiny fruits emerge, growing to the size of apples, ready for harvest in early or late fall. Two types are adapted well to California. Astringent types must be completely ripe before eating because the tannins pack pucker power. Nonastringent types are the same color and the apple-crisp flesh can be eaten before peak ripening.

When, Where, and How to Plant

Plant in January from bare rootstock, or in spring or summer from 5- or 15-gallon containers. Protect from drought and cold, strong winds. Persimmons need a soil with a pH of 6.5–7.0. The soil should be well drained and sandy so that water percolates down and through the root zones. If the soil is heavy and clayey, amend with organic matter and gypsum. Space 6–10 ft. apart for dwarf or semidwarf types, 15–20 ft. if a standard type. Build a watering basin 4–8 ft. in diameter for dwarf and semidwarf varieties, 10–15 ft. for standards; cover with 2 in. of organic material. See Planting Techniques, p. 20.

Growing Tips

Soak deeply after planting and water about once a week, adjusting for the climate and growing conditions. As a general rule, water regularly from fruit set to harvest, making sure its root system does not dry out, then decrease or withhold watering during dormancy. Fertilize in late winter with a complete organic granular food.

Advice and Care

For high-quality fruit, nonastringent varieties (apple-shaped) need warmer climates than astringent (heart-shaped) types. At planting, prune sparingly and cut away any broken or injured roots. For large fruits, prune to train a central leader with well-spaced laterals. Keep birds away from fruit with bird netting (if practical) and use a canola-based horticultural oil if mealybugs or scale infestations are extensive.

Companion Planting and Design

Use these ornamental trees as attractive background plants or in front of evergreens. Train them as shade umbrellas above lawns or as espaliers in patio containers, or plant a row along a fence for a visual screen.

Try These

Self-fruitful 'Fuyu' has large, round, flattened fruit with reddish orange skin. It is nonastringent with excellent, applelike flavor, and is a heavy producer ripening in November, bearing as a young tree. 'Izu' and 'Coffee Cake' are nonastringent, flat-shaped, apple-crisp persimmons (100–200 chill hours). Self-fruitful, 'Hachiya', 'Chocolate', and 'Tamopan' are acorn-shaped and astringent. Although labeled as self-fruitful, most cultivars will produce more abundantly with cross-pollinaters.

Pomegranate

Punica granatum

Bloom Period and Seasonal Color
Red-orange flowers in spring through summer with reddish to light yellow fall foliage.

Mature Height × Spread 10–20 ft. × 8–15 ft.

Botanical Pronunciation
POO-nik-ah GRAH-nah-tum

Zones 9–11

We live in an area with a year-round mild climate, but pomegranates remind us that seasonal changes occur even without sharp fluctuations in weather. In early spring, small clusters of glossy green foliage bush out the shrublike trees; in spring and summer, bell-shaped red-orange flowers wave greetings in the gentle breezes. Leaves take on a reddish or bright yellow tint in autumn, and soon decorative balls of crimson fruit appear, holding on to bare limbs from late fall through winter. Thick leathery rinds with membranous compartments of pink, white, or scarlet seeds have a nutty, tart-sweet flavor. They thrive in areas where summers are hot and dry, tolerate freezing temperatures when dormant, and once established, withstand periods of drought and dry winds.

When, Where, and How to Plant
Plant in December or January from bare rootstock or, in spring or summer, from 5- or 15-gallon containers. Pomegranates do best in deep loam, well-drained soil, pH 6.5–7.0, but also grow in sandy or adobe-clay soils. Space dwarf varieties 4–6 ft. apart, standards 20 ft. apart. Build a watering basin 4 ft. in diameter for dwarf varieties, 10 ft. for standards. See Planting Techniques, p. 20.

Growing Tips
Although established pomegranates are drought tolerant, they will produce better if watered regularly every seven to ten days, especially through the growing season until fall. Decrease or withhold water during winter. Once established, fertilize with a complete organic granular food in late winter or early spring.

Advice and Care
Pick pomegranates when the fruit is plump and heavy for its size. Their crowns should give when pressed slightly and their rind should be shiny rather than dull. Few diseases or pests seriously affect pomegranates, but as a preventive, remove old fruit from the trees during pruning, and keep a watchful eye out for mites and leaf rollers. If damage is extensive, pick off the damaged foliage and fruit or apply a canola-based horticultural oil.

Companion Planting and Design
Pomegranate trees not only bear delicious, healthy fruit, but they are beautiful ornamentals for backyard gardens and canyon lots. They are exceptional for water-thrifty landscapes as well as Mediterranean-style gardens. If trimmed regularly, it is a wonderful choice for a courtyard focal specimen and of course perfect in fruit orchards or kitchen gardens. For hot summer areas with difficult soils, pomegranates will adapt and continue to produce good fruit.

Try These
'Wonderful' is the most commonly grown of all the pomegranates, but other cultivars are gaining popularity with improved taste. 'Ambrosia' (150 chill hours) bears large, pale pink-skinned, sweet-tasting pomegranates. 'Desertni' produces large orange rinds with deep red, dessert-sweet seeds (100 hours), and 'Eversweet' has clear nonstaining juice (150 hours). 'Angel Red' grows only 10 ft. with bright red fruits, less pulp, and higher juice content; its seeds are soft enough to eat.

Scarlet Flowering Eucalyptus

Eucalyptus ficifolia

Bloom Period and Seasonal Color
Red, pink, orange, or white flowers in summer followed by capsules.

Mature Height × Spread 18–40 ft. × as wide

Botanical Pronunciation
YEW-kah-lip-tus FI-sih-fole-ee-ah

Zones 10–11

Eucalyptus ficifolia (syn. *Corymbia ficifolia*), the scarlet flowering eucalyptus, has astonishingly beautiful vermilion, pink, or white flowers that are really clusters of stamens and anthers. Following its summer bloom, unusual woody, urn-shaped capsules appear. This relatively slow-growing evergreen tree has a spreading, dome-shaped crown covered with elliptic leaves that are leathery, dark green, and stiff, with light veins. The reason eucalyptus trees are so common in California is their adaptability to diverse environments. The lignotuber, a swollen portion of the root flare located just above- or below-ground, is a moisture and nutrient storage reservoir during drought. Even after a natural disaster such as a fire, the lignotuber allows it to regenerate. This tree handles most adverse conditions except extended periods of freezing temperatures.

When, Where, and How to Plant
Plant in spring from 5- or 15-gallon containers. These trees like full sun and an acidic soil with a pH of 6.5–7.0. They prefer a loam-textured soil because it permits good percolation. Space 30 ft. apart. Build a watering basin with a diameter of 10 ft. and mulch the surface with 2–3 in. of organic material such as humus mulch or compost. Thoroughly soak the root zone to collapse any air pockets. Refer to the Planting Techniques for additional information, p. 20.

Growing Tips
Water once a week, then reduce to every ten to twenty-one days once established; adjust watering schedule for climatic and growth conditions. Fertilize in winter with a complete organic granular food.

Advice and Care
Prune for shape or to remove dead wood. When tree is immature, prune off the heavy seed capsules to prevent weighing down the slender branches. It resists most diseases and pests, including the eucalyptus longhorned borer.

Companion Planting and Design
Eucalyptus trees are perfect for less-manicured landscapes that have natural habitat themes. These are excellent trees in combination with other drought-tolerant plants. They work well with many native shrubs and groundcovers that thrive in cycles of winter rains, such as California lilac, dwarf coyote bush, and manzanita.

Try These
Look for new grafted introductions in the future under the reclassification of the genus/species, *Corymbia ficifolia*: 'Lollypops' (powder puff pink), 'Dwarf Orange', 'Baby Scarlet' (red), and 'Little Sweetie' (cerise pink). They will be much smaller at maturity, about 16–20 ft. and since they are grafted, their size and colors are stable. For non-grafted scarlet flowering eucalyptus, purchase when it's blooming if color is important, because it can vary from red, to pink, to orange, to white. *E. citriodora*, lemon-scented 45–90 ft. eucalyptus, has pungent, citrus-scented foliage; smooth white bark; and white flowers that bloom in fall and winter. *E. polyanthemos*, silver dollar eucalyptus, has unusual oval, gray-green foliage that makes it popular in cutflower arrangements. It resembles an aspen tree, as it moves in the wind, and is deer resistant.

Tabebuia

Tabebuia spp.

Bloom Period and Seasonal Color
Pink, yellow, purple blooms in late winter
to spring.

Mature Height × Spread 25–50 ft. × as wide

Botanical Pronunciation TAB-eh-bew-yah

Zones 9–11

Tabebuia or trumpet tree is a rounded, semievergreen tree with an open and spreading canopy growing more than 20 ft. tall and as wide, but what makes this tree so appealing is its bright clusters of large (1–4 in. wide), trumpet-shaped flowers in pink, yellow, or purple with contrasting throats against the backdrop of deep green foliage measuring up to 6 in. in diameter. This showy tree with the gorgeous flowers heralds the spring season and a fresh beginning in the garden like few other blossoming trees. However, do not be surprised by its slow-to-bloom nature. It may take five to seven years before gifting a garden with its colorful buds, but as it matures, the clusters of blossoms become larger and more floriferous.

When, Where, and How to Plant
Plant in spring or fall from containers and keep 30 ft. away from structures or paved areas. Provide full sun in well-draining, loam-textured, slightly acidic soil. Refer to Planting Techniques, p. 20, for more information.

Growing Tips
Water weekly until roots extend outward into the surrounding soil; thereafter, water every ten to fourteen days or longer, depending on weather and growth conditions. Once mature, it is drought tolerant, but will flower more profusely if watered regularly. Feed with a complete organic fertilizer or cottonseed meal before its buds swell, usually in late February to early March and again in June for the first three years. Once mature, fertilize once in late winter or early spring.

Advice and Care
If lower-growing branches become a problem, shorten or remove them either in early spring before the flower buds form or after the flowering season is past. Otherwise, prune to shape and remove any interfering or diseased branches. Since the tree is resistant to insects, its wood, marketed as ipè, is used for outdoor decks. However, if thrips ruin the flowers, apply a systemic insecticide that is formulated for thrips and other pests around the perimeter of the tree once a year.

Companion Planting and Design
Tabebuias are showy, semievergreen specimen trees planted as colorful accents along driveways, in expansive lawns, or in containers on patios. Smaller species make lovely patio trees.

Try These
The yellow flowering deciduous *T. chrysotricha*, golden trumpet tree, is a low-branching tree with a rounded shape, hardy to approximately 25 degrees Fahrenheit and reaching 25–30 ft. tall. The blossoms appear on bare branches in late winter to early spring, followed by dark green foliage. Its white-, pink-, or purple-flowering cousin, *T. impetiginosa*, grows to a similar height in late winter or early spring, but often blooms again in late summer or fall. A taller species, *T. heterophylla*, grows 40 ft., bearing pinkish purple, pink, or white flowers primarily in spring, but also on and off throughout the year. It can be pruned into a shrub.

Tulip Tree

Liriodendron tulipifera

Other Name Yellow poplar

Bloom Period and Seasonal Color
Spring blooms in lime with orange centers
followed by yellow fall foliage.

Mature Height × Spread 60–80 ft. × 60 ft.

Botanical Pronunciation
LEER-ee-oh-den-drun TEW-lip-ih-feh-rah

Zones 6–10

Elegant specimens of *L. tulipifera* stand over 70 ft. tall with ramrod-straight trunks, strong branching structures, and broad crowns. In a home landscape, these trees normally grow to about 40–50 ft. Unique light green, four-lobed leaves, appearing as if they have been cut off at the top, turn into rich buttery yellow foliage that shimmers in autumn breezes. In late spring, their flowers are the color of limes with orange centers, resembling the blossoms of a magnolia. After the blossoms are spent, clusters of conelike seeds appear and remain on the trees long after the leaves are gone. Tulip trees tolerate temperatures as low as -10 degrees Fahrenheit and gusty winds, but they are fast growing, so they do not withstand drought or high temperatures without adequate moisture.

When, Where, and How to Plant
Plant in fall, from 5- or 15-gallon containers, or in December through January when bare-root trees are available. Select a sunny location with a well-drained loam soil with a pH of 6.7–7.0. Space 40–60 ft. apart and at least 50 ft. from structures or paved areas. Never, ever plant above or near leach lines. To encourage rapid development of lateral root systems, build 12–15 ft. diameter watering basins and mulch the surface with 2–3 in. of organic material. Also see Planting Techniques, p. 20.

Growing Tips
Water thoroughly after planting by filling the basin two or three times. Water every three to seven days for two weeks, then adjust the amount and frequency according to climatic and growing conditions, about once every seven to fourteen days. Provide additional water during drought, dry winds, and high temperatures. Fertilize in late winter or early spring with a complete organic granular food.

Advice and Care
Removing dead wood is usually all that is necessary. As tender foliage emerges in spring, sucking and chewing insects such as aphids and leafhoppers can cause problems. Spray with a strong stream of water and if infestation is severe, apply a systemic with imidacloprid.

Companion Planting and Design
A stunning shade tree in a large landscaped area, this North American native provides fall color and is similar in appearance to eastern oaks, without their chill requirement. Combine tulip trees with evergreens such as Japanese mock orange, deciduous trees such as saucer magnolia, or ornamental or fruit-bearing cherry trees.

Try These
L. tulipifera 'Arnold', Arnold's tulip tree, has many short, ascending branches giving it a compact look; it grows 25–50 ft. × 10–15 ft. and flowers by its third year. 'Aureomarginatum', aka 'Majestic Beauty', has variegated green leaves with yellow edges and matures at 40–60 ft. × 15–25 ft. 'Emerald City' has yellow with orange flowers and grows to 55 ft. × 25 ft. 'Little Volunteer'™ grows quickly in zones 4–9 to just 30 ft. × 15 ft. with orange-green blooms.

Victorian Box

Pittosporum undulatum

Bloom Period and Seasonal Color
Spring to early summer blossoms in creamy white.

Mature Height × Spread 20–30 ft. × 30 ft.

Botanical Pronunciation
PIT-oh-spore-um un-DOO-lay-tum

Zones 9–11

Victorian box is a dense, bushy-crowned standard tree or large shrub growing up to 30 ft. The trunk has gray bark that resembles coarse sandpaper with long, narrow, glossy, dark green leaves. Creamy bell-shaped flowers bloom in spring and early summer. The flowers are as fragrant as orange blossoms, and the seasonal warm breezes infuse the air with their perfume. Once the flowers are spent, bright orange capsules form, containing black seeds covered with a sticky resin. Victorian box trees are native to the tropics of Queensland and temperate areas of Brisbane along Australia's east coast, attesting to their adaptability in high- and low-rainfall regions, in mild winds, and in heat, if enough moisture is available. They withstand freezing temperatures for short periods only.

When, Where, and How to Plant
Plant in spring or fall from a 1-, 5-, or 15-gallon container. Select a full-sun or partial-shade area and plant in a loam soil with good drainage and a pH of 6.7–7.0. Site a single tree at least 20 ft. from buildings or paved areas; if grown in groups, space 12–15 ft. on center. Build a watering basin 10 ft. in diameter and mulch the surface with 2–3 in. of organic material. See Planting Techniques, p. 20.

Growing Tips
Water deeply once a week until established; thereafter water every ten to fourteen days, depending on growth and weather conditions. Fertilize in late winter or early spring with a complete organic granular fertilizer or cottonseed meal.

Advice and Care
If you grow it as a standard tree, remove its lower foliage and branches to expose its trunk and to encourage canopy growth. Prune for shape or when unsightly suckers appear at the bottom of the trunk, in late winter or early spring. When flowers and new foliage emerge in spring, aphids and brown soft scale populations can explode quickly. These sucking pests secrete a sticky substance called honeydew, which attracts ants. If this situation persists, a fungus known as black sooty mold will cover the leaves. To avoid extensive damage, wash off the foliage with a strong stream of water or use a canola-based horticultural oil.

Companion Planting and Design
Victorian box is a popular landscape tree; ours is growing under a large jacaranda near a cork oak and a mulberry. Whether as a screen, hedge, or focal landscape tree, combine with Japanese mock orange, pink Indian hawthorn, and laurustinus. Hummingbirds love its nectar and other birds enjoy the fruit.

Try These
'Variegatum' bears leaves with undulating white margins. *P. phillyreoides* is the desert willow. It is a slow grower to 20–25 ft. × 10–15 ft. with a weeping, airy habit and very fragrant yellow flowers in late winter to early spring.

Weeping Bottlebrush

Callistemon viminalis

Bloom Period and Seasonal Color
Red blossoms heavily in spring, continued throughout the year.

Mature Height × Spread 15–20 ft. × 10–15 ft.

Botanical Pronunciation
ka-LIS-the-mon VIM-in-ah-lis

Zones 8–11

Callistemon viminalis, an evergreen with a willowlike growing habit, is commonly called the weeping bottlebrush tree because of its long, downward-arching branches tipped with flower spikes resembling bottlebrushes. As a small tree, its canopy is narrow with a densely domed crown. In the native habitats, callistemon grow in low-lying areas such as creek beds or the bottoms of canyons where water tables are high. This makes them excellent choices where percolation is poor, along drainage swales, or near the bottoms of cut or filled banks. Their flowers are rich with ambrosia and attract many different species of birds, butterflies, and bees. Bottlebrush tolerates short durations of freezing temperatures, endures wind and heat if sufficient moisture is available, and withstands brief periods of drought once trees are mature.

When, Where, and How to Plant
Plant in fall or spring from 5- or 15-gallon containers. They do best in full sun, but can adapt to partial shade. *C. viminalis* prefers porous soils with a neutral pH of 7.0, but can tolerate dense clay to loam soils. If planting as a group, space the trees 12–15 ft. on center; locate a single specimen at least 15 ft. from structures or paved areas. Build a watering basin 6 in. high and 8 ft. in diameter, and mulch the surface with 2–3 in. of organic material. See Planting Techniques for more information, p. 20.

Growing Tips
Soak thoroughly immediately after planting, then water once a week for the first season, reducing frequency once established, adjusting for weather and growth factors. Fertilize in early spring with an organic granular food.

Advice and Care
Prune for shape after flowering in summer. Deadheading is not necessary; as the stamens drop off, woody capsules form on the stems, and new foliar and branch growth emerges at the tips. If left to grow naturally, *Callistemon* species develop branches close to the ground. Remove all branches below 4 ft. if you want to train it into a standard-form tree. Prune off any emerging growth from the trunk's base. They are relatively impervious to disease or insect infestation.

Companion Planting and Design
Since they are shallow rooted, they are used as street, parkway, or patio trees, and as visual screens. They're perfect for water-thrifty or desert gardens, as a hummingbird attractant, hedge, or in the middle of a border. Plant with other water-thrifty plants such as rock rose and pride of Madeira.

Try These
C. viminalis 'Red Cascade' has a profusion of large, rosy red, brushlike flowers, blooming most heavily in spring and growing 20–25 ft. tall. The shrub *C. yiminalis* 'Little John' is for the smaller garden at 3 ft. tall × 5 ft. wide and once established, needs little water. 'Canes Hybrid' grows 10 ft. × 15 ft., with new foliage tinted pink and pink blooms in early spring and summer.

Western Redbud

Cercis spp.

Bloom Period and Seasonal Color
Magenta flowers in spring.

Mature Height × Spread 15–20 ft. × 15–20 ft.

Botanical Pronunciation SIR-sis

Zones 8–10

Western redbud is found throughout the southwestern United States among foothills and along rocky slopes. In early spring, the western redbud's abundant clusters of magenta-red flowers blanket every bare branch. Growing to 15 ft., this deciduous tree is one of the most dazzling members of the pea family. Even when tightly budded, it creates a showy display. Once its elegant blossoms are spent, lush, heart-shaped, bright green foliage bursts forth, covering all its branches. Delicate, flat seedpods dangle in the soft spring and summer breezes. Although similar in growth to the eastern redbud, it tends to be shrubbier in habit. For a smaller tree, *C. canadensis* 'Forest Pansy' grows 12–20 ft. and about 15 ft. wide with bright red-purple leaves maturing into a softer purple.

When, Where, and How to Plant
Plant in fall for optimum root development; the second-best time is in spring. Select 1- or 5-gallon container plants. If planting in a group, space 12–15 ft. apart; locate a single tree 10 ft. from structures or paved areas. Choose a full-sun site for maximum bloom production, although partial sun will do. Redbuds need a porous soil with a neutral pH of 7.0. Plan the location carefully because redbuds do not like to be transplanted.

Growing Tips
Construct a watering basin to encourage the development of deep roots and mulch its surface with 2–3 in. of organic material. See p. 20 for more planting details. Water weekly the first growing season to establish a deep, extensive root system; thereafter water every ten to fourteen days, depending on weather and growth conditions. Withhold water during winter dormancy. Fertilize with a complete organic granular or a slow-release food in late winter before new growth begins in spring.

Advice and Care
To grow as a multitrunk specimen, select three strong, main stems to be the leaders, pruning away all other lateral branches below 4 ft. in winter or immediately after bloom season is over. If leafhoppers or grasshoppers persistently destroy the foliage, spray with an organic insecticide. Control scale by applying a canola-oil based horticultural oil.

Companion Planting and Design
Redbuds are excellent for lawns, woodland landscapes, or wherever a more naturalized look is desired. Add to beds and borders or as a specimen to create a distant focal point. Whether planted as a specimen or in groups, in small landscape areas or large estates, they are a good choice for shadier, understory sites. They also blend well with California lilac, manzanita, and California poppies.

Try These
Western redbuds need winter chill for prolific blooms, but *C. canadensis* 'Forest Pansy' adapts to mild winter areas. With 'Forest Pansy', deep pink, white, or lavender spring blooms are replaced with scarlet-purple heart-shaped leaves that morph in a blaze of autumnal hues. It's the perfect specimen tree for small gardens or large containers. *C. occidentalis* 'Claremont' bears deep red blossoms.

White Alder

Alnus rhombifolia

Bloom Period and Seasonal Color
Yellow catkins in spring and summer; fall yellow fall foliage.

Mature Height × Spread 25–40 ft. × 40 ft.

Botanical Pronunciation
ALL-nus ROM-bih-fole-ee-ah

Zones 6–10

White alders are useful in problem areas that have poor drainage or nutrient deficiencies. They are also appealing for their attractive, distinctive white bark, upright shape, and contrasting deep green, glossy foliage that covers slightly weeping branches. In winter, its bare appearance only enhances the delicate form; in warmer months, the serrated leaves quiver with the slightest breeze. The flowers are unisexual, appearing as catkins that blossom on the trees periodically throughout the year, except winter. Keep in mind that alders are found naturally in areas where soil is deep and constantly moist, such as riverbanks, canyon floors, or marshes. These trees tolerate temperatures as low as -10 degrees Fahrenheit, but need supplemental moisture during drought, high temperatures, and dry winds.

When, Where, and How to Plant
Select 5- to 15-gallon containers, but make sure these fast-growing plants are not rootbound. It's best to plant in fall or early spring. For optimum development, plant in full sun where the soil has adequate access to moisture and the pH is 6.5–7.2. If planting in a group, space 20–30 ft. apart. If planting a single tree, plant at least 30 ft. from the nearest structure or paved area, and never plant near leach lines. To establish trees as quickly as possible, encourage lateral root development by building a watering basin well beyond a tree's drip line and mulching the basin's surface with 2–3 in. of compost or humus mulch. Also see p. 20 for planting techniques.

Growing Tips
Because these trees are "water babies," it is almost impossible to overwater them, especially if there is good percolation throughout their root zones. Withhold or decrease water during winter dormancy, but do not allow the soil to dry out completely. The most efficient time to fertilize is in early spring and fall, with an organic granular food.

Advice and Care
If white alder is a focal point in the garden and a standard tree form is desired, prune for shape early. Remove all but a single trunk and any branches below 4–5 ft., as well as suckers and interfering or damaged branches. There are few diseases or pests that invade these trees, but be on the lookout in summer for migratory, chewing insects. Control chewing insects with spinosad, or if that's impractical because of the tree's height, use a systemic containing imidacloprid.

Companion Planting and Design
White alders are widely used as fast-growing shade trees, as windbreaks, along waterways for erosion control, and as background trees. White alder grows well with other woodland plants that love moist soils, including hydrangeas, Japanese iris, and leopard plant (*Farfugium*).

Try These
A. glutinosa, black alder, is slower growing to 70 ft. × 30 ft. with a dense crown and foliage growing low on the tree. 'Imperialis' has deeply cut, dark green leaves.

TROPICAL PLANTS

FOR CALIFORNIA

W hat is it about orchids, plumerias, hibiscus, angel's trumpet, and other tropicals that leaves us awestruck? Perhaps it is because they express themselves in such different forms, hues, perfumes, and structures. Or is it because languorous landscapes transport us to dreamy visions of faraway South Seas islands?

Orchids, the Stuff of Tropical Dreams

Besides palms, few plants evoke visions of the tropics better than orchids. Their alluring, yet strangely gnarled roots, variety of leaf shapes, and of course their elegant and extraterrestrial flower forms and limitless colors have inspired plant hunters to risk their lives in search of these exquisite beauties, the obsessive object of their dreams. Once the nature and specific needs of orchids is understood, however, gardeners do not have to be obsessed plant hunters or "orchid thieves" to unravel the orchid mystery and successfully grow these beauties.

Bloom and Growth Categories

Orchids can be categorized into three groups according to bloom period: cool-season flowering, warm-season flowering, and continuously flowering varieties. After flowering, orchids generally enter a resting state for one to two months, followed by several months of a vegetative growth period. Depending on environmental factors and the orchid variety, this entire process will take from eleven to fourteen months.

Orchids can also be categorized into four groups according to their growing conditions: epiphytic, which thrive in rainforest canopies; terrestrial, which grow in soil; geophytic, which grow on rocks; and saprophytic, which grow on decaying organic material. Epiphytic and terrestrial orchids are the varieties most commonly available to California gardeners.

More Tropical Plants

Beside otherworldly orchids and swaying palms, there are more plants that are found in lush jungle-scapes, such as fragrant plumerias; nodding angel's trumpets, which announce their perfumed presence in the evening hours; and neon-colored hibiscus, some as large as dinner plates. They provide a panorama of brilliant foliage and spectacular flowers. It's also different to ignore the breathtaking beauty of orchid cactus.

Hibiscus add tropical drama to a garden.

Tropical Oasis in Cooler Zones

For Californians in USDA zone 9 or higher, there are dozens of tropical plants from which to choose, but even those living in cooler zones can create a tropical oasis by planting cold-tolerant varieties.

The exotic canna lily looks at home under a Hawaiian sunset, but can survive freezing weather by dying back to the ground and resprouting from its roots. Epiphyllums are epiphytic rainforest plants, but they also adapt to the shade canopies of trees in Southern California. The unusual banana shrub is hardy down to zone 8; its intense banana perfume can be fully appreciated in spring when planted close to walkways or entries. Even more cold hardy, Chinese ground orchids adapt to a wide range of temperatures from zones 6–11 and resemble mini cattleyas.

Plant sensitive tropicals in containers to move them easily into temporary winter quarters such as a greenhouse, conservatory, enclosed courtyard, atrium, or protected entryway.

The Story of Understory Plants

Many tropicals come from rainforests as understory plants thriving in dappled light, making them adaptable to moving indoors during inclement weather. However, they require 50–60 percent humidity, a condition difficult to replicate if the human residents are to be comfortable. A simple solution to increasing humidity around the plants while keeping the rest of the house comfortable for human habitation is to use humidity trays. Buy them at your local garden center or make your own. Fill a waterproof container such as a saucer or tray with coarse gravel, decorative pebbles, or marbles, and add water up to the gravel surface. Place a brick, rack, or wood block on the gravel and set the potted plant on top to keep the pot from sitting in water. Humidity trays, as well as misting plants around the soil and under the leaves with a spray bottle, help to create a continuous column of humidity.

So dare to dabble in orchids and other tropicals—you will be in for an exciting journey that will captivate all your senses.

Angel's Trumpet

Brugmansia suaveolens

Bloom Period and Seasonal Color
Pink, white, or yellow flowers.

Mature Height × Spread 8–12 ft. × 8 ft.

Botanical Pronunciation
BRUGH-man-see-ah SWAV-ee-oh-lenz

Zones 8–11

A member of the nightshade family of plants, angel's trumpet (syn. *Datura suaveolens*) is a large bush that can be pruned into a small tree. Each leaf of its lovely blue-gray foliage measures 6–10 in. in length and width and has a fuzzy surface. Angel's trumpet has spectacular pendulous, funnel-shaped flowers that range in color from white, pink, and peachy orange to yellow. A cautionary note: Its leaves and flowers are toxic and the entire plant is a narcotic. Never use it in cutflower arrangements or plant in your garden if you have small children or pets. The beauty of the flower and its citrusy-musk perfume are well worth the extra care. Angel's trumpet is easy to maintain if you have selected the correct growing environment.

When, Where, and How to Plant
The best time to plant is in spring, from 1- or 5-gallon containers, in a frost-free location protected from wind because wind tears the foliage. Plant in full sun in loam soil with a slightly acidic to neutral pH of 6.5–7.0. If you want to plant several, space them 6–10 ft. apart. Use a preplant fertilizer, 2–10–6, following manufacturer's directions. Provide shade in desert regions. For more information on soil preparation refer to Planting Techniques, p. 20.

Growing Tips
Water deeply once or twice a week depending on weather conditions and maturity of the plant. Reduce or withhold water in winter. Two in. of organic material such as humus mulch or compost will minimize moisture loss. Fertilize three times from spring to fall with an organic granular food or cottonseed meal.

Advice and Care
To develop this plant into a small tree form, remove the lateral branches up to 4 ft. with pruning shears. Since this plant is toxic, use latex or other waterproof gloves when pruning and wash the shears afterwards using warm water with liquid detergent, then dry them. Before new growth emerges in spring, remove damaged, weak, or crowded stems. Control aphids by washing them off with a stream of water or by applying a canola-based horticultural oil. Spray with spinosad for chewing insect damage.

Companion Planting and Design
Angel's trumpet contrasts well with plants such as canna lily and banana shrub. It can also be used to great effect as an accent plant in a large container.

Try These
B. × cubensis 'Charles Grimaldi' is a fast-growing hybrid 10–12 ft. × 10 ft. with pale orange-yellow, very fragrant flowers. Also 10–12 ft., *B. × insignis* 'Frosty Pink' has large, 8–10 in. pink blooms, while 'Betty Marshall' is more compact at 6–8 ft. and has white flowers. *B. versicolor* 'Equador Pink' is a spectacular cultivar with pastel pink-and-white flowers. 'Double White' bears creamy white, 8–12-in. double flowers with long grayish green leaves. 'Cherub' grows to 7 ft. tall and wide and has very fragrant salmon pink blooms.

Banana Shrub

Michelia figo

Bloom Period and Seasonal Color
Creamy yellow blossoms in spring to
early summer.

Mature Height × Spread 6–12 ft. × 4–12 ft.

Botanical Pronunciation mig-KEE-lee-ah FY-go

Zones 8–11

Michelia figo is native to western China and was introduced to the U.S. in the 1700s, becoming a popular evergreen in the old South. It is closely related to the genus *Magnolia* and commonly known as the banana shrub because of its intensely distinctive sweet banana-scented flowers. Emerging from fuzzy brown bracts, small creamy yellowish flowers shaded with a purplish tint burst open from late spring through summer. The small, 1½-in. flowers are composed of six waxy petals thinly outlined in a deep crimson red. It is an evergreen, woody, shrubby plant bearing narrow, glossy leaves. At maturity, its rounded form may reach 15 ft. tall and as wide. Despite its common name, be aware that no part of the plant is edible.

When, Where, and How to Plant
Available in 5-gallon or larger containers; transplant into humus-rich, slightly acidic, well-draining soil in full sun along coastal regions and part shade inland. Protect from windy conditions. If planted in the ground, construct a watering basin that is about three to four times the diameter of the plant's original container and soak thoroughly to collapse any air pockets. Refer to Planting Techniques, p. 20, for more information. If planting in a container, use a commercial well-draining acid potting medium and add an additional 20 percent perlite to the mix.

Growing Tips
Water regularly once a week from spring to summer, or more often during heat waves, but decrease frequency during fall to winter. Fertilize with cottonseed meal before and after the bloom cycle.

Advice and Care
For a formal look, shear once a year after flowering; left unpruned it grows into a looser, more open and rounded form with multiple stems and branches. There are few pests or diseases except mealybug, aphid, or scale infestations. Spray with a strong stream of water or use a canola-based horticultural oil. Root rot may be a problem if there is poor-draining soil. Add products containing saponin and humic acid to improve drainage.

Companion Planting and Design
Place it close to walkways or entries where its intense banana perfume can be appreciated during spring. Or plant it in a pot and place on a patio, by a swimming pool, or near a fountain. Create a hedge for privacy, or plant near windows or doors to allow its fragrance to waft indoors for aromatherapy. Ideal for shade gardens or as an understory plant under the protective canopy of taller trees, it also blends well with bird of paradise, bougainvillea, and hibiscus. Its branches make perfect perches for visiting songbirds and its dainty flowers can be used in leis, rivaling the fragrant plumeria.

Try These
Michelia figo 'Purple Queen' bears purple flowers and is a slow grower just like its species cousin. *M. figo* var. *skinneriana* is larger, growing 30 ft., with 3-in. pale cream flowers with pink or maroon centers.

Canna Lily

Canna × generalis

Bloom Period and Seasonal Color
Red, white, pink, yellow, or orange flowers bloom in spring and summer.

Mature Height × Spread
3–6 ft. (rhizotomaceous, clumping)

Botanical Pronunciation KA-nah JEN-er-ah-lis

Zones 9–11

A must-have for a tropical garden, include a bed of cannas to display their lush, bold foliage and burgeoning flowers of eye-popping reds, oranges, yellows, and pinks. In summer, their foliage runs the color gamut from plain green, red, purple, and bronze to a rainbow of variegation. Spectacular 4–6-in. flowers spread their fiery hues from sturdy clumps of 2–8 ft. These exotic hybrids add snap to an otherwise bland foliage border. Canna resembles ginger and banana plants, having what appear to be thick stalks that are actually tightly rolled leaves emerging from surface rhizomes. It's heat tolerant if sufficient humidity and moisture are present, but cannas do not withstand drought; hot, dry winds; or severe cold. In mild-winter regions, cannas naturalize.

When, Where, and How to Plant

Plant rhizomes in spring after the last frost from 1- or 5-gallon containers, spacing 1–2 ft. apart. Select a sunny site, in rich, moisture-retaining, slightly acidic soil that has a pH of 6.5–7.0. Build a watering basin twice the diameter of the original container and mulch with 1 in. of organic material such as humus or compost.

Growing Tips

Cannas are almost impossible to overwater; water once a week or more, especially in warm weather. Fertilize in early spring after the last frost with a complete organic granular or water-soluble food.

Advice and Care

To prevent seed formation and encourage a longer flowering season, remove spent blooms. Where extended winter freezes are common, prune 6–8 in. in the fall and dig up the rhizomes; wipe them off and place in dry peat. Maintain at a temperature of 45–50 degrees Fahrenheit in a dry, dark place with good air circulation, and let them rest for the winter. In temperate zones, allow cannas to naturalize in your garden. Control giant whitefly with an organic insecticide such as spinosad or a systemic product containing imidacloprid. For slugs and snails, apply an organic iron phosphate bait, handpick, or, in Southern California, use decollate snails.

Companion Planting and Design

Thirsty cannas show off best when massed as accents beside a pool or water garden. Don't squeeze the statuesque cultivars into tiny beds with more mundane salvia, ageratum, or marigolds. Instead, add to roomier beds and borders as contrasts in forms, color, and texture along with daylily, bird of paradise, and passionflower vines.

Try These

Some newer varieties of tall cannas, growing 6–8 ft. tall, are: 'Tropicana', with orange blooms and purple leaves striped with green, yellow, pink, and red; 'Black Canna', which has deep red blooms with black-bronze foliage; and 'Bengal Tiger', which bears bright orange blooms emerging from deep green-and-yellow-striped leaves. Smaller dwarf types growing 24–30 in. tall are 'Yellow Futurity', with green foliage and yellow blooms, and 'Red Futurity', with deep red flowers and striped green leaves.

Chinese Ground Orchid

Bletilla striata

Bloom Period and Seasonal Color
Magenta, yellow, pink, white blooms in spring.

Mature Height × Spread
12–20 in. × 12–20 in.

Botanical Pronunciation
BLEH-tee-ah STRY-ah-tah

Zones 6–11

Remember those large, magenta, or white cattleyas in the 1940s–1960s? They were the orchids of choice for special-occasion corsages. Unless grown indoors, few California gardens are hospitable enough for cattleyas, but there is a hardy, terrestrial species that is its miniaturized version. It bears flowers, often as many as twenty, resembling mini cattleyas atop wiry spikes rising from pleated, straplike foliage. Native to western China and other parts of northern Asia, bletillas have been cultivated in the U.S. for more than fifty years, most commonly *Bletilla striata*. In a partially shaded, well-draining space, bletillas are one of the easiest terrestrial orchids to grow even for a beginner, and are adaptable to most California gardens, although some protection in the winter for zones 6–7 is recommended.

When, Where, and How to Plant
This is a very hardy orchid to grow in containers or in the ground. Provide part shade and plant the pseudobulbs with tips up, about 1 in. below the soil surface. Where winter freezes are common, plant 2 in. below the surface and mulch around the plant. This plant needs humus-amended, well-draining, slightly acidic soil and spacing 6–8 in. apart. In pots, use a commercial organic potting mix and plant in 6 in. or larger pots.

Growing Tips
Keep soil moist, but not soggy, spring through summer while flowering; decrease water after flowers are spent fall through winter. During winter dormancy, do not water. Feed potted orchids monthly at half recommended strength with an organic liquid fertilizer such as liquid kelp, once a month from spring to mid-summer, or add a slow-release fertilizer once in spring. For bedded plants, fertilize with cottonseed meal once just before the flowers emerge.

Advice and Care
Plants can be divided easily by hand from clumps and replanted in early spring before new growth begins, but they flower more profusely when crowded. Cut off flowering spikes once blossoms are spent. Protect from snails and slugs with an organic iron phosphate bait or handpick. For aphids and other sucking insects, spray with a canola-based horticultural oil or wash off with a strong stream of water.

Companion Planting and Design
Bletilla is a perfect choice for a low-maintenance orchid in a shade garden, woodlands, or in a pot in dappled light. Plant with other shade-loving perennials such as ferns, hellebores, and clivias and set toward the front of the beds.

Try These
Besides the common *B. striata* with lovely lavender blooms, *B.s. albostriata* has green-and-white-striped leaves with rosy purple flowers, while 'Alba' blooms are white. 'Murasaki Shikibu' bears bluish lavender flowers and *B. s. ochracea* grows up to 20 in. tall with lovely, star-shaped yellow flowers. 'Big Bob' has taller 2–3-ft. stalks with up to twenty rose-lavender flowers that have white and dark lavender highlights; it doesn't need much fertilizer and is hardy in zones 6–9.

Cymbidium Orchid

Cymbidium × hybrida

Bloom Period and Seasonal Color
Winter to spring blooms in all the colors of the rainbow and combinations.

Mature Height × Spread 12–48 in. × 8–36 in.

Botanical Pronunciation
SIM-bid-ee-um

Zones 9–11

Cymbidiums are found in far-flung areas from the Himalayas to China, Japan, Southeast Asia, the Philippines, and Australia. Growing on erect or arching spikes, their flowers range from petite to 3-in. beauties, in hues including green, white, yellow, orange, red, and purple, with contrasting streaks, splashes, and speckles. Popular for their spectacular beauty, but also because they are relatively easy to grow and maintain, they bloom from winter to spring in huge sprays, although the miniature forms flower from fall to winter. There are few orchids that can equal their longevity as cut flowers. Arising from pseudobulbs, long, narrow, evergreen foliage serves as a draping backdrop to flowering spikes. For hanging baskets, there are cymbidiums that even cascade over the confines of their containers.

When, Where, and How to Plant
Unless the soil drains very well, you should plant cymbidiums in containers using a commercial orchid mix available at garden centers. Place in partial shade or in full sun as long as the foliage does not burn; and provide good air circulation. Flowering spikes develop when night temperatures dip into the 50s outdoors. As long as temperatures are no higher than 85 degrees Fahrenheit in summer and no colder than 45 degrees Fahrenheit in winter, cymbidiums will be happy outdoors.

Growing Tips
From spring through summer, keep soil moist, but decrease watering during winter, providing just enough water to keep the pseudobulbs plump. When high temperatures prevail or during hot, dry winds, also mist the foliage with water. Feed a complete, organic liquid fertilizer every two to three weeks or granular fertilizer once a month from winter to fall.

Advice and Care
Although cymbidiums bloom best in crowded conditions, divide them about every three to five years when the bulbs completely fill the container. Select at least three healthy bulbs with their foliage per division. Bring indoors during extended winter frost or to enjoy the blossoms. Control slugs and snails by handpicking or using iron phosphate bait.

Companion Planting and Design
Upright cymbidium adds winter to early spring beauty under the shaded canopy of a tree and can be brought indoors to enjoy their clusters of spiking blossoms. Miniature cymbidium is ideal for small spaces and cascading varieties are lovely in hanging baskets.

Try These
There are thousands of cymbidium hybrids, so select the ones that "sing" to you, such as 'Sweetness', a crystal clear white with red spotted lips, or 'Beauty Stripes', with vivid bronze-striped petals. 'Vintage' has melon-colored petals with deep apricot lips, while 'Lime Delight' is bright, knock-your-eyes-out chartreuse. For basket displays, consider Sarah Jean 'Ice Cascade' (packed clusters of cascading white flowers) or Sarah Jean 'Helen' (deep pink with contrasting lips). Peter Pan 'Greensleeves' is a fragrant miniature with pale green petals and maroon lip that blooms in the fall.

Epidendrum

Epidendrum × *hybrida*

Other Name Terrestrial orchid

Bloom Period and Seasonal Color
Orange, yellow, pink, red, lavender, and white blooms year-round in temperate climates

Mature Height × Spread 8–36 in. × 8–36 in.

Botanical Pronunciation EH-pih-den-drum

Zones 9–11 or indoors

Another easy-to-grow terrestrial orchid, the epidendrum bears globular clusters of small blooms atop reed stems arising from thin pseudobulbs. Found in the warmer climates of Florida, Mexico, the West Indies, and Central and South America, it is commonly known as the crucifix orchid because of its showy labellums. Most are red, orange, yellow, pink, lavender, white, and bicolors, and bloom continuously in warm weather. Despite their easy care, epidendrums are one of the most underappreciated among orchid growers. Unlike their more shade-loving cousins, they are more partial to sun and will be happy planted in garden beds or containers. Our first epidendrum quickly grew from a single cutting taken from a friend's garden into a rambunctious plant bearing vibrant orchid-colored flowers.

When, Where, and How to Plant
Classified as a cool-growing orchid, epidendrums do best when daytime temperatures are between 60–75 degrees Fahrenheit and evening temperatures range from 50–55 degrees Fahrenheit. Where winter freezes are common, plant them in containers and move indoors to protect them. Plant in a commercial orchid potting mix and provide some shade in the afternoon, particularly in inland regions to avoid burning the foliage. Along the coast, plant their roots in the shade and faces in the sun. When growing in the ground, provide well-draining, humus-rich soil and mulch around the plant with humus or compost, leaving a 2–4-in. space around its base.

Growing Tips
Water every five to seven days, depending on growth and weather conditions. If in containers, or during a heat wave, water more frequently. Use a complete liquid organic fertilizer (half the recommended rate) when watering about every other time for plants in containers during the growth period and for those in the ground, about once a month. Another option is to apply a slow-release fertilizer formulated for orchids following the recommendations for containers and for in-ground plants.

Advice and Care
Cut spent flowers down to one or two leaf nodes above the soil in order for another flower stem to form. Control aphids, mealybugs, and scale with a canola-based horticultural oil. Use an organic iron phosphate bait to keep snails and slugs at bay.

Companion Planting and Design
If specific colors are important, make selections when in flower so you can see what you are getting. Although epidendrum can grow directly in planting beds, especially in cooler climates, its needs are better met if grown in a container.

Try These
E. atropurpureum blooms in late spring and its flowers are a mixture of green and mahogany hues with crimson-striped or white lips. *E.* × *obrienianum* have 1–2-ft. stems that continuously bloom in warm weather. Its cattleya-like flowers are red. *E. ibaguense* are native to Columbia.

Hibiscus

Hibiscus rosa-sinensis

Other Name Chinese hibiscus

Bloom Period and Seasonal Color
Red, white, pink, yellow, blue, purple, or orange flowers bloom late spring to fall.

Mature Height × Spread 4–10 ft. × 4–6 ft.

Botanical Pronunciation
HI-bis-kus ROE-sah sin-EN-sis

Zones 10–11

Native to tropical areas of Asia, *H. rosa-sinensis* plants are evergreen shrubs that produce vibrant flowers in a wide range of brilliant colors. Some of the hybrids have spectacular 8–10-in. diameter blooms as single or double-flowered forms. While it is unfortunate that each flower usually lasts for only a day, the continuous and abundant bloom cycle, from late spring to fall, more than compensates for each single flower's short life span. Hibiscus plants have glossy green foliage with slightly serrated edges. Since they are tropical plants, they withstand heat as long as there is plenty of humidity and moist soil, but they need protection from the wind and must be in frost-free areas. They make excellent hedge screens if allowed to reach full height.

When, Where, and How to Plant
The best time to plant is in spring so they will have the long summer and fall growing period to establish their root systems. They can survive in partial shade, but for maximum bloom production, full sun is best. Hibiscus plants require an acidic pH, 6.5–7.0, with a rich, organic loam soil that is kept adequately moist. If you select 1- or 5-gallon containers, be aware they will grow much larger, and space them so their mature canopies do not touch each other. Plant 6–8 ft. on center. If you want to use hibiscus for hedges, plant them closer together. Bloom and growth cycles stop when temperatures fall below 50 degrees Fahrenheit. See Planting Techniques, p. 20.

Growing Tips
Hibiscus are tropical plants, and must have sufficient moisture about once every five to seven days,

especially during the warmer months. Decrease watering during the cool seasons, but do not allow to dry out completely. Fertilize twice a year, in spring and in early summer, with an organic granular food or cottonseed meal.

Advice and Care
Prune for shape in the early spring and when unruly new branches appear above the canopy. Deadheading is unnecessary. Giant whitefly produce cotton candy–like white strands underneath the leaves. Control by spraying with spinosad every seven to ten days until the problem is remedied or use a systemic insecticide with imidacloprid.

Companion Planting and Design
Hibiscus adds an important component to the tropical and cottage-garden landscapes. Versatile as a hedge, screen, background specimen, or in containers, they bloom almost continuously in frost-free areas.

Try These
H. rosa-sinensis 'Crown of Bohemia' has petals in deep orange with a red throat. *H. rosa-sinensis* 'Hula Girl' has large single yellow blooms with a touch of bright red in its throat. 'Mongon' is fiery red with ruffled petals. Grafted selections with large 8–12-in. blossoms, like 'Rainbow Christie', with pink flowers and carmine red eyes; 'Dragon's Heart', in deep burgundy; or 'C'est Bon' with ruffled, rose-pink petals edged in white, grow 4–8 ft. tall in the ground and 3–4 ft. in containers.

Moth Orchid

Phalaenopsis amabilis

Other Name Butterfly orchid

Bloom Period and Seasonal Color
Magenta, lavender, pink, white, pale green, yellow, brown, and red blooms year-round.

Mature Height × Spread 8–12 in. × 12–18 in.

Botanical Pronunciation
FAE-lee-en-op-sis AH-mah-bih-lis

Zones 11 or everywhere indoors

The loveliest of all spray orchids, epiphytic moth orchids come in a dazzling palette of magenta, lavender, pink, white, pale green, yellow, brown, and red shades, as well as contrasting patterns of spots, splashes, streaks, and stripes. From deep green, tongue-shaped, leathery leaves come flowering spikes laden with four to ten blooms that last two to three months. A mature *Phalaenopsis* can remain in bloom for up to eight to ten months and form two or three budding offshoots. Despite their fragile, exotic appearance, they are great for beginners because they are one of the most forgiving orchids. The ideal temperature range is from 65 degrees Fahrenheit in the evening to 75 degrees or higher during the day, provided there is adequate moisture and good air circulation, making them ideal houseplants.

When, Where, and How to Plant
Repot about every two years when the plants are in an active stage of growth. Use a fir bark mixture, fine-grade ¼ in. for seedlings, ½–⅝ in. medium-grade for larger sizes. Filtered light is best most of the year; in winter, provide a bit brighter light. Keep them away from heat, air conditioning, cold drafts, and direct sunlight. Remove dead and decaying roots and place a layer of Styrofoam peanuts at the bottom of a lightweight plastic pot for drainage.

Growing Tips
To allow the injured roots time to heal, do not water for a couple of days after planting, then soak deeply, watering before noon to let the plants dry by night. Thereafter water every seven to ten days, allowing the medium to dry out slightly. Fertilize with every watering during the growth and bloom cycles with a complete water-soluble organic food at half-dosage strength or use a controlled-release food formulated for orchids.

Advice and Care
When flowers wilt, leave spikes so additional buds form. If a spike tip dies back, cut off at the nearest bump or node on the stem and a lateral shoot should emerge in about four weeks. Or cut entire stem for vigorous new growth. In fall, keep temperatures around 61 degrees Fahrenheit for four to six weeks to stimulate flower spike development. Thrips, scales, aphids, mealybugs, and spider mites can be problems. After washing off with soapy water and rinsing with tepid water, keep an eye out for subsequent infestations. Should damage continue, use a systemic insecticide formulated for orchids or houseplants.

Companion Planting and Design
Moth orchids are best grown indoors during the cooler months in bright, indirect light and taken outdoors to a shady area during the warmer months of late spring to summer. To raise humidity, especially while indoors, set on a tray filled with gravel and water and use a block to keep the plant from sitting in water.

Try These
P. amboinensis has star-shaped flowers with brown markings. *P. equestris* is a compact plant with small deep rose flowers. It is a prolific bloomer.

Orchid Cactus

Epiphyllum hybrids

Bloom Period and Seasonal Color
Spring, summer, or fall blooms in white, yellow, pink, red, orange, lavender, magenta, and bicolors.

Mature Height × Spread 2–6 ft. × 2–6 ft.

Botanical Pronunciation eh-pih-FI-lum

Zones 10–11

Epiphyllums, or "epis," are tropical succulents growing mainly in the crooks of trees and forming flat, leaflike, spineless green stems with scalloped edges growing about 2–6 ft. long. Not a climber, it leans on a tree or other sturdy support. Although the stems are interesting, epis are grown for their spectacular and large 4–10-in. flowers blooming from spring to fall. Attached to the end of a long tube emerging from the side of a stem, a large cup opens up to flaring silky petals centered with many filament-like stamens and a stigma. The species flower opens at night and closes during the day, but most hybrids bloom during the day and come in every color of the rainbow except blue; some are even fragrant.

When, Where, and How to Plant
In spring or summer, plant from cuttings or pots in rich, well-draining, slightly acidic soil such as a commercial cactus mix. Without a well-draining medium, epis are prone to root rot, so it is best to plant in containers. From 6–12-in.-long cuttings, allow the ends to callus over for several days, then dip in a rooting hormone before planting in a moistened cactus mix. Tie loosely to a support such as a stake. Withhold water for several weeks before beginning a regular watering regimen, but do not allow it to dry out completely. Provide partial shade or morning light and begin fertilizing once it is established and new growth is evident, in about one year. For areas where winter freezes are common, move epis indoors where there is bright light or into a greenhouse.

Growing Tips
Although considered succulents, epis are tropical plants, not drought-tolerant cacti, and require regular water, about every five to seven days. Keep roots moist but not soggy. Use an organic granular food or cottonseed meal before and after bloom cycles.

Advice and Care
There's no need to deadhead. Control scale with a canola-based horticultural oil and keep slugs away from foliage. If rodents are a problem, use manual traps or battery-operated traps that electrocute them.

Companion Planting and Design
The long, arching stems with spectacular blossoms show off best in hanging baskets, large tubs, or pots. Combine indoors with other tropical plants such as schefflera or succulents like jade plants, or outdoors on a partially shaded deck or under the protective canopy of trees.

Try These
Excellent for hanging baskets, 'Gold Charm' bears small yellow-and-white flowers, but its fragrance and color more than compensate for its lack of size. Another epi showing off best in a basket is 'Blue Paradise', a blend of vibrant pink, orange, and violet growing 1–2 ft. 'Golden Fleece' is pale yellow with a dark midstripe. 'George's Favorite' is a spidery flat bloom in rich carmine red with an orange midstripe.

Plumeria

Plumeria rubra

Other Name Frangipani

Bloom Period and Seasonal Color
White, yellow, red, pink, orange, and multicolored blooms in spring to autumn.

Mature Height × Spread 6–40 ft. × 10–15 ft.

Botanical Pronunciation
PLOO-meh-ree-ah ROO-brah

Zones 10–11

Plumeria, also known as frangipani, have large, 6–24-in. thick, leathery leaves that are heavily veined and found at the edges of candelabra-like branches. Long-tubed, perfumed flowers with five often-overlapping petals appear as clusters. When the buds open, they reveal corollas that can tinged with pink and yellow, solid or bicolored. Their fragrances are as varied as their colors, with scents akin to gardenias, honeysuckle, coconut, citrus, rose, peach, apricot, or indescribably unique. It is the iconic flower of choice for leis. Some people refer to the plumeria's unusual form with grayish white limbs as "awkward antlers festooned with nosegays," especially when deciduous. But others will find plumeria architectural in the winter garden, and while in leaf and flower, the crown jewels of the tropical garden.

When, Where, and How to Plant
Three prerequisites for optimum growth include a climate that is frost-free or nearly frost-free, well-draining soil, and 6–8 hours of sunshine. Also make sure humus or compost has been added to the native soil. If clayey, add a product containing saponin and humic acid to improve drainage or plant in containers using a commercial cactus mix. Where winters are cold and wet, containers are best so that the plants can be moved to drier, more protected locations to avoid root rot. Plant from cuttings or containers and space 6–10 ft. apart.

Growing Tips
Water every five to seven days during growth and bloom periods, allowing the soil to dry out slightly before watering again. Withhold water when dormant, but keep roots moist if there is an extended drought. Although somewhat drought tolerant once established, plumeria thrive best with a regular watering regimen. Feed with a granular organic fertilizer such as cottonseed meal or use a controlled-release food following the manufacturer's directions from spring to fall.

Advice and Care
Prune in late spring or summer for shape or to remove damaged branches. Before bringing containers indoors during inclement winters, prune lightly. Take 18–24-in. cuttings from ends of branches that are not in bloom in late spring to summer. Allow cut ends to callus over for several days in a shaded, dry spot. Plant in cactus mix and keep moist, but not soggy. Control white flies with a strong stream of water or use an organic insecticide such as spinosad.

Companion Planting and Design
Since plumeria bear generous clusters of fragrant flowers, set near entryways or walkways to enjoy their perfume. And of course, combine with hibiscus, epidendrums, and cannas to complete the tropical look in mixed beds or by a pool or pond.

Try These
'Daisy Wilcox' produces huge 4½-in. flowers in pastel pink blending to white with yellow. 'Candystripe' bears deep pink, yellow, and white blossoms. 'Guillot's Sunset' is in pink and white with a yellow center, while yellow, gold, and orange hues are in 'Hawaiian Yellow', 'Aztec Gold', and 'Tangerine', respectively.

VINES
FOR CALIFORNIA

Clematis vine their way upward into a landscape.

Whether they are casting cool shadows, creating privacy, twining up a fence, or arching over a gate, vines can be flamboyant flower factories or sedate evergreen shingles. When space is limited, think about gardening up walls, trellises, arbors, posts, or any other structure that begs for highlighting or camouflage. Rambunctious vines can even weave their way through shrubs and trees.

Training Your Vines

To keep vines from smothering their supports, other plants, or each other, pinch tender shoots about once a month during their growth cycle, saving the heavy pruning for dormancy. If you prefer a lush, more overgrown look, then relax and subscribe to a laissez-faire style of gardening.

Mandevillas and clematis are easy to train in small places, but other vines such as wisteria, bougainvillea, scarlet trumpet vine, and passion vine fill larger spaces such as walls and fences. Creeping fig and Boston ivy are self-supporting vines with the help of holdfasts, tendrils with disklike suction cups, or rootlets that enable them to attach to just about anything. Bear in mind that even aggressivevines can be curtailed and confined with annual pruning and frequent pinching back.

Most vines have a natural tendency to grow upward, branch into a tangled mass at the top, and leave their "bottoms" bare. To prevent these growth habits, train and tie their branches horizontally until the desired width is reached. Cover a wall or trellis by laterally spreading and securing the runners, but wrap an arch by training runners upright and spreading them when they reach the top. If multiple branching or denser growth is desired, pinch back regularly, just above the buds—this also promotes more blooms, as the flowers normally emerge at the tips of branches. Once the plant's framework is established, vines can be sheared like a hedge for a dense, compact appearance, or clipped to thin out for an open look. To encourage more growth at the base, bend some shoots down and train them to fill in the gaps. Check nearby nurseries or look around your neighborhood to determine how specific vines perform—as a rule, the milder your climate, the wider your choices.

Cultivation and Care

Bougainvillea and wisteria vines are not self-supporting, grow very large, develop a lot of weight, and must have a sturdy structure on which to grow. Carolina jessamine, Madagascar jasmine, and passion vines climb by twining or with tendrils, and they grow best up wires or narrow slats. If you use supporting wires, make sure they are insulated; otherwise, they might burn the tender vines in full-sun areas.

For adequate air circulation between a trellis and a wall, allow 3–4 in. of space, which makes pruning and tying easier and promotes healthier growth. Use insulated wire or rubber tree ties to train and support heavier vines, and stretch plastic or twist-ties for lightweight vines, but check and loosen all ties a couple times a year to prevent any girdling of the stems.

Vines serve as natural screens for sun and wind, create inviting entryways, highlight special architectural features, promote privacy, and camouflage unsightly walls or fences. Grape vines not only provide cool shade during hot summers, but bear generous clusters of sweet, juicy fruit. Once established, vines forgive neglect, rebound after overzealous pruning, and often survive short bouts of drought and frost. With proper cultivation and care, they become lush havens that beckon us during glorious springs, sweltering summers, tranquil autumns, or blustery winters.

A New Zealand Memory

On our spring visit to New Zealand, few sights were more impressive than the sprawling white clematis vines weaving their 40-ft. tresses in and out among the canopies of aged trees. As we strolled by these trees, masses of star-shaped, creamy white flowers released their vanilla fragrance in the warmth of the late-morning sun. Memories like this remind us that vines not only weave their way into landscapes, they cling to heartstrings.

Boston Ivy

Parthenocissus tricuspidata

Bloom Period and Seasonal Color
Crimson, scarlet, and aubergine fall foliage.

Mature Length 30–60 ft.

Botanical Pronunciation
PAR-then-oh-sis-sus TRI-kus-pih-dah-tah

Zones 4–11

One memorable autumn morning we strolled around the stately grounds of Harvard University. Boston ivy, with serrated, 8-in., three-lobed leaves that morph from shades of shiny green, had exploded into fiery fall hues of crimson, scarlet, and aubergine. Now we always associate fall color with our memory of Boston ivy and how it enlivened the staid brownstones with its blazing autumnal curtains. In addition to its fall beauty, we appreciate the late-summer clusters of plum-colored, grapelike fruits attached to vermilion stems. Shoots of branched tendrils attached to adhesive pads or suckers create a vigorous climber. Boston ivy (syn. *Ampelopsis tricuspidata*) withstands frost and, once established, short periods of drought, but needs protection from severe wind. Heat is not a problem as long as there is adequate moisture.

When, Where, and How to Plant
Plant in spring from rooted cuttings in flats, or from 1-gallon containers. For optimum color display, grow Boston ivy in partial shade or on freestanding structures that are exposed to dappled sunlight. They prefer well-drained soil with good moisture retention and a slightly acidic pH of 6.5–7.0. If planting against a large structure such as a freestanding or retaining wall, space 8–10 ft. on center. Build a watering basin 4 ft. long and 1 ft. out from the wall's base, and mulch the surface with 2 in. of organic material such as humus mulch or compost.

Growing Tips
Immediately after planting, soak thoroughly and deeply. Once established, water every seven to ten days, but decrease or withhold during winter dormancy. Fertilize in early spring with a complete organic granular food or cottonseed meal.

Advice and Care
Prune at regular intervals to control rampant or errant growth or to lace out dense vines. Because of the invasive habit of its root system, make sure the freestanding structures on which you plant Boston ivy are solidly built. Do not use Boston ivy to cover exterior walls of wood, stucco, or brick buildings. Prune regularly to prevent the tenacious vines from growing into rooftops, under eaves, or around window frames. Some people are sensitive to the fruit pulp—wear gloves as a precaution when handling or cutting the fruits. Aside from the usual spring pests of aphids, snails, and slugs, few pests or diseases affect this vine.

Companion Planting and Design
Boston ivy vines are excellent for covering large, unsightly structures, for growing over pergolas and fences, and for weaving in and out of small but sturdy trees, shrubs, and hedges. Ginkgo, sweet gum, and crapemyrtle trees are ideal companion plants for Boston ivy.

Try These
P. tricuspidata 'Lowii' and 'Veitchii' have smaller leaves and are more docile in their growth. *P. quinquefolia* is also known as Virginia creeper or woodbine. It has compound leaves with five leaflets.

Bougainvillea

Bougainvillea hybrids

Bloom Period and Seasonal Color
Red, pink, white, or orange bracts appear in summer.

Mature Length 15–30 ft.

Botanical Pronunciation
BOO-gahn-vil-ee-ah

Zones 10–11

ougainvillea's intense coloration is due not to its flowers but to the three bracts that surround one to three clusters of tiny, tubular white flowers. The bracts of this sprawling plant range from white to hot pink to golden orange to brilliant red to vivid lilac. Soft, forest green, heart-shaped, ovate leaves provide a lush background. Although bougainvillea does not have tendrils to support itself, curved thorns located at the base of its leaves enable it to climb. After about five years it tolerates drought and heat, but dislikes windy, cold locations where temperatures dip below 45 degrees Fahrenheit. Reduce watering to stress the plant in summer and fall months; this simple procedure will maximize bloom production and intensify bract color.

When, Where, and How to Plant
Plant in spring from a 1- or 5-gallon container in an area free from frost, in full sun, and protected from wind. Although not particular about soil, it thrives with good drainage and a pH of 6.7–7.2. It has sensitive roots (meaning it also does not transplant well), so carefully cut the container away to keep the sensitive roots intact. Construct a 1 × 4 ft. watering basin. See Planting Techniques, p. 20.

Growing Tips
Immediately after planting, fill the watering basin two or three times to collapse the air pockets in the root zone. Deeply soak twice during the first week, and once established water every ten to fourteen days in spring. Reduce watering during summer to winter, adjusting frequency and amount according to the weather and growth conditions. Fertilize in early spring with a complete organic granular food.

Advice and Care
Prune *after* flowering because the next season's bloom is on new growth. To reduce the size of a mature plant, prune out all the dead wood and reduce its canopy by one-third. Few diseases or pests affect this plant, except the bougainvillea looper, a 1 in. long yellowish, green, or brown caterpillar. Spray with spinosad every seven to ten days until this problem is eradicated.

Companion Planting and Design
Bougainvillea is shown off to best advantage on trellises, against a wall or fence, on pergolas or arbors, and as brambles on slopes. As a shrub, it can also be used effectively in large containers or raised planters. This plant grows well with many other specimens, including pride of Madeira or bird of paradise.

Try These
B. spectabilis 'San Diego Red' is a vigorous grower, reaching lengths of 30 ft. It is the variety with the most brilliant red coloration. 'Mary Palmer's Enchantment' has showy masses of crisp, clear white bracts while 'California Gold' has deep golden yellow bracts. Hot pink bracts adorn 'Camarillo Fiesta', and 'Purple Queen' is smaller—it can grow to 15 ft. with supports or can be used as a groundcover. Plant the Bambino™ series, growing only 4 ft. tall, for smaller spaces or containers.

Carolina Jessamine

Gelsemium sempervirens

Bloom Period and Seasonal Color
Yellow flowers bloom spring to fall.

Mature Length 20 ft.

Botanical Pronunciation
gel-SEM-ee-um sem-pur-VY-renz

Zones 7–11

On a walking tour through Charleston, we noticed many decorative wrought-iron fences festooned with twining branches laden with funnel-form, sweetly fragrant, yellow flowers against a backdrop of glossy rich green foliage. Carolina jessamine is an evergreen that blooms heavily from spring to early autumn. Despite their beauty, they had a more sinister reputation in the past. All parts of the vines are toxic and were used by the villainous to commit nefarious deeds of murder. Fortunately today we appreciate their ornamental value. Once established, vines survive temperatures below freezing as long as they have long, hot summers to develop hardy canes. They prefer a wind-protected location, but tolerate wind and withstand drought. With time, their watering needs are not as demanding as other, more tropical vines.

When, Where, and How to Plant
Plant in early spring from a 1- or 5-gallon container in full sun to maximize flower production (it will tolerate partial shade, but will flower less). It prefers well-drained soil and needs a pH of 6.7–7.0. Space plants 12–30 ft. on center. Construct a watering basin 1 ft. × 6 ft. and cover with 2 in. of organic material such as humus mulch or compost. Consult Planting Techniques, p. 20, for more information.

Growing Tips
Immediately after planting, soak deeply and thoroughly. Water twice the first week, but once established water moderately in spring and summer, about every seven to ten days, and sparingly in fall and winter, adjusting frequency and amount according to weather and growth conditions. Fertilize in late winter with a complete organic granular food.

Advice and Care
When older wood develops, in about two or three growing seasons, the vines are mature enough to prune hard after their bloom cycle to keep them in bounds. Since all parts of these vines are poisonous, wash your pruning shears carefully after use, and wear protective gloves as a precaution. There are few diseases or pests that affect Carolina jessamine, except mealybugs, scale insects, and whitefly during the warmer months. Control them with a canola-based horticultural oil or use a systemic containing imidacloprid.

Companion Planting and Design
Carolina jessamine vines, also called evening trumpet flower, are lovely and fragrant on trellises, pergolas, fences, and walls, and as brambling groundcover. Ideal companions are crapemyrtle, European olive, and golden mirror plant. Since all parts of the vine are toxic, keep it away from small children and pets.

Try These
'Pride of Augusta' is double flowering and adapts to partial shade. It climbs 15–20 ft. and blooms from mid-spring to midsummer. 'Margarita' is semideciduous, making it hardy in zone 6. It has larger, more prominent clear yellow blooms. *G. rankinii*, swamp jessamine, is smaller in stature than *G. sempervirens* and grows more compactly. It is unscented and doesn't mind boggy conditions.

Clematis

Clematis hybrids

Bloom Period and Seasonal Color
Late spring in a rainbow of colors and bicolors.

Mature Length 3–25 ft. depending on variety

Botanical Pronunciation
kleh-MA-tis

Zones 8–11

The uses of clematis are limited only by your imagination. When new clematis foliage emerges, it is a rich bronze color; it then transforms into a deep green with a leathery texture. Masses of star-shaped flowers open in the spring and some release a lovely scent. These are thirsty plants that need their toes in cool, moist soil and their heads in the sun. Although some are evergreen, other species will go dormant in the fall to winter, giving the plant a forlornly bare appearance. Prune the canes back 4–6 ft. in fall or late winter so new growth emerges from the base. You may lose a bloom cycle, but the plant will appear more vigorous.

When, Where, and How to Plant
Plant in spring from 1- or 5-gallon containers. Clematis prefers to have its root system in a cool, moist location, but as it matures, its canopy should be in full sun for maximum bloom and fragrance. Clematis prefers a porous, well-drained soil with a normal to slightly alkaline pH. Build watering basins 4–6 ft. in diameter and mulch the surface with 2 in. of organic material such as humus mulch or compost. If you plant against a south-facing wall, space the plant 18 in. away from the wall base to avoid damage from heat buildup and dry conditions. Consult Planting Techniques, p. 20, for more information.

Growing Tips
Protect from the damaging effects of drought, wind, and heat by providing adequate moisture. Water clematis once a week in spring to summer, less in fall to winter, adjusting frequency and amount for climatic and growth conditions. Fertilize in spring with a complete organic granular food.

Advice and Care
Do not prune in late winter or you will remove the buds that emerge in spring. Prune immediately after the bloom cycle. Few diseases or insect problems bother clematis, but it can be susceptible to clematis wilt. Purchase varieties most resistant to clematis wilt.

Companion Planting and Design
Use clematis to embrace fences; cover trellises; cascade over pergolas, walls, and arbors; bramble over the ground; or train on supports in pots. Clematis is deer resistant. Raymond Evison's Patio Collections are bred to be in containers, while others such as 'Avalanche' can weave through trees, roses, and tall shrubs. Bearded iris and climbing roses are great companions and for structural support, use Victorian box and Grecian laurel.

Try These
Masses of large-flowered (some fragrant) hybrids are available in every imaginable color or shape; some such as 'Evijohill' ('Josephine') are double-flowered 4–5 in., bearing three-dimensional lavender petals with deep rose-pink stripes. This 8–9-ft. variety needs minimal pruning. *C. armandii* 'Apple Blossom' has apple blossom–like, blush pink blossoms with a vanilla scent, and is a robust 15-ft. evergreen. *C. armandii* 'Snowdrift' has a delicious almond and honey-scented white bloom, growing to 25 ft.

Creeping Fig

Ficus pumila

Bloom Period and Seasonal Color
Evergreen.

Mature Length 20–30 ft.

Botanical Pronunciation
FIY-kus pew-MIL-lah

Zones 9–11

With large concrete-block retaining walls in a landscape, it can be a challenge to soften the massive, uninviting structure and to create a more temperate environment by deflecting some of the intense heat generated by the concrete surface. Creeping fig (syn. *Ficus repens*) solves these dual problems very well. The leaves of juvenile plants are small, leathery, dark green, and shaped like small hearts; once established, larger, deep green, oblong-shaped leaves emerge from the mat of the juvenile foliage. Its stems nimbly climb a support by means of aerial roots that appear at leaf junctures. Despite its tropical heritage, creeping fig is surprisingly hardy. Like other ficus species, this vigorous vine dislikes wind, drought, and extended periods of cold temperatures, but enjoys heat with enough humidity and moisture.

When, Where, and How to Plant

Plant in spring, after the last frost, from 1-gallon containers. Creeping figs grow equally well in full sun or shade, but make sure the soil drains well and the pH is slightly acidic, 6.6–7.0. We do not recommend planting creeping fig close to wood, brick, or stucco surfaces because its invasive root system may cause damage. It may burn if planted in full sun on south- or west-facing walls. If using as wall covers, space 8–10 ft. apart. Build a 1 × 4 ft. watering basin and mulch the surface with 2 in. of organic material such as humus mulch or compost. For additional information, see Planting Techniques, p. 20.

Growing Tips

Soak deeply after planting. Water weekly until established; thereafter water every fourteen days, adjusting frequency and amounts according to weather and growth conditions. Fertilize in spring with cottonseed meal.

Advice and Care

If you see errant growth falling away from its support, prune it off, discard, or plant elsewhere. Cut creeping fig back to the ground every few years and deadhead fruits to keep its size manageable. Spray support walls with water if you want to encourage the finer and flatter immature growth. Pinch back terminal (tip) growth to increase lateral (side) branch development. Aside from slugs or snails, quickly controlled by an iron phosphate molluscicide, few disease or insect problems affect creeping fig.

Companion Planting and Design

Creeping fig thrives on warm, protected walls; as groundcover over a rock garden; as a houseplant; shaped as topiaries; or as a trailing container plant. Pink Indian hawthorn, bronze loquat, and silverberry are ideal planting companions.

Try These

F. pumila 'Quercifolia', also known as oak leaf creeping fig, has foliage shaped like lobed oak leaves. 'Variegata' has marbled white to cream leaves and 'Sonny' has green foliage with white edges. *F. pumila* 'Minima' grows to 40 ft. in full sun and part shade in zones 7–11, with smaller leaves that retain their size longer, even into maturity.

Grape

Vitus vinifera hybrids

Bloom Period and Seasonal Color
Pale green blooms in spring, fruit late summer through fall.

Mature Length 8 ft. × spreading

Botanical Pronunciation
VY-tus vin-IH-fur-ah

Zones 6–11, depending on cultivar

Edible grape vines are so ornamental that it seems a waste of time and space to plant the strictly ornamental species. While visiting family in Italy during the heat of summer, grape vines festooned with clusters of dangling fruit provided a welcome shaded respite from the relentless sunshine. And eating their sweet fruit out of hand was a refreshing thirst-quencher. Besides table grapes, there are ornamental cultivars of wine grapes including *V. vinifera* 'Incana' with attractive white veins marking the foliage, as well as 'Purpurea', morphing from green to deep purple foliage in autumn. To help them climb, grape vines use tendrils to hold fast to structures or to themselves. Even dormant, the woody vine's prominent trunk and branches provide winter beauty.

When, Where, and How to Plant
Bare-root, year-old vines are available in winter. Plant in well-draining, sandy loam soil and provide full sun on a slope or sturdy support for good air circulation. Space 6–8 ft. apart. Cut newly planted vines' topgrowth to two or three buds. One grape vine can cover an arch or arbor, so select carefully.

Growing Tips
Drip irrigation is the most efficient method of providing regular moisture without splashing water on the grape foliage (necessary to control powdery mildew). While it's important to provide regular watering during the growth cycle, once they have set fruit, decrease to prevent fruit from cracking and withhold water during winter dormancy unless there is an extended drought, then supplement occasionally. Feed in early spring with a complete organic granular food.

Advice and Care
For the first summer, do not prune; wait until winter, then choose the thickest shoot for the trunk, tie to a sturdy support (vertical or horizontal), and prune all shoots, leaving three to four of the lowest buds. To continue the trunk, select the most vigorous, upright, 6–8 inch shoot in spring and tie to support; cut off all other shoots. To train on a fence or wired trellis, also choose two lower shoots for arms and tie to horizontal support. Pierce's bacterial disease, spread by the glassy-winged sharpshooter insect, causes (particularly in European wine grape vines) leaves to brown and wilt, and eventually kills the vine. Contact the Cooperative Extension Office for control suggestions and/or remove the infected vine. Control powdery mildew or mealybug with a canola-based horticultural oil.

Companion Planting and Design
Plant on a trellis, arbor, pillars, fence, or any structure that is sturdy enough to support its woody trunk and bountiful harvest.

Try These
Red, seedless, self-fruitful European grape 'Flame' needs hot summers, and fruits early to midseason. Let soil go drier as it sets fruit to encourage ripening and to reduce new foliage and vigorous growth. 'Perlette' tolerates milder summers, and produces pale yellow grapes early in the season. For coastal and inland valleys, select self-fruitful wine cultivars 'Cabernet Sauvignon' (warm summers) but where summers are cool, try 'Chardonnay'.

Madagascar Jasmine

Stephanotis floribunda

Bloom Period and Seasonal Color
White flowers bloom in summer.

Mature Length 10–20 ft.

Botanical Pronunciation
STEF-ah-no-tis FLOR-ih-bun-dah

Zones 10–11

Bruce's parents lived on the brow of a hill overlooking Mission Bay, and had an atrium garden filled with many vining plants, including one of our favorites—the evergreen Madagascar jasmine. Its heavy, woody stems twine ropelike around a trellis against a wall that is shaded from the midday heat by the eaves. The dark silky sheen of the elliptic leaves enhance the elegance of the blooms. Madagascar jasmine has triple clusters of fragrant, ivory, tubular-shaped blossoms on trailing stems of deep green leaves. Once established, they form seedpods that resemble bladders, but their development takes two to three years. Madagascar jasmine appreciates cool soils and warm but shaded areas. This vine does not care for blustery winds, extended drought, or freezing temperatures.

When, Where, and How to Plant
Plant in the spring, after the last frost, from 1- or 5-gallon containers. Locate your vine in a partly shady or shady frost-free location. It needs good drainage with rich, organic, loam soil and an acidic pH of 6.5–7.0. Be very careful not to disturb the rootball, because it suffers from transplant shock easily. Where winter frosts are common, plant in a container and move indoors into bright indirect light and take outdoors during the warmer months. If grown on a trellis or fence, space the plants 10 ft. apart. Construct a watering basin 3–4 ft. in diameter. For more information, see Planting Techniques, p. 20.

Growing Tips
Water frequently, every three to seven days, during the first growing season to establish a deep root system. Once established it needs only occasional supplemental water depending on climatic and growth conditions. For example, water generously when in growth, but reduce watering in the winter months. Fertilize in spring with cottonseed meal.

Advice and Care
Prune in late winter or early spring before the growth cycle to thin out dense vines. Tie the vines for support since it is not their nature to twist around anything that is more than 2 in. in diameter. If you want to share your plant with a neighbor, propagate by layering, cuttings, or air layering. Few diseases or pests affect this vine, except soft scale and mealybugs. Benign remedies include washing off the leaves with water or applying canola-based horticultural oil.

Companion Planting and Design
In addition to being used as cut flowers and in wedding bouquets, they are equally spectacular when planted on obelisks, trellises, or pergolas in a patio or entryway, although they must be tied for support since their stems become quite heavy. Hibiscus, plumeria, and mystery gardenias make ideal tropical companions.

Try These
S. floribunda 'Variegata' has beautiful, glossy green-and-yellow leaves with white fragrant blooms from spring to summer. Grow outdoors in zones 10 and 11 or grow in a pot indoors, maintaining growth of 2–3 ft.

Mandevilla

Mandevilla hybrids

Bloom Period and Seasonal Color
Pink, red, white, and bicolor flowers bloom late spring to summer.

Mature Length 15–20 ft.

Botanical Pronunciation
man-de-VIL-le-a

Zones 10–11

Named after Henry John Mandeville (1773–1861), the British prime minister in Buenos Aires, this plant's hybridizers have since made improvements in vigor, color, and growth habit. Flowers on this twining vine come in pastel pink, deep rose, white, red, and bicolors emerging from glossy, emerald green, oval foliage. Its showy flowers, resembling giant periwinkles, have five lobes that form from tubular throats. True to their tropical heritage, mandevillas prefer warm weather, but most hybrids will tolerate evenings that dip into the 50s. Where nights typically fall into the 40s, it is best to plant them in containers so they can be moved indoors during the winter. Although cultivars are typically not fragrant, their bold looks and fresh green foliage more than compensates for their lack of perfume.

When, Where, and How to Plant
Plant in spring after the last frost, or in fall, from 4–8-in. pots or 1- or 5-gallon containers, in full sun or partial shade. Provide humus or compost-amended, slightly acidic soil. In frost-free locations, plant directly in the ground, but where freezes are common, plant in containers filled with a well-draining commercial potting soil such as cactus mix. Move containers indoors during winter and take outdoors after danger of frost is past. Provide a trellis, stake, or other form of support.

Growing Tips
Water every five to seven days during the first growing season to establish a deep root system. Once plants are established, decrease watering to seven to ten days during warm weather. Water container plants more frequently. Fertilize in spring with cottonseed meal.

Advice and Care
Prune in late winter or early spring before the growth cycle, to thin dense vines. Tie the vines to supports because tendrils need help when beginning to climb; pinch back new growth to encourage a bushier habit. While indoors, tendrils can be snipped off without damaging the plant. Mandevillas are susceptible to aphids and spider mites. Wash plants with a strong stream of water and if problems persist, spray with a canola-based horticultural oil for aphid control and use a systemic miticide for a severe infestation of spider mites.

Companion Planting and Design
Mandevillas are spectacular when planted in the center of an obelisk, trellis, or pergola in a patio, entryway, or by a fountain or pool. Since most are not fragrant, plant with plumeria, gardenias, Carolina jessamine, or Madagascar jasmine to add the perfume of the tropics.

Try These
Dozens of evergreen hybrids have been bred, including 'Alice du Pont', which bears pastel pink flowers with a cherry red throat and grows 10–12 ft. The Sun Parasol series plants come in an amazing range of colors, forms, and floral sizes, like 'Pink Parfait', with double pink flowers; 'Giant Crimson', with red blossoms; 'Pretty White', which bears smaller flowers; and more demure-sized plants appropriate for smaller gardens.

Passion Vine

Passiflora hybrids

Bloom Period and Seasonal Color
White or blue flowers bloom all summer; closed on overcast days and at night.

Mature Length 6–10 ft.

Botanical Pronunciation
PASS-ih-flor-ah

Zones 10–11

Our first memory of the beautiful and mysterious passion vine occurred many years ago while we were window-shopping in Little Tokyo in the middle of downtown Los Angeles. In such a polluted urban environment of total neglect, you'd think this vine would be struggling to survive, but it was flourishing, with lush, 3-in.-long, light green foliage and elegant, 4-in. wide white flowers lightly tinted with pink blush. In temperate climates passion vine is evergreen, but in cooler zones it will lose its leaves, only to grow them again as the weather warms and the days lengthen. It does not like cold or wind, but when it's mature, it blooms profusely during short periods of drought or moisture stress and loves heat, provided there is enough humidity.

When, Where, and How to Plant
Plant in spring from 1- or 5-gallon containers. It needs a full-sun location in well-drained, slightly acidic soil, pH 6.6–7.0. Space 10–15 ft. apart if using on a fence or wall. Build a 1 ft. × 4 ft. watering basin and cover with 2 in. of organic material such as humus mulch or compost. See Planting Techniques, p. 20.

Growing Tips
Soak deeply after planting. Water three times the first week; thereafter, adjust frequency and amount to weather and growing conditions. Fertilize in spring with a complete organic granular food.

Advice and Care
After the second year, prune annually in late winter or early spring to lace out and clear away dead inner woody vines. Root-pruning is a simple procedure to increase flower production. Sever the root system by pushing a pointed shovel 8–10 in. into the ground and 2–3 ft. from the base of the plant. Another way to increase blooms is to confine the roots by building an underground brick barrier 1–2 ft. deep and 2 ft. in diameter. This is probably why that neglected passion vine triumphed over such adverse conditions in downtown Los Angeles. It actually *liked* being in a confined space with poor soil conditions. Few diseases or pests affect it, but watch for snails and aphids in spring and summer. If caterpillars are hungry enough, they will dine on the vine's tender leaves. Control these chewing pests with *Bacillus thuringiensis* (B.t.), a natural pesticide.

Companion Planting and Design
Passion vine's climbing tendrils are easily supported by wires, plastic netting, or posts, and its beauty is best displayed on trellises, walls, or sunny foyers. Southern magnolia, hibiscus, and bird of paradise are ideal companions for a tropical garden.

Try These
P. × *belotii* has white flowers shaded with pink and purple and is least subject to caterpillar damage. 'Lavender Lady' is a heavy bloomer with unscented 4½ lavender flowers. *P. caerulea*, blue crown passion flower, goes dormant in colder regions; it has greenish-white, slightly fragrant flowers.

Scarlet Trumpet Vine

Distictis buccinatoria

Bloom Period and Seasonal Color
Red to orange-red flowers in summer.

Mature Length 20–40 ft.

Botanical Pronunciation
dih-STIK-tis BOOK-sin-ah-to-ree-ah

Zones 9–11

A s a youngster, Bruce's family greenhouse was our own secret fortress, with thick-stalked vines covering the structure. Throughout the warm months of spring and summer, the most spectacular feature of these dense vines was the explosion of 4-in. long, blood red to orange-red, trumpet-shaped flowers with bright yellow throats. These evergreen vines have lance-shaped, dull green, 3-in.-long compound leaves. Grasping suction cup–like appendages located at the ends of wispy, three-forked tendrils enable these vines to be self-clinging as long as the support structure has a rough surface. *D. buccinatoria* (also known as *Bignonia cherere*), the scarlet trumpet vine, loves heat if there is sufficient humidity and moisture but defoliates and recovers during short periods of drought, strong winds, or cold temperatures.

When, Where, and How to Plant
Spring is the best time to plant, from 1- or 5-gallon containers. If you want your vine to be covered with flowers, plant in full sun in porous loam soil that has a pH of 6.6–7.0, spacing 20 ft. apart. Build a watering basin that is 6 ft. in diameter and mulch the surface with 2 in. of organic material such as humus mulch or compost. Consult Planting Techniques, p. 20, for more information.

Growing Tips
Immediately after planting, soak deeply and thoroughly, then water twice during the first week. After that, adjust watering frequency and amount according to the climate and growth conditions. Fertilize in spring with a complete organic food.

Advice and Care
As the vines mature they become woodier, and it may be necessary to lace out their canopies so sunlight can stimulate new growth. Otherwise, prune just to remove dead wood. Prune in the late winter or early spring, before the flush of new growth, because they flower from current-season growth. Chewing insects such as caterpillars can be a problem, especially during the warmer months, but they are easily controlled with applications of B.t. (*Bacillus thuringiensis*), a natural larvaecide. Generally speaking, there are few diseases or insects that affect these vines.

Companion Planting and Design
For brilliant summerlong color on gazebos, arbors, walls, fences, pergolas, and in large planters with trellises, scarlet trumpet vines are the oohs and aaahs of garden ornamentals. Although their floral fragrance is mild, their nectar attracts all the local bees and hummingbirds. Using these beautiful vines on freestanding supports such as trellises and arbors is recommended, but avoid planting them to cover house walls because their tenacious clinging tendrils and attaching disklike organs can pose problems in the future. Butterfly bush, pride of Madeira, and jacaranda make ideal planting companions.

Try These
Royal trumpet vine, 'Rivers', has mauve to purple blooms with yellow to orange throats. *D. laxiflora*, vanilla trumpet vine, is less rambunctious, with vanilla-scented, violet fading to lavender blooms.

Star Jasmine

Trachelospermum jasminoides

Other Name Confederate jasmine

Bloom Period and Seasonal Color
White flowers in summer.

Mature Length 10–15 ft.

Botanical Pronunciation
TRAKE-ee-oh-spur-mum JAZ-min-oye-deez

Zones 9–11

At our home we had an unsightly west-facing wall with a narrow planter in front of it. For years the wall remained barren until we constructed a 5-ft.-high by 15-ft.-long redwood trellis and planted four 1-gallon containers of star jasmine. Normally it is not necessary to plant so many, but we wanted the trellis to be completely covered in a short period. Now, from spring to early summer, we are rewarded with intensely fragrant, star-shaped, pure white flowers that drape over vines blanketed with shiny, dark green, oval foliage. In addition, the local honeybees, Anna hummingbirds, and monarch butterflies appreciate our star jasmine's spring bounty. Star jasmine plants do not tolerate cold, drought, or hot, dry winds, but thrive in heat if there is sufficient humidity and water.

When, Where, and How to Plant
Plant in spring after the last frost from 1- or 5-gallon containers. Star jasmine does best in full sun but can tolerate partial shade. For optimum growing conditions, the soil should be slightly acidic (pH 6.6), but they survive in most soils, even slightly alkaline, provided the soil is rich, deep, well drained, and warmed by the sun. Space 4 ft. on center. Build a watering basin 3 ft. in diameter and cover with 2 in. of organic material such as humus mulch or compost. See Planting Techniques, p. 20.

Growing Tips
Immediately after planting, soak thoroughly and deeply. Water twice the first week; thereafter, adjust frequency and amount according to weather and growth conditions. Fertilize in late winter or early spring with a complete food, 10–10–10.

Advice and Care
Prune to remove dead or errant growth and to direct growth. Like many other plants that are related to the Apocynaceae family, it exudes a milky sap when the stems are cut that can irritate your skin. Wear a long-sleeved shirt and gloves, and wash off your pruning shears. Few diseases affect star jasmine, but brown soft scale and giant whitefly occasionally colonize their tender leaves in spring and summer. Neem oil is an excellent control for these pests. Sometimes alligator lizards seek shelter among the vines and they provide a natural pest solution by dining on whitefly.

Companion Planting and Design
Use star jasmine as an evergreen groundcover, slope plant, and shrub; on trellises, gazebos, pergolas, and arbors; and in hanging baskets and raised planters. Pink Indian hawthorn, golden mirror plant, and lavender starflower are ideal as companions.

Try These
'Variegatum' has white-edged and blotched leaves. 'Madison' grows to 12 ft. as a vine or to 1 ft. tall if used for a fragrant groundcover. It is more cold hardy growing in zones 7–10. *T. asiaticum*, yellow star jasmine, has the same growth characteristics as those of star jasmine with smaller creamy yellow flowers that bloom in summer.

Wisteria

Wisteria sinensis

Other Name Chinese wisteria

Bloom Period and Seasonal Color
White or lavender flowers in spring.

Mature Length 60–100 ft.

Botanical Pronunciation
WIS-the-ree-ah SIN-en-sis

Zones 5–11

Gnarled trunks laden with pendulous bluish purple to lavender-mauve clusters of aromatic wisteria languidly top garden walls and outline entryways. Their early spring-blooming bunches of sweet pea–shaped flowers release a perfume like a mixture of lilacs and honey. Once flowers are spent, a curtain of feathery, compound, light green, elliptic foliage blankets the twisted, bare canes. We must warn you that the seeds and pods of this plant are toxic. They contain a glycoside known as wisterin, which causes gastroenteritis. Wisterias dislike hot, dry winds but survive short periods of drought. They thrive in heat, provided there is sufficient humidity and soil moisture, and tolerate temperatures as low as 0 degrees Fahrenheit. *W. sinensis* twists clockwise as it grows upward, unlike *W. floribunda*, whose vines twine counterclockwise.

When, Where, and How to Plant
Plant in late winter or early spring from bare root-stock or 5- to 15-gallon containers. Plant in full sun, though they will also survive in partial shade. They prefer well-drained, slightly acidic soils with a pH of 6.6–7.0; space them 15–20 ft. apart. Construct a watering basin 6 ft. in diameter and cover with 2 in. of organic material such as humus mulch or compost. See Planting Techniques, p. 20, for more information.

Growing Tips
Immediately after planting, soak twice, deeply and thoroughly. Water twice during the first week; thereafter, adjust watering frequency and amount according to weather and growth conditions.

Fertilize in late winter or early spring with a complete food, 6–10–4.

Advice and Care
In fall, after the vines are dormant, prune back the flexible new, young growth, leaving two to four buds for next spring's blooms. Few fungi or virus problems attack wisteria, and any damage is usually cosmetic. During spring, aphids and brown soft scale may settle on tender foliage and young canes, but you can easily control them with Neem oil or insecticidal soap. Birds enjoy eating the flower buds, and they may be the cause of poor bloom production, so be on the lookout for ravenous birds.

Companion Planting and Design
As one of the most spectacular flowering vines, wisteria can be used to cover pergolas, gazebos, shaded walkways, and patios; it can even be pruned and miniaturized as a prized bonsai container plant. Butterfly bush, saucer magnolia, and European olive make ideal planting companions.

Try These
'Alba' has white blooms. 'Prolific' blooms at an early age. 'Caroline' and 'Cooke's Purple' are grafted and have lilac-purple blooms. *W. floribunda*, commonly known as Japanese wisteria, has pendulous flower clusters that are 2–3 ft. in length. It blooms in mid-spring and comes in many shades of blue, purple, lavender, white, and pink. Japanese wisteria blooms while the vine is leafing out with soft new foliage in early spring; it gives less instant floral impact, but blooms over a longer period.

WATERWISE PLANTS
FOR CALIFORNIA

L imited water supply, recurring drought, dry summers, and firestorms are some of the challenges of living in our golden state. Fortunately, there are many native and nonnative plants that are not only waterwise and fire resistant, but also add unique beauty and provide welcoming bird, bee, and butterfly habitats to our California gardens.

Average annual rainfalls in California vary greatly from region to region: Redding traditionally receives 33 in., San Francisco normally has 20 in., San Diego receives a mere 10.77 in., and Los Angeles County gets anywhere from 13–20 in. With global warming, experts are predicting extended periods of drought for California.

With drought comes the danger of wildfires and the critical issue of home safety. Local fire departments suggest creating a 100-ft. line of defensible space. Their recommendations are listed on p. 27.

Additionally, much of the state relies on the Sierra Nevada snowpack, particularly during summer. If Northern California's mountains experience light snowfall and a warm, dry, and early spring, water supplies are compromised even more by lack of snow, early thaw, and runoff.

Unlike other natural disasters such as floods, earthquakes, and fires, which require an immediate

Waterwise plants can add color and texture to the landscape.

response with little time to prepare, droughts occur slowly over a number of years. Rather than forget about the bad times during years of plentiful rainfall, incorporate plants that adapt to arid environments into your landscape design as a first line of defense against future episodes of dry weather and firestorms.

Beautiful and Colorful Waterwise Plants

Despite the efforts of water departments and other water conservationists, myths abound when it comes to waterwise plants. They are not just prickly cacti sticking out of concrete or gravel beds, nor are they limited to the blah color spectrum from lackluster brown to gloomy gray. Instead of barren landscapes and windswept sand dunes, water-thrifty plants create colorful and beautiful gardens with lower water demands.

Besides stunningly colorful or fragrant California natives, many exotic species with similarly low water and fertilizer needs endemic to Australia, New Zealand, South Africa, and the Mediterranean are adaptable to our soil and climate. When you combine natives with compatible out-of-towners, you lengthen the flowering season and brighten up the landscape.

There are additional reasons to consider water-thrifty plants. Many, such as sage, have resins that saturate the surrounding air with their fragrance on sultry afternoons, encouraging you to inhale nature's aromatherapy and exhale all of life's tensions. Others are nectar and seed factories that advertise their bounty to birds and butterflies. Butterfly bush and pride of Madeira will lure so many winged flutterers your garden may look like a wildlife refuge.

Problems Solved

Drought-tolerant species are also problem-solvers. Kinnikinnick or dwarf coyote bush stabilize slopes. If there are swaths of dry, light shade, calandrinia and California lilac will happily bloom for you in hot inland areas. Near windswept coastal areas and salt spray, butterfly bush and silverberry are ideal choices. For high elevations at 6,000–7,000 ft., flannel bush has survived for 60 million years while meeting additional challenges such as dry, granitic slopes and rocky ridges. There are others such as red hot poker, agave, or aloe that are attractive, water-efficient succulents able to thrive in the desert and other areas that average fewer than 10 in. of annual rainfall.

Be Waterwise

Indigenous plants offer a striking range of color for the drought-tolerant landscape and diverse plant groups have adapted well to California's seasonal rhythms of wet winters and dry summers. They all can be very useful in designing an easily maintained, drought-tolerant, fire-resistant landscape.

When planning a new landscape or renovating part of an existing one, consider plants that do not require much water or maintenance, and yet are just as colorful and interesting as more water-thirsty plants. Hopefully, this chapter will inspire you to incorporate more waterwise plants that are also known for their "oohs-and-aahs" beauty.

Aeonium

Aeonium hybrids

Bloom Period and Seasonal Color
Yellow, pink, red, and white blooms from spring to summer, depending on the hybrid.

Mature Height × Spread 6–18 in. × 4 ft.

Botanical Pronunciation
EYE-own-ee-um

Zones 9–11

If you're looking for an evergreen plant that produces rosettes of distinctive leaf colors and textures, aeoniums are must-haves. Originally from the Canary Islands and Morocco, the rosettes emerge on the ends of stems that may be ¼ in. or more, depending on the variety or cultivar. And the color choices, oh my! From burgundy-black to rose, bright green and yellow, and myriad variegations, the spoon-shaped, leafy rosettes bear conical stalks of petite, primarily yellow flowers (although some hybrids offer other floral hues) in the spring or summer. The branch that bears the flower stalk will die once the blooms are spent. Being cool-season growers, they are dormant during the summer months, but will revive and grow when cooler temperatures return.

When, Where, and How to Plant
Plant from containers anytime from spring to summer, or in fall where winters are mild. Provide full sun along the coast, but morning sun inland, and plant in a well-draining cactus mix. They are also easy to plant from cuttings, but hold off on cutting until the cooler months. Allow cuttings to dry for 48–72 hours, then plant in cactus mix, keeping the medium slightly moist until new growth emerges.

Growing Tips
Allow soil to dry slightly before watering, especially in the summer months, about once a month or more to avoid rot. Also water around the plant and not in the crown's center. Supplement water during winter only if there is an extended drought. No fertilization is necessary.

Advice and Care
Keep compact by pruning back leggy branches from fall to spring if desired. Remove dead leaves, and deadhead the spent flowers. Wash off aphids and mealybugs with a stream of water. If the problem persists, use a systemic with imidacloprid formulated for succulents.

Companion Planting and Design
Considered a mainstay in water-thrifty gardens and wide, shallow containers, it goes well with other waterwise plants. Low-growing, mounded aeonium is also decorative in rock gardens or in the front of borders. Spiral aloes (*Aloe polyphylla*), which grow 1 ft. × 2 ft., and artichoke agave (*Agave parryi* v. *truncata*), which grows 3 ft. × 4 ft., complement the symmetrical rosette shape of aeoniums.

Try These
'Kiwi' grows to 15 in. × 2 ft., with rosettes of fleshy bright green leaves and yellow centers that progressively transition from lime green to pink and edged in red streaks, bearing pale yellow flowers. *A. arboreum atropurpureum* 'Zwartkop' bears dark burgundy, 10-in. rosettes decorating the ends of tall stems and growing up to 5 ft. × 2 ft. For a more diminutive, low-clumping burgundy variety with a stunning green eye, select 'Voodoo' at 10 in. × 10 in. Clustering rosettes of unusual chocolate brown and green are the hallmark of 12 in. × 24 in. 'Blushing Beauty' while *A. decorum* grows into a 1 ft. mound with pale green leaves with red edges and small pink flowers.

Agave

Agave hybrids

Bloom Period and Seasonal Color
Blue-green foliage year-round.

Mature Height × Spread 2–5 ft. × 2–5 ft.

Botanical Pronunciation
ah-GAH-vay

Zones 7–11

gaves include quite a few fibrous-leaved speci-mens, often with stiff, swordlike leaves tipped with sharp points and thorns along the margins, and arranged in tight rosettes. With cream to gold flowers aligned on tall floral stalks, agaves produce either pups (offsets at the plant base) or plantlets along the flower stalk. Typically the mother plant dies after flowering, but that may take years. Most agaves available to Californians come from species endemic to Mexico or the southwest, but some are tropical and subtropical, while others survive harsh winters. Most tolerate drought and poor, alkaline soils. Whether upright in habit, such as the tequila agave, or clumping, like the artichoke agave, they all make bold, architectural statements in the landscape, but should be planted away from pathways.

When, Where, and How to Plant
Plant from containers anytime from spring to summer or in fall where winters are mild. Provide full sun along the coast, but morning sun inland, and plant in well-draining cactus mix for optimum growth. Wear thick, protective gloves whenever handling agaves because of its sharp tips and thorns along the margins and the irritating sap, which can cause a severe rash.

Growing Tips
Soak after planting, then water about every four days until established, if planted in the heat of summer. Once established, wait until soil dries out slightly before watering again, about once a month in cool weather and every other week in summer. Withhold water completely or water sparingly during winter dormancy. Check the tag for fertilizing

needs because most do not need additional food, with the exception of tropical species, which might appreciate a timed-release or water-soluble organic food such as liquid kelp at half the recommended dosage once a year.

Advice and Care
To avoid the possibility of disease, avoid pruning healthy, living foliage and remove only dead leaves or spent flowers. Agave snout weevil lays eggs at the base of the plant. Use a grub control with imidacloprid formulated for succulents.

Companion Planting and Design
Agaves add structure to containers, as single specimen focal points, or planted in rock gardens with other water-thrifty plants. Plant the spiral form, such as artichoke or Queen Victoria agaves, in wide, shallow containers because they are so beautiful when viewed from above. They can also be grown with perennials since agaves tolerate some summer irrigation. Large agaves make stunning silhouettes in front of walls and boulders, while smaller varieties are fantastic massed in garden beds.

Try These
'Blue Glow' is 2 ft. tall with blue-tinted spines and leaves edged in red. 'Sharkskin' bears smooth, bluish gray, sharklike skin and 3-ft. upright leaves tipped in black. *A. bracteosa*, the spider agave, does not die after blooming. It grows 12 in. × 24 in. with twisting pale green leaves and has creamy white blooms. Since it has no spines or teeth, it is a great choice for containers.

Aloe

Aloe hybrids

Bloom Period and Seasonal Color
Winter to spring orange, red, yellow, or cream flowers but some species bloom summer or fall.

Mature Height × Spread
8 in.–5 ft. × 8 in.–5 ft., depending on the hybrid

Botanical Pronunciation a-LOE

Zones 9–11

Primarily from South Africa, aloes are bold perennials that look stunning in coastal to low-desert landscapes. They range in size from elfin 6-in. varieties to statuesque trees with succulent green or grayish green leaves arranged in rosettes or spirals, in clumping, sprawling, or semiclimbing habits. Although some are edged with teeth, they are not as sharp or thorny as agaves. The most common floral flourishes occur in the middle of winter to summer, but many bloom during other months. Their flowers come in a variety of colors, and the leaves also come banded or streaked in contrasting colors. They're ideal where there are no extended periods of frost. Where winter freezes are common, plant aloes in containers and move to more protected areas.

When, Where, and How to Plant
Plant from containers any time from spring to summer, or in fall where winters are mild. Provide full sun along the coast, but morning sun inland, and plant in well-draining cactus mix. Even though they will tolerate rocky, native soil, they will be much happier in well-draining soil.

Growing Tips
Soak thoroughly after planting, then water about every seven days for the first few weeks, if there is no rainfall. Once established, allow soil to dry out slightly before watering again, about once every two to three weeks in winter if no rainfall, and once every one to two weeks during the heat of summer. No supplemental fertilizer is necessary.

Advice and Care
Since fresh cuts increase the possibility of disease, avoid pruning healthy foliage and remove only dead leaves and spent floral stalks. To control ants, mealybugs, and mites, use ant baits; wash off mealybugs with a strong stream of water; and for mites, apply a miticide formulated for succulents.

Companion Planting and Design
Hybrids are available with beautiful variegation of green to reddish foliage and add rich colorful texture to containers or rock gardens. Use larger or taller varieties as focal points in perennial or dry shade gardens.

Try These
There are so many species and hybrid varieties available that the following are but a few selections. The 12 in. × 24 in. spiral aloe (*Aloe polyphylla*) exhibits the mathematical Fibonacci spiral, which makes its green-blue form so breathtaking when viewed from above. Climbing aloe (*Aloe ciliaris* 'Firebreak') grows 24 in. × 72 in. and its fast-growing clump makes it an ideal fire-retarding plant. For a miniature 6 in. × 10 in. aloe, consider 'Firebird' because it blooms almost year-round. The medicinal aloe (*Aloe vera*) belongs in every garden because of its use for sunburn and minor skin scrapes. 24 in. × 18 in., it has stiff upright leaves and yellow flowers in spring. Tree aloe (*A. barberae*) is a slow-growing, 20–30 ft. × 10–20 ft. species with rosette leaves and late winter blooms in rose pink.

Bird of Paradise

Strelitzia reginae

Bloom Period and Seasonal Color
Orange flowers bloom in spring and fall.

Mature Height × Spread
3–5 ft. (clumping)

Botanical Pronunciation
streh-LITS-ee-ah RAY-gin-aye

Zones 10–11

There are few flowers more dramatic in form and color than that of the bird of paradise. Its pointed, waxy beak, three erect orange petals, and blue spiked corolla resembling a crown of plumage makes it a superb cut flower with longevity and a spectacular form. This is a clumping herbaceous plant with large, deep green, glossy leaves growing from the base. The leaves are 3–4 ft. long with distinctive ribs. Although bird of paradise does not tolerate cold, it is still an easy plant to maintain since it withstands drought, heat, and wind. It's best to plant from a 5-gallon container; if you choose a 1-gallon container plant, be patient because it will take about two or three years to bloom.

When, Where, and How to Plant
Plant from 5-gallon containers just about any time, but spring and fall months are best, as is a site in full sun for abundant flowering. It prefers porous, well-drained loam soil but will survive in denser, clay soil. Soil pH needs to be a bit on the acidic side, 6.5–7.0. Space 6 ft. on center. Build a watering basin 4 ft. in diameter with a berm 4–6 in. high. Mulch the basin's surface with 2 in. of compost or humus mulch. See Planting Techniques, p. 20.

Growing Tips
For optimum bloom, these plants do best when watered deeply and thoroughly every seven to ten days in summer, but water every two to three weeks in winter. Fertilize twice a year, early spring and early fall, with a complete organic granular food or cottonseed meal.

Advice and Care
Remove spent flowers and stems all the way down to the base, and any tattered or dead leaves. Divide the plant every five to seven years before it takes a jackhammer to divide. Control snails with the pick-and-squish method or use an organic molluscicide, such as iron phosphate.

Companion Planting and Design
It makes a colorful addition and accent to any tropical garden. You can display these plants in large terracotta pots and use them as colorful architectural focal points in your patio or entryway, provided there is full sun. Pink powder puff, mystery gardenia, and hibiscus are tropical plants that go well with the bird of paradise. If you use it in a floral display, do not throw a cut flower away when the initial bloom is spent; simply remove the old flower, reach in, and carefully lift the new flower out of the sheath.

Try These
Strelitizia juncea has grayish green, reedlike foliage with similarly colored flowers and cold hardiness down to 25 degrees Fahrenheit as *S. r.* does, but it grows 4–6 ft. tall and wide. *Strelitizia nicolai*, the giant bird of paradise, reaches a height of 10–20 ft. and a diameter of 6–8 ft. with summer-blooming, greenish blue and white flowers.

Butterfly Bush

Buddleja davidii

Other Name Summer lilac

Bloom Period and Seasonal Color
Dark violet, pink, white, red, and purple flowers bloom in summer.

Mature Height × Spread 5–15 ft. × 5–15 ft.

Botanical Pronunciation
bud-LAY-ah DAY-vid-eye

Zones 6–11

As winds carry brilliant orange- and black-edged monarch and yellow- and orange-dotted swallowtail butterflies toward their destination, they light on our butterfly bush, decorating the flowers with pulsing wings. Bumblebees and honeybees buzz industriously, red-crowned and ruby-throated hummingbirds whir their wings in a blur, and lucky us, we get to watch all this beauty. To enjoy such visitations, plant this shrub with its clusters of delicate, fragrant, spiked flowers. It is a wonderful choice for a summer-blooming plant because of its vibrant color. The 6–10-in. leaves are dark green and felted underneath. The butterfly bush thrives in almost any growing condition, including seaside exposures. This is a hardy, cold-tolerant shrub; it is deciduous, but its upright structure provides a picturesque silhouette in winter.

When, Where, and How to Plant
You can plant butterfly bushes anytime of year, but the best times are fall or early spring in full or part sun. Prepare the planting pit with 20–30 percent organic material mixed with the native soil to encourage rapid root development. Plant this vigorous-growing plant at least 10–15 ft. on center, especially if planting in groups. As the plant continues to grow, increase the size of the watering basin so that its diameter is slightly beyond the drip line, just beyond the edge of the outermost branches. For more planting information, see p. 20.

Growing Tips
Irrigate thoroughly every seven to ten days depending on weather and soil conditions until established.

Once the soil dries out, water regularly from spring until fall or winter rainfall. Once established, butterfly bushes are drought tolerant and require little supplemental water except an occasional deep watering in summer. Fertilize in early spring and early summer with an organic granular food.

Advice and Care
Remove spent flowers to promote and extend the blooming season. Since flowers develop on the current season's growth, prune back the canes 75–90 percent in late winter. Once the flush of new growth occurs in spring, pinch back the tips of the growth to encourage new flowering branches to develop at a lower level for a fuller plant and more abundant blooms. Control aphid infestations with a strong stream of water.

Companion Planting and Design
Combine butterfly bush with other nectar-rich plants like pride of Madeira, crapemyrtle, and California lilac. Place in the back of beds or use as a visual screen. Butterfly bush is also lovely in cottage-style gardens.

Try These
'Black Knight' bears dark purple-violet panicles of flowers and grows 4–6 ft. while 'Harlequin' grows the same height, but shows off raspberry blossoms and variegated foliage. The Petite series is more compact at 5 ft., and 'Monrell' (or Strawberry Lemonade) grows 6–8 ft. × 4–6 ft., with variegated pale yellow and green leaves with bright pink 5–10-in.-long blossoms.

Calandrinia

Calandrinia grandiflora

Other Name Rock purslane`

Bloom Period and Seasonal Color
Magenta flowers from spring to fall.

Mature Height × Spread 1–3 ft. × 2–3 ft.

Botanical Pronunciation
KAL-in-drin-ee-ah GRAND-ih-flore-uh

Zones 8–10

While visiting the Water Conservation Garden at Cuyamaca College in El Cajon, California, we came upon a group of calandrinia planted *en masse* for a breathtaking display of brilliant magenta flowers. They rested atop tall, wiry stems that waved and danced in the gentle breeze. Naysayers who claim succulents have little to recommend them except water-thriftiness must never have seen a calandrinia. Even though the satiny, cup-shaped flowers are short-lived (24 hours), there are several buds on 18–36-in. stems that open up one at a time, for a very long bloom period. Found along the coastal areas of North and South America, this succulent has a low, dense mounding habit, spreading to 3 ft. with thick, grayish green, narrow, pointed leaves.

When, Where, and How to Plant
Plant from containers in fall or spring. Even though calandrinia will grow in poor soil, for optimum bloom and growth, provide humus or compost-amended, well-draining soil. Also, site the evergreen in full sun, except in areas where summer temperatures are consistently above the 90s, then provide some afternoon shade. Space 2–3 ft. apart if planting in multiples of three or more. Refer to p. 20 for additional planting information.

Growing Tips
Soak thoroughly after planting, then water regularly every five to seven days until established. Thereafter allow to dry out slightly before watering again about once every two weeks, but withhold water during winter dormancy unless there is no rainfall. Feed with a controlled-release fertilizer in early spring.

Advice and Care
Propagate by cuttings in spring. Allow the cuttings to callus over for several days, then plant in a commercial cactus mix, keeping the medium slightly moist, and keep in partial shade. It can be transplanted when new growth emerges, preferably in spring or fall. Remove spent flower stems down to the base of the plant for a neat appearance. There are few pests, but root or crown rot may develop as the result of overwatering or poorly draining soil.

Companion Planting and Design
Plant calandrinia *en masse* in front of borders, in rock gardens as a focal point, or in containers for a punch of brilliant color. Make sure companion plants have low water needs—rock rose, aloes, agaves, and butterfly bush are good choices. Calandrinia is also a wonderful addition to a butterfly garden.

Try These
C. spectabilis grows only 10 in. × 36 in., but has the vivid purple flowers on tall stems. *C. umbellata* is known as rock purslane, and is treated as an annual in cold-winter regions, but grown as a perennial where winters are mild, with tight 6 in. mounds of gray-green foliage and crimson blooms that peek just above the leaves. 'Shining Pink' bears glossy, hot pink flowers from blue-green foliage measuring 8–12 in. tall and wide; it blooms from spring-frost.

California Lilac

Ceanothus tomentosus

Other Name Woolly leaf mountain lilac

Bloom Period and Seasonal Color
Blue flowers bloom in spring.

Mature Height × Spread 6–12 ft. × 10 ft.

Botanical Pronunciation
SEE-ah-no-thus TOE-men-toe-sus

Zones 7–11

Covering the Southern California foothills is a California native species, *C. tomentosus*, commonly called California lilac. Its thick, spiked, lilac-blue blossoms form a spectacular carpet when compared to its more camouflaged companions. Providing a showy contrast to these blue spikes is dark green foliage the texture of crepe paper, with serrated margins. When mature, these plants grow into large shrubs, reaching heights and widths of 10 ft. Since they tolerate windy conditions and temperatures below freezing, as well as the other extreme of high 90s and even, for short periods, temperatures in the 100s, California lilacs are adaptable to many otherwise adverse environments. Be sure the soil is well drained because lack of adequate percolation is a common reason this native will perish.

When, Where, and How to Plant
Fall is the best season to plant because it is at the beginning of the rainy season and the flush of root growth occurs during this time; the second-best season is spring. Select a 1- or 5-gallon plant and plant in full sun or partial shade. Make sure the location has well-draining soil and is just beyond the limits of the sprinkler pattern. Space plants 10 ft. on center in a triangular or rectangular pattern. Mulch the surface of the ground immediately after planting to conserve moisture, stabilize the temperature, and limit the growth of weeds. Refer to Planting Techniques, p. 20.

Growing Tips
Once established, Mother Nature provides adequate moisture and nutrients, provided there is an average amount of rainfall during the months of November to March. Since infrequent deep watering is the rule, make sure California lilac is apart from plants that need more frequent watering, or root rot may result. Fertilize once a year in December or January with an organic granular or slow-release food.

Advice and Care
There is no need to deadhead, and prune only to shape the plant or to avoid an unruly canopy after the bloom cycle. To control whitefly, spray with spinosad; for aphids, spray with a canola-based horticultural oil.

Companion Planting and Design
When landscaping a drought-tolerant area with California lilac, plant it behind medium-sized shrubs and groundcovers because of its width and height. Combine with other natives that are water-thrifty and thrive in full sun, such as red clusterberry cotoneaster, silverberry, and rock rose.

Try These
'Blue Jeans' is one of the toughest (tolerates heavy soil and drought) of ceanothus hybrids with spring-blooming lavender-blue flowers against the backdrop of glossy, small, hollylike foliage growing to 6 ft. × 6 ft. 'Dark Star', with its deep blue flowers, grows to 6 ft., and the 9-ft. 'Concha' bears magenta buds that mature into dark blue flowers; it does well in mountain and beach landscapes. The 8-ft. 'Tuxedo' blooms summer to fall with lavender-blue flowers contrasting with dramatic, almost black foliage.

Carmel Creeper

Ceanothus griseus

Bloom Period and Seasonal Color
Blue flowers bloom in spring.

Mature Height × Spread 4–6 ft. × 6–10 ft.

Botanical Pronunciation
SEE-ah-no-thus GRIS-ee-us

Zones 8–11

Carmel creeper is a bushy plant with bright, shiny, crinkled leaves. Like many other California native plants, it is drought and seaside tolerant, and once established requires little maintenance. At the end of the rainy season, large, bright blue, flowering spikes appear that are 2–3 in. in length. Once mature, they survive several adverse conditions, including cold, wind, and heat, but they cannot tolerate clay soils or sites where soil aeration is poor. The ideal percolation rate for Carmel creeper is 1 inch per hour, to avoid root rot caused by saturated soils over an extended period. Although this is another species of ceanothus, many of these species make ideal groundcovers, compared to the larger *C. tomentosus* shrubs described in the previous profile.

When, Where, and How to Plant
In fall, select 1- or 5-gallon plants that are not root-bound. Plant in full sun along the coast, but provide partial shade inland. Soil pH should be neutral, 7.0. If the soil dug from the planting pit is soft and friable, there's no need to amend the backfill. Just eliminate large rocks and dirt clods. If the soil needs amendment, use one-third humus mulch, compost, or planting mix, and two-thirds loam soil. Plant 10 ft. apart and cover with a 2–3 in. layer of mulch. See Planting Techniques, p. 20.

Growing Tips
Do not use an automatic irrigation system unless your system has many zones keyed to specific plant grouping needs. Although a mature plant will survive on natural rainfall, infrequent deep watering is essential for a young plant. Water about every seven to ten days, unless there is a drought or period of heavy rainfall—then adjust watering accordingly. Fertilize in late summer and early winter, just before the plant's two growth cycles, with a complete organic granular or slow-release food.

Advice and Care
There is no need to deadhead or prune Carmel ceanothus because the plant's natural form is open and graceful. Control aphids by washing the critters off with a strong stream of water or by applying a canola-based horticultural oil.

Companion Planting and Design
Use Carmel ceanothus with other native or drought-tolerant plants. Try not to mix native plants with tropicals or subtropicals because of their different water requirements. Rock cotoneaster, rock rose, and dwarf coyote bush are good companions for ceanothus groundcover cultivars. Use it to stabilize slopes and as a fire retardant.

Try These
'Horizontalis' grows up to 2–3 ft. in height and has clusters of blue flowers in spring. 'Horizontalis Diamond Heights' (1 ft. × 4 ft.) has chartreuse or golden yellow leaves splattered with dark green, its variegation most prominent in warm climates and full sun; if in shaded areas or in winter, the green will be more dominant. 'Yankee Point' stands at 2–3 ft. × 8–10 ft. and is an excellent groundcover, with spring-blooming, darker blue flowers.

Crimson Bottlebrush

Callistemon citrinus

Bloom Period and Seasonal Color
Red flowers bloom in spring and summer.

Mature Height × Spread 6–10 ft. × 8 ft.

Botanical Pronunciation
ka-LIS-tih-mon sit-REE-nus

Zones 8–11

Crimson bottlebrush (syn. *Callistemon lanceolatus*) is a large plant bearing feathery red flowers that bloom from late spring to summer; the masses of bristlelike stamens (flowers) give the plant its common name. When you crush the leaves, they release a wonderful lemon scent, and cut-up leaves can be used as a potpourri when mixed with dried citrus rind. The narrow green foliage is stiff with an erect structure, and new growth extends beyond the flowers. Native to the dry areas of Australia, these plants are wind and drought tolerant and have few insect or disease problems. Deer usually leave the plants alone because they find the stiff leaves unpalatable. To screen an area in a short period with a low-maintenance plant, consider crimson bottlebrush.

When, Where, and How to Plant
Select 1- or 5-gallon specimens and plant in fall or spring in full sun. They do well in most types of soils, and tolerate slightly alkaline soils with a pH of 6.5–7.0, but their root systems develop most rapidly in porous rather than clay soils. Space these large plants 10–12 ft. apart. Once planted, mulch the ground's surface with 2 in. of organic material. See Planting Techniques p. 20.

Growing Tips
For established crimson bottlebrush, water infrequently and deeply, about once every seven to ten days. Fertilize twice a year, early spring and early summer, with a slow-release food or cottonseed meal for optimum growth and blooms.

Advice and Care
Little pruning is necessary if you want to use these plants as large shrubs. If you prefer the form of small trees, however, train the trunks vertically to 5 ft., then allow the canopy to develop naturally. Few pests and diseases affect crimson bottlebrush, but wash them off periodically to clean out accumulated debris.

Companion Planting and Design
Use this spreading shrub to cover up a foundation or other unsightly structure, as well as in desert landscapes, fire-resistant and hummingbird gardens, and in the middle of mixed borders. Line up for a hedge or group together in hot areas where other plants might not thrive. Combine with other water-thrifty plants like cotoneasters, rock rose, and ceanothus.

Try These
Two other varieties of *C. citrinus* that add interest to the landscape are 'Perth Pink' (10 ft.), with unusual pink flowers, and 'Violaceus' (6 ft. × 4 ft.), bearing red-purple blooms. 'Little John' is a dwarf bottlebrush growing to 3 ft. in height and width with blood-red flowers that bloom most heavily in spring and sporadically through the summer. The soft new growth develops into handsome, blue-green, narrow leaves and its diminutive size also makes it ideal for containers.

Firethorn

Pyracantha coccinea

Bloom Period and Seasonal Color
Cream flowers in spring; red, yellow, and orange berries late summer to winter.

Mature Height × Spread 2–12 ft. × 2–12 ft.

Botanical Pronunciation
PIE-rah-kan-thuh KOKE-sin-ee-ah

Zones 5–10 depending on cultivar

Valued for its fall to midwinter vivid orange, red, or yellow berries and prolific delicate white blooms in spring, pyracantha attracts local and visiting birds to feast on its fruits. When in flower, it is a magnet for bees and butterflies. Adaptable to a wide variety of uses, this evergreen to semievergreen (in cold regions) shrub or groundcover grows fast, is tolerant of most soil types, and does not like to be overwatered. True to its common name, the berries are not only the color of fire, but have sharp thorns often camouflaged amid its glossy, deep green leaves, making it an effective barrier. Ours grows just outside our office, and we particularly enjoy watching the birds' inebriated antics after feasting on the fermented berries.

When, Where, and How to Plant
Plant from containers in spring or in fall where winters are mild. Provide full sun and well-draining, slightly acidic soil. For spreading groundcover types, space 4–5 ft. apart. If there is a preference for color, purchase during its berry season.

Growing Tips
Water deeply and regularly during the first growing season to establish a deep, extensive, and healthy root system, but once established, allow to dry out before watering again, about once every two to three weeks, depending on growth and weather conditions. Remove withered berries and clean out debris with a strong stream of water. Feed with a complete organic granular fertilizer before new growth in spring.

Advice and Care
Prune only for errant growth in spring, keeping in mind that hard pruning lessens berry production. Pyracanthas look better when they're left alone. Control aphids and scale with a canola-based horticultural oil and use a miticide for spider mites.

Companion Planting and Design
Firethorn's dense, thorny growth is perfect for barriers against unwelcome intruders, hedges, windbreaks, and visual screens, and can also be trained as an espalier on walls or as topiaries. The sprawling varieties are used as colorful groundcovers and are excellent as firebreak plants. Birds and flower arrangers love the beautiful clusters of berries, but because of its sharp thorns, it is deer resistant.

Try These
'Kasan', with its long-lasting, orange-red berries, grows 8–10 ft. tall and 6 ft. wide while 'Lowboy' stands 2–3 ft. with a 6–8-ft. spread, making it a great groundcover with orange berries. A perfect low hedge, 'Rutgers' grows to 3 ft. × 5 ft. with paler orange berries and has some disease resistance. The hybrid 'Silver Lining' is a small 3 ft. shrub with silver-and-white-variegated foliage that morphs into a bronze pink in autumn and has minimal berry production. For a statuesque variety growing up to 12 ft. tall, select 'Mojave', a disease-resistant hybrid and prolific producer of huge orange-red berries that remain on the plant for a long time.

Flannel Bush

Fremontodendron spp.

Other Name Fremontia

Bloom Period and Seasonal Color
Bright yellow flowers in spring.

Mature Height × Spread 4–20 ft. × 6 × 40 ft.

Botanical Pronunciation
FREE-mon-toe-dehn-dron

Zones 8–11

While visiting the renowned gardens at Vita Sackville-West's Sissinghurst in Kent, England, we were surprised to see the common flannel bush, native to California, Arizona, and Baja, Mexico, growing with sprawling abandon against one of the aged brick walls. It was stretching about 20 ft. tall and 10 ft. wide. The leathery foliage was a deep green topside and grayish green fuzziness underneath. It was spring and the plant was covered with large, saucer-shaped, five-petaled, golden yellow flowers that would be replaced in summer to autumn with rust-colored, ciliated seed capsules. Known to be fast growing and found in dry woodlands, canyons, and along the slopes of mountains, flannel bush are drought tolerant. Because its roots are shallow, stake initially to keep it from being blown over during windy conditions.

When, Where, and How to Plant
Plant from containers in fall or spring, providing full sun and excellent-draining, sandy loam, slightly alkaline soil. Allow plenty of room for it to stretch and protect it from wind. Stake while still young for extra support. In chilly climates, place against a sunny wall for extra warmth. Where drainage is a problem, plant on a slope. Provide a 2–3-in. layer of mulch. See Planting Techniques, p. 20.

Growing Tips
Water thoroughly when planted, then allow to dry out before watering deeply about every ten to fourteen days during the first fall and winter if there is little or no rainfall. Once established, water only during periods of extended drought, because

overwatering can kill it. Do not fertilize, but to encourage the proliferation of beneficial aerobic soil microbes and prevent anaerobic microbes, apply a product rich in humic acid twice a year.

Advice and Care
Stake young plants for extra support and protection during windy periods. To control size and encourage more branching, pinch back new growth regularly. To prevent root rot, make sure the soil drains well and is not too soggy. It is best to wear gloves when handling flannel bush because the fuzz on leaves and pods irritates the skin.

Companion Planting and Design
Depending on the variety, flannel bushes are tree-sized, large shrubs, or low, mounding groundcovers. Plant with other water-thrifty plants such as ceanothus—its sparkling bluish purple flowers contrast dramatically with the yellow flowers of flannel bush. Can be planted *en masse* as an informal hedge or espaliered in a more formal setting.

Try These
F. californicum is the California native with bright yellow blooms. Most others offered are hybrids. 'California Glory' is one of the largest, quickly maturing to 20 ft. tall and wide with a long bloom period. 'Ken Taylor' is a midsized flannel bush, growing to 6 ft. × 12 ft. with a cascading habit, and bearing yellowish orange cupped flowers from late winter to summer. A smaller-growing hybrid, 'Dara's Gold' matures at just 4 ft. × 8 ft. and flowers from late winter to late spring.

Glossy Abelia

Abelia × *grandiflora*

Bloom Period and Seasonal Color
White flowers bloom all summer and even early fall, with lingering purplish or bronze sepals.

Mature Height × Spread 4–10 ft. × 5–8 ft.

Botanical Pronunciation
ah-BEEL-ee-ah GRAND-ih-flore-uh

Zones 6–11

Whenever a client requests a low-maintenance shrub, this is one of our top suggestions. Glossy abelia is a hybrid of *Abelia chinensis* and *A. uniflora*, and grows in every part of California, even where temperatures dip below freezing for short periods of time. Its sweetly scented, bell-shaped white flowers on gracefully arching branches can be an attractive accent in an otherwise humdrum yard. The bloom period is exceptionally long, from June through November in temperate climates, when few other shrubs are in flower. In addition, the lingering sepals are a beautiful purplish or bronze hue. Glossy abelia is an excellent shrub for both the beginning and experienced gardener, and its bright, shiny foliage glistens and sparkles in landscapes, especially when combined with more matte-colored plants.

When, Where, and How to Plant
Plant from 1- or 5-gallon containers in early spring, in a full sun location. While glossy abelia prefers loam soils with a pH of 6.5–7.0, it tolerates a wide range of soil textures, as well as seaside exposures. Consult the Planting Techniques, p. 20.

Growing Tips
Water one to two times a week when newly planted, but once established, water every ten to fourteen days, adjusting amount and frequency according to climatic and soil conditions. Use a complete organic granular or slow-release fertilizer in early spring.

Advice and Care
Glossy abelia can be pruned for shape at any time, but preferably after it has finished blooming. It should be periodically laced to stimulate new growth by allowing light to reach the center of the plant. The more you lace out in winter or early spring, the more open the plant will be with next year's growth. Deadheading is not necessary. Although largely pest free, keep an eye out for aphid infestations. Wash off aphids with a strong stream of water; if they persist, use a canola-based horticultural oil.

Companion Planting and Design
Plant several different species or varieties of glossy abelia *en masse*, and you will have a showy display. Structurally, they make ideal dense hedges (perfect for those who think good hedges make good neighbors), and can be planted along a foundation or in front of large evergreens. Japanese mock orange and rock rose make ideal companion plants.

Try These
'Edward Goucher', with lilac-pink flowers, grows a little smaller and more compact (3–5 ft. × 3–5 ft.) than the species. *A. grandiflora* 'Prostrate White' grows low and spreading (18–24 in. × 4–5 ft.) with white flowers, and is ideal groundcover and good for erosion control on slopes. 'Kaleidoscope' is compact, growing to just 2–3 ft. × 3–4 ft., with white flowers against the backdrop of yellow variegated leaves that shows some fall foliage color. The deer-resistant 'Ruby Anniversary' has ruby-red new growth and fall color, and grows 4–6 ft. × 4–6 ft.

Jade Plant

Crassula argentea/ovata

Bloom Period and Seasonal Color
Pink or white blooms appear in fall.

Mature Height × Spread 1–9 ft. × 2–4 ft.

Botanical Pronunciation
KRAS-oo-lah AR-jen-tee-ah/OH-vah-tah

Zones 10–11

Just as its name indicates, the foliage is light jade green in color. Shiny in texture with red margins and, like many succulents, high in moisture content, the jade plant is a branching shrub with sturdy stems and a stout trunk. Its stems have thick, delicate, star-shaped clusters of pale pink or white blooms that appear in the fall to spring. Since they are native to South Africa, they are drought, wind, and heat tolerant, but they cannot withstand temperatures below freezing because of their succulent foliar structure. Interestingly, their leaves redden when temperatures dip or when drought conditions persist. The plant can stretch to 9 ft. if left alone, but it also adapts to the confined quarters of a container to remain a smaller, more manageable size.

When, Where, and How to Plant

Plant anytime, but fall or spring months are best. Jade plants in the ground can be in full sun, partial shade, or shade. They tolerate a wide pH range, from 6.5–7.2, and prefer loam soils that provide good drainage (but they will survive in clay soils). Space about 18 in. on center from any sized container, although a 1-gallon size is more than adequate, or transplant into another container using a commercial cactus mix. Also see Planting Techniques, p. 20.

Growing Tips

Keep soil moist but not soggy until established; thereafter, allow it to dry out before watering again, about once every two to three weeks. For a better and longer bloom season, fertilize in spring and fall with a balanced organic granular food or cottonseed meal.

Advice and Care

Pruning is unnecessary because the form of the plant is naturally symmetrical, but cut off the spent flower clusters for a neat appearance. Propagation is easy. Air dry cuttings for a day or so to allow the cut ends to callus over, dip the ends in a rooting hormone, and place the cuttings halfway down into a cactus mix. Transplant into containers, or directly into the landscape when new growth appears. Use an iron phosphate molluscicide to control snails and slugs.

Companion Planting and Design

Dwarf jade plants make ideal border plants, as well as specimens for rock or desert gardens. They also do very well in containers because they are attractive and require little maintenance. Rockspray cotoneaster and other succulents such as aloes and agaves are good companions.

Try These

For the shire, why not plant dwarf cultivars such as 'Hobbit', with small leaves that curl back on themselves, and 'Gollum', with tubular leaves that are tipped with flattened ends, resembling suction cups? Both grow to 1–3 ft. × 1–2 ft. 'Crosby's Compact' is even smaller, forming a dense mass 1 ft. tall and wide. For variegated color, select 'Sunset' (yellow with a touch of red) and 'Tricolor' (green, white, and pale pink).

Lavender Starflower

Grewia occidentalis

Bloom Period and Seasonal Color
Lavender-pink flowers bloom in spring, summer, and fall.

Mature Height × Spread 6–10 ft. × 6–10 ft.

Botanical Pronunciation
GROO-yah OCK-sid-en-tah-lis

Zones 10–11

Lavender starflower is a fast-growing shrub with tiered branches that makes a great espalier plant. If you have a limited space in an enclosed area that receives full sun, we recommend it as an excellent container plant. Since every plant has a front and a back side, position your lavender starflower so that its foliage and blossoms are exposed to the direct sunlight and its more barren side is up against a wall, trellis, or fence. Throughout the summer, its striking 1½-inch, lavender, star-shaped flowers will be beautifully displayed against the shiny green foliage. Its foliage is leathery in texture and has serrated edges. Like other established plants from South Africa, it tolerates drought, wind, and full sun, but cannot tolerate extended freezing temperatures.

When, Where, and How to Plant
Plant in the spring or fall months from 1- or 5-gallon containers. Some 5-gallon container plants are already trained as espaliers. For maximum bloom production, locate in full sun in slightly acidic or neutral soil, 6.5–7.0 pH. Keep in mind that they prefer a porous soil. If you use them as espaliers on walls or fences, space them 8 ft. on center. If you use them as shrubs, space them 6 ft. on center. After planting, mulch the ground's surface with 2 in. of compost or humus mulch. Consult Planting Techniques, p. 20, for more information.

Growing Tips
Water every five to seven days until established; thereafter water deeply about every ten to fourteen days, or longer once established. Fertilize in the spring and fall with a complete organic granular food or cottonseed meal for lush foliage and profuse blossoms throughout the summer. Use an iron supplement if foliage becomes chlorotic.

Advice and Care
It is unnecessary to deadhead the flowers since they fall to the ground naturally after they are spent. Prune for shape after flowers are spent in late fall, either as a single-trunked tree, clipped into a hedge, or espaliered. Pinch back new growth for a denser habit. Lavender starflower is susceptible to root rot in poor-draining soils. To encourage the proliferation of beneficial soil microbes, add a product with humic acid and add more humus mulch or compost to improve soil drainage. Few other diseases or pests bother the lavender starflower.

Companion Planting and Design
Train as an espalier against a wall, fence, or trellis, or plant as an upright single-trunked tree and surround with low-growing annual color companion plants such as alyssum or cascading petunias. As a privacy screen or hedge, it is ideal and can be trained to cover an arbor. Also grow a wonderful addition in a butterfly/hummingbird garden.

Try These
G. caffra is the other name sometimes used for lavender starflower, but this is an entirely different species bearing yellow flowers, rarely in cultivation, and only occasionally found growing in the wild. There are no other cultivars for *C. occidentalis*.

Matilija Poppy

Romneya coulteri

Other Name Fried egg plant

Bloom Period and Seasonal Color
White blooms in spring through summer.

Mature Height × Spread 8–10 ft. × 3 ft.

Botanical Pronunciation
RAHM-nee-ah COLE-ter-eye

Zones 7–10

Native to chaparral and coastal sage habitats along the mountains and valleys of Southern California, from Santa Barbara to Baja, matilija poppy is considered the giant among poppies because it develops multiple 8-ft.-tall or taller thick stalks with greenish blue foliage. Also known as the "fried egg plant" due to its spectacular 4–9-in. diameter, chalk-white flowers with golden eyes, its flower petals resemble crepe paper and emerge in late spring to summer. Its plate-sized blooms are the largest of any California native, but the caveat is this perennial is not recommended for small gardens. If there is room, few natives are as exuberantly spectacular in the warm-season landscape; watch for "pups" that can develop a distance from the mother plant.

When, Where, and How to Plant
Plant from containers in spring or fall. Provide full sun and well-draining soil for optimum growth and development, but it will tolerate many types of soils. Since propagating from seed is very challenging, it is much simpler to dig up "pups" (rooted suckers that develop from the spreading root system) to get more plants. To keep plants within a confined area while allowing sufficient space for development, use root barriers 6–8 ft. from the rootball. Be careful when removing the plant from its original container to avoid disturbing its sensitive roots. After planting, apply a root stimulator containing indolebutyric or naphthaleneacetic acid following manufacturer's directions. Vitamin B-1 products sold for root growth are ineffective.

Growing Tips
Water deeply every five to seven days during its first summer, but once established, no supplemental water is necessary, especially when it is dormant in fall to winter. New growth will emerge after winter rains. To control rampant growth, withhold water during successive summers as well. Since this native is found in nutrient-poor soils, no fertilization is necessary.

Advice and Care
Cut down the plant's stalks close to the base about 3–4 in. in late fall; wear protective gloves to avoid skin irritation. Matilija poppies are deer resistant. If infestations of mealybugs or aphids need control, use a strong stream of water to knock them off or use a canola-based horticultural oil.

Companion Planting and Design
Matilija poppies are excellent for erosion control on slopes; in expansive, water-thrifty gardens; or near the back of wide borders. Since it can be invasive, combine with other vigorous plants such as pride of Madeira or salvia. When it's planted *en masse*, sit back and enjoy the butterfly and bee visitations. They're lovely in cutflower arrangements (but again, wear protective gloves when handling).

Try These
'White Cloud' is very vigorous, with prolific, large flowers, while 'Butterfly' is multibranched with smaller flowers. *R. trichocalyx*, commonly known as coast matilija poppy, has smaller leaves and is somewhat less aggressive.

Pride of Madeira

Echium candicans

Bloom Period and Seasonal Color
Blue flowers bloom in spring and summer.

Mature Height × Spread 5–8 ft. × 6–12 ft.

Botanical Pronunciation
EH-kee-um kan-dih-KANZ

Zones 10–11

While visiting Hanbury Botanic Garden in La Mortola, Italy, we saw the most spectacular pride of Madeira, growing in all their massive glory on steep bluffs exposed to the hot Mediterranean sun and blustery winds. It was late spring, and their dramatic spiked panicles of purplish blue flowers looked like candles blowing in the wind against a backdrop of grayish green leaves covered with fine hairs. The shrubs grow tall and spread widely, so give these plants enough space. Although heat and cold will affect their rate of growth, they can easily survive such conditions, as well as tolerate drought and wind. If you use them as cut flowers, make sure you remove all the foliage that might stand in water to prolong its beauty.

When, Where, and How to Plant
Spring or fall are the best times to plant and provide full sun. A pH of 6.5 is ideal, but they will tolerate pH ranges up to 7.2. They do well in dry, poor soil, but need porous well-draining soil. Plant at least 8–10 ft. on center from 1- or 5-gallon containers. To encourage rapid maturation of root systems, make watering basins at least 6 ft. in diameter and 6 in. high and mulch its surface. See Planting Techniques, p. 20.

Growing Tips
Deeply soak pride of Madeira immediately after planting, then water about once a week until established; thereafter, water when soil dries out slightly, about once every two to three weeks, withholding water during seasonal rains. Fertilize in late winter or early spring with an organic granular fertilizer.

Advice and Care
Prune to control size and shape in fall. After the bloom cycle is complete, remove the spent panicles. If you want to propagate these plants, allow the panicles to remain until their seeds mature, then cut the panicles, shake out the seeds, sow them in starter pots filled with a seed-starting mix, and keep moist. Few diseases or pests affect these plants. In fact, their pubescent foliar texture discourages chewing insects.

Companion Planting and Design
Pride of Madeira's stature and spectacular spikes of clustered lavender-blue flowers are excellent for steep slopes, butterfly/hummingbird gardens, and seaside areas. It also makes an excellent background plant with butterfly bush, glossy abelia, and matilija poppy. It is dramatically effective against a wall and can be used in cutflower arrangements.

Try These
E. candicans 'Star of Madeira' has beautiful gray-green foliage edged in creamy white. 'Starburst' is also variegated, with irregular white stippling throughout the leaves. Both have the classic blue floral spikes in spring and grow 6 ft. × 6–8 ft. *E. wildpretii* (*E. bourgaeanum*), tower of jewels, has long narrow leaves with spikes of funnel-shaped flowers that are salmon in color. It is a biennial, meaning it takes two years from seed germination to flowering, followed by death.

Red Clusterberry Cotoneaster

Cotoneaster parneyi

Bloom Period and Seasonal Color
White flowers bloom in summer with deep red berries fall through winter.

Mature Height × Spread 6–8 ft. × 8 ft.

Botanical Pronunciation
ko-TONE-ee-as-ter PAR-nee-eye

Zones 8–11

Cotoneaster parneyi differs from our other cotoneaster species because it is much larger and less dense in structure. Its foliage is dull gray-green with a coarse texture, and the leaves are 2–3 in. long. The underside of each leaf is tomentose, meaning it is fuzzy in texture, another distinguishing characteristic. In contrast to its evergreen foliage, the deep red clusters of berries make an outstanding display of color from fall through winter, and often into spring months. Its loose-growing form and size create an ideal visual screen. Once established, it is drought tolerant and withstands wind, heat, and cold temperatures as low as 20 degrees Fahrenheit. Birds perch and feast on its arching branches when they are laden with berries.

When, Where, and How to Plant
Plant in the spring and fall from 1- or 5-gallon containers. Like other cotoneaster species, red clusterberry cotoneaster does best in full sun, but can survive in partial shade. The production of flowers and berries, however, will be much reduced in shaded areas. A neutral soil pH of 7.0 is ideal for these plants. Make sure the soil is porous enough to allow adequate percolation. Space them about 10–12 ft. on center for optimum results. Mulch with compost or humus mulch 3 in. deep in a watering basin that is 4 ft. in diameter. Make sure the watering basin is twice the diameter of the plant's canopy. Refer to Planting Techniques, p. 20, for more specific planting directions.

Growing Tips
Thoroughly water the root zone immediately after planting, then water every seven to ten days until established; thereafter water once every two to four weeks, depending on weather and growth conditions. If necessary, fertilize in late winter or early spring with a complete organic granular food.

Advice and Care
Prune only for the purpose of shaping or removing dead wood. Deadheading the flowers is unnecessary. To increase bloom and berry production, pinch back the ends of the branches about 10 percent for the first and second growing seasons. This will increase the development of more branches as well as flowers and berries. Like the other species of cotoneasters, it has few insect or disease problems.

Companion Planting and Design
Use as a visual screen and plant with other water-thrifty plants such as silverberry and butterfly bush. The colorful branches create striking fresh arrangements for the home from fall to winter.

Try These
C. acutifolius, Peking cotoneaster, is deciduous and hardy in zones 4–8, growing to 10 ft. and bearing red flowers followed by black fruit, with stunning fall foliage splashed in oranges and reds. *C. glaucophyllus* is evergreen, growing 6–8 ft. tall and wide. It has an arching branch form with white flowers and dark red berries. *C. salicifolius* is the willow-leaf cotoneaster, another evergreen or semievergreen, maturing to 15–18 ft.

Red Hot Poker

Kniphofia hybrids

Bloom Period and Seasonal Color
Red, orange, peach, yellow, white, and pale green flowers in summer, spring, or winter.

Mature Height × Spread 1½–8 ft. × clumping

Botanical Pronunciation
NEE-foe-fee-ah

Zones 5–9

For an exotic, easy-to-grow plant, red hot pokers have few equals. Most of today's hybrids have been developed from South African species and come in a rainbow of colors. Out of sharp-edged, grasslike clumping foliage emerge the spiky blooms, which are shaped like torches. Another name is torch lily. The brightest-colored cultivars bear tubular flower buds at the top of each inflorescence that give a fiery glow, illuminating the garden, unlike other perennials. As the buds open from the bottom to the top, they fade and turn brown, giving the inflorescence a bicolored appearance. Depending on the cultivar, the flowering upright stalks grow between 3–5 ft. tall and are a favorite nectar source for hummingbirds.

When, Where, and How to Plant
Plant red hot poker plants in fall or spring from containers. Provide full sun or part shade and well-draining soil. *Kniphofia* cannot survive in water-logged soils. To improve drainage, amend with humus or compost, and add a product containing saponin. Space 2–8 ft. on center depending on mature size of the cultivar. See Planting Techniques also, p. 20.

Growing Tips
Water every seven days until established; thereafter, wait until the soil dries slightly before watering again. During the rainy season, withhold watering. Feed with an organic granular fertilizer in late winter or early spring before new growth begins.

Advice and Care
After the flowering cycle is over, cut off the spent stalks but leave the foliage alone. The leaves are needed to continue photosynthesis, which strengthens the plant. As cooler weather arrives, the plant will go dormant for a few months before beginning the next growth period in spring. Where winters are mild, the foliage will remain green. Where winter freezes are common, tie leaves over their clumps in autumn or allow to yellow and die back. Red hot poker has few disease or pest problems and is deer resistant.

Companion Planting and Design
Plant red hot poker close to the house for a colorful vertical accent, as well as for fire resistance. Its height and dramatic bold spikes of torchlike flowers lend a tropical and architectural focus to a sunny landscape. Unless it's a dwarf form, most are not suitable for containers because mature specimens expand into large clumps 2–4 ft. or more in diameter.

Try These
'Christmas Cheer' has bright orange buds and yellow flowers that bloom from fall to late spring where winters are moderate, but from fall to first freeze in other regions. Allow space for its 6–8 ft. × 6–8 ft. mature growth. Sending out 4-ft.-tall spikes is 'Percy's Pride' in greenish yellow. Shorter types at 2–3 ft. that are ideal for smaller gardens include 'Flamenco', with spikes of red, orange, and yellow; 'Little Maid', with white and pale yellow blooms; and 'Toffee Nosed', which has white blooms with orange tips.

Rock/Rockspray Cotoneaster

Cotoneaster spp.

Bloom Period and Seasonal Color
Rock: small, flesh-pink flowers in spring.
Rockspray: white flowers in late spring or
early summer.

Mature Height × Spread 2–4 ft. × 4–6 ft.

Botanical Pronunciation ko-TONE-ee-as-ter

Zones 6–11

otoneaster *horizontalis*, rock cotoneaster (deciduous), and *C. microphyllus*, rockspray cotoneaster (evergreen) are so named because they are native to hillside areas where there are rugged outcroppings of rocks. Rock cotoneaster has a fanlike spreading habit and thickly intertwining prostrate branches, making it an excellent groundcover. Rockspray cotoneaster is compact and moundlike with a thick, dense structure, making it ideal for rock gardens and banks, or for pruning into formalized shapes. In spring, shiny dark green leaves provide a lovely backdrop to small flesh-pink and white (respectively) spring flowers. Fall foliage is a grayish green to reddish orange or purplish bronze, followed by brilliant red berries. Both are excellent for fall color and cold locations where temperatures drop to -10 degrees Fahrenheit.

When, Where, and How to Plant
Plant from 1- or 5-gallon containers in fall or early spring. Full sun is best; it will adapt to shadier areas, but it will produce fewer blooms and berries. The soil should provide even percolation and have a neutral pH of 7.0. If soil is clayey, amend with humus or compost and add a product containing saponin. Space about 4–6 ft. on center and add a 2 in. layer of mulch. Mix a preplant fertilizer, at manufacturer's recommended rate, with the backfill soil.

Growing Tips
Thoroughly water the root zone immediately after planting, then water once a week until established; thereafter, wait until soil dries slightly before watering

again once every two to three weeks. Withhold water during the rainy season. Fertilize in late winter or early spring with a complete organic granular food.

Advice and Care
Prune only to remove the dead wood on rock cotoneaster, because the form maintains itself. When pruning rockspray for formal shapes, lace the canopy from the inside out so that sunlight reaches the latent buds, stimulating new growth. Do not deadhead the flowers. Control aphids by washing them off with a strong stream of water or applying a canola-based horticultural oil.

Companion Planting and Design
Both species are ideal for waterwise groundcovers and cascading over rocks. Use also where there is a difference in elevation, such as a terraced area or bank, and plant as a fire-retarding zone 30 ft. around a home. For formal landscapes, floribunda and shrub roses, silverberry, and other species of cotoneaster blend well with this plant. Birds will feast on the berries.

Try These
C. horizontalis 'Perpusillus', ground cotoneaster, is more compact and smaller, with dark shiny leaves that turn orange to red in fall and red flowers in spring; it is semievergreen in colder areas. *C. h.* 'Variegatus' is prostrate, with green leaves edged in white. *C. microphyllus* 'Cochleatus' is an ideal miniature for rock gardens, with a mounding habit to 1 ft. across. *C.m.* 'Thymifolius' grows to 1½ ft. and is used for hillside planting because of its dense structure.

Rock Rose

Cistus × purpureus

Bloom Period and Seasonal Color
Pink, white, and purple flowers bloom in spring.

Mature Height × Spread 4 ft. × 6 ft.

Botanical Pronunciation
SIS-tuhs pur-pur-REE-us

Zones 9–11

 ☀

R ock rose comes from the Mediterranean region and the Canary Islands, where annual rainfall is minimal. They are planted on our slope next to our street, and although we watered regularly during their first two years, once they established themselves, we left them alone. Rock rose are mound-shaped shrubs with leaves that are ovate and green in spring. As summer progresses, the leaves begin to dry and turn a dull grayish green. Single-petaled flowers with a crepe-paper texture peak in mid-spring in colors ranging from pink, to white, to purple. Established rock rose plants are extremely drought tolerant and even if their foliage wilts during the summer heat, they will revive when the rains return in fall.

When, Where, and How to Plant
You can plant in fall or spring, but fall is best. Start with young 1- or 5-gallon plants. Select plants that are not rootbound in their containers, because the new root system needs to web into the soil that has been backfilled into the planting pit. Carefully turn the container over to make sure the roots are not matted. Plant in full sun; if in partial shade, they will not bloom as profusely and their growth will be scraggly. They prefer a neutral pH of 7.0 and a well-drained soil so that their roots are not saturated. Space 6–8 ft. on center and mulch the surface of the ground with 2 in. of compost or humus mulch. See Planting Techniques, p. 20, for more information.

Growing Tips
Water every seven to ten days until established, then water once every two to thirteen weeks. Withhold water during fall to winter rains. Fertilize with a complete organic granular food in late winter or early spring.

Advice and Care
Deadheading flowers is unnecessary, but lightly prune for shape in late winter. Very few diseases or pests affect these plants.

Companion Planting and Design
Rock rose plants are deer and fire resistant, and tolerant of cold ocean winds and salt spray. Use them as low dividers, on dry banks, as fillers in beds; larger varieties make excellent background shrubs. Plant with other water-thrifty plants such as matilija poppy, ceanothus, and pride of Madeira.

Try These
C. × *pulverulentus* 'Sunset' ('Brilliancy'), which grows 2–3 ft., has clear magenta-pink flowers in early summer and a low-growing, mounding habit. 'Purple' or 'Orchid' bears rose-purple blooms with maroon spots emerging from compact shrub at 4 ft. × 4 ft.; it is considered one of the best rock rose plants for coastal conditions because of its high tolerance for salt spray. 'Bennet's White' is a big flowering white variety on a large, fast-growing, 4–6 ft. × as wide shrub. *C. ladanifer maculatus*, brown-eyed rock rose, has very showy white flowers with crimson spots in summer on a sturdy shrub 3–5 ft. × 3–5 ft. It's very cold hardy to zones 7–10.

Sage

Salvia officinalis

Other Name Garden sage

Bloom Period and Seasonal Color
Purple, red, and white flowers in
late spring-summer.

Mature Height × Spread 1–3 ft. × 1–2½ ft.

Botanical Pronunciation
SAL-vee-uh oh-fi-shi-NAH-lis

Zones 5–11

There are hundreds of sage species, as well as many hybrids and selections with an ever-widening range of temperature tolerances, sizes, and flower and foliar colors, with or without floral or leaf fragrance. Despite their differences, there are similarities: all bear two-lipped flowers arranged in tight or loose spirals around square stems. Sage belongs to the largest genus in the mint family, but we will focus on the garden sage, *S. officinalus*. Endemic to the Mediterranean, it is the sage of choice for culinary and medicinal purposes and can root wherever their stems rest on the soil. The species have oval to oblong, grayish green, and aromatic foliage on multiple branches. Up to 12-in. stems bear spiking clusters of lavender, blue, violet, reddish violet, pink, or white blossoms.

When, Where, and How to Plant
Plant from seed, cuttings, or containers in spring, or in autumn where winters are mild. If planted directly in the ground, provide full sun in well-draining, slightly alkaline soil with good air circulation and space 6–12 in. apart. Where climate is intensely hot, provide afternoon shade. Once planted, water deeply and cover with a 2–3-in. layer of mulch, kept away from the base of the plant. Sage also does well planted in containers in a commercial cactus mix.

Growing Tips
For its initial spring, water once a week; by summer, water twice a week where temperatures are hot and dry. In cooler-summer areas, allow soil to dry slightly before watering. Once established, water once every seven to fourteen days during its growth

cycles, but withhold water during winter unless there is no rainfall, then water about once a month. Do not fertilize because salvia does well in nutrient-poor soil.

Advice and Care
After flowering, cut sage back 20 percent and when new growth begins again, prune about 50 percent or just above fresh growth. After about four years, if it becomes woody with sparse growth, consider replacing it with a new plant. It's prone to mildew and root rot if planted in soggy, clay soil with poor air circulation. Improve clayey soil with a product containing saponin or plant in a container. For aphids or mildew, spray with a canola-based horticultural oil.

Companion Planting and Design
Some garden sage such as 'Aurea' (golden sage), is an ideal companion with cool-season annuals, while others such as 'Purpurascens' or 'Tricolor' tolerate hot summers and are pretty additions to butterfly, mixed-flower, and herb gardens. Use garden sage in containers, in the middle of sunny borders, planted *en masse* along pathways, or near windows or doors, where their aroma can be appreciated.

Try These
'Aurea', golden sage, has bright yellow-and-green-variegated leaves. Both 'Purpurascens' (2 ft. × 3 ft.) with purplish gray foliage and 'Tricolor' with white, rose, and green leaves tolerate hot summers. 'Berggarten', growing 16 in., is longer lived than the species.

Senecio

Senecio spp.

Other Name Blue chalk sticks

Bloom Period and Seasonal Color
Green-blue, gray-blue, or powder blue leaves year round.

Mature Height × Spread
12–18 in. × 12–18 in.

Botanical Pronunciation
seh-NEE-cee-oh vi-TAL-is

Zones 8–11 or treat as an annual

*S*enecio species are an odd mix, from dusty miller to cineraria, but two South African evergreen species are truly unique: think three shades of blue-grayish blue, bluish green, and powdery blue. *S. vitalis*, commonly known as blue chalk fingers, has delicate, fingerlike, gray-blue foliage lightly dusted with a chalky hue. Its graceful, upright leaves are densely packed and emerge in a symmetrical manner from sprawling fleshy stems. The shorter cultivar 'Serpent' has a more pronounced blue-green coloration with smaller leaves, but *S. mandraliscae*, blue chalk sticks, is the bluest, a powder blue with 3–4-inch cylindrical leaves encircling long, tubular, trailing stems. All have a waxy white coating that protects them from hot, sunny, and dry conditions. They are drought tolerant, but will accept irrigation.

When, Where, and How to Plant
Plant from containers in spring or fall, spacing 8–10 in. apart. Provide full sun or part shade and excellent-draining, sandy soil, although they will adapt to heavier soils if watered sparingly. For heavy soils, amend with humus or compost and add a product containing saponin or plant in a container using a commercial well-draining planting medium such as cactus mix. Pick a site in partial shade in the desert, full sun elsewhere. Propagate from cuttings, but allow cut ends to dry for a few days in a protected, shady spot before planting in cactus mix. Add about 20 percent perlite to the mix; keep planting medium moist but not soggy until there's new growth and transplant in spring or fall.

Growing Tips
Keep moist until established; thereafter water once every two weeks from spring to fall in desert regions, once a month in cooler areas, and allow to dry out slightly before watering again. If planted with plants that require more water, it will adapt, but grow much more rapidly. There's no need to fertilize.

Advice and Care
The smallish insignificant flowers can be cut off. Keep it away from small children or pets because it's toxic if eaten. Few pest or disease problems affect senecio, except overwatering and poorly draining soils often lead to root rot.

Companion Planting and Design
S. vitalis and 'Serpent' are stunning in mixed-succulent containers and waterwise planting beds, and can be acclimated to indoor conditions as a houseplant in bright, indirect light. The powder blue color of *S. mandraliscae* is an eye-popping contrast with other low-water plants in a sunny spot or as edging, planted *en masse*, over a wall, or tumbling over a pot with other succulents.

Try These
S. mandraliscae has chunky leaves growing on stems 12–18 in. × 24 in. and is perfect wherever a powder blue color is needed to brighten a landscape area. *S. vitalis*, 12 in. × 12 in., and *S.vitalis* 'Serpent' (6 in. × 12 in.) are more upright, with slender leaves that show off best in containers or in front of borders.

Silverberry

Elaeagnus pungens

Other Name Thorny elaeagnus

Bloom Period and Seasonal Color
White or cream flowers appear in autumn with red berries in winter.

Mature Height × Spread 6–8 ft. × 6–8 ft.

Botanical Pronunciation
EL-ee-ag-nus PUNJ-enz

Zones 8–11

Silverberry is a large evergreen shrub known for its natural, loose-growing form. The foliage has a medium texture with a dull green coloration on top; underneath, it is a dull silvery white color with brown spots. In autumn, fragrant silvery white or cream-colored flowers resembling tiny, elongated bells form. After flowering, it produces single-seeded berries, called drupes, that transform from brown to red in the late fall and early winter months, providing an excellent food source for wildlife. Once established, it tolerates drought, and its leathery foliage resists moisture loss even in windy locations. Amazingly, silverberry can survive temperature ranges from subzero to 100 degrees Fahrenheit for short periods of time. Its silvery, olive green foliage contrasts nicely against a backdrop of solid green plants.

When, Where, and How to Plant
Although fall and spring are best, silverberry can be planted anytime. Since they grow 20–30 percent in a year, a 1- or 5-gallon plant is a good choice. Plant in a sunny or shady location, although it will not grow as quickly in shadier spots. Tolerant of seaside conditions, wind, and drought once established, it prefers a neutral pH of 7.0 with good percolation, ensuring rapid root development. Plant 6–8 ft. on center. Create a 6-ft.-diameter watering basin and mulch its surface with 2–3 in. of organic material such as humus, leaving a 2–4-inch space around the plant base. Soak thoroughly after planting.

Growing Tips
Water every seven to ten days until established; thereafter, water when soil dries slightly, about once every two to three weeks depending on weather and growth conditions. Fertilize in spring and fall with a complete organic granular fertilizer.

Advice and Care
Little pruning is necessary because of its rigid stems. Errant new growth makes it look disheveled, so prune selectively for shape. Deadheading the flowers or removing the berries is unnecessary. It is deer resistant, but control rust with a canola-based horticultural oil.

Companion Planting and Design
Its size, loose-growing habit and twiggy, spiny growth is ideal for barrier planting, a visual screen, or as a background plant, especially if left to develop out in its natural form. It is also an effective addition to formal gardens and hedges if sheared. Silverberry is an excellent choice as part of the palette of low-maintenance shrubs along with rock rose, bottlebrush, and glossy abelia.

Try These
Cultivars of the species have been developed for a brighter appearance as compared to the duller, more matte olive green shade of *E. pungens*, but may be less hardy. 'Fruitlandii', fruitland silverberry, is an average height and width at 8 ft., with large, pronounced silvery-colored leaves. The green leaves of 'Variegata' are edged in yellowish white, while 'Marginata' is edged in silvery white. 'Maculata' is unusual, with leaves that have a single large gold splotch in the center.

Stonecrop

Sedum spp.

Bloom Period and Seasonal Color
Yellow flowers in summer.

Mature Height × Spread 4 in. × 2 ft.

Botanical Pronunciation
SEE-dum

Zones 4–11

Since sedums are found in many different parts of the world, some are cold hardy while others are fair weather–only varieties. Their size, habit, and color are also variable, from diminutive and trailing to larger and more upright, with petite, star-shaped blossoms to ample clusters of flowers. The smaller varieties are wonderful as groundcovers, tumbling and cascading in rock gardens, or as special container plants popular with collectors. The donkey or burro tail (*S. morganianum*) shows off the best when grown in a hanging basket, because of its long, 3–4-ft. trailing stems with overlapping leaves resembling braided tails. Bigger specimens are used in borders as well as pots, with pink, rose, red, and cream flowers that are bee, butterfly, and hummingbird magnets.

When, Where, and How to Plant
Plant from containers in spring or fall, spacing 2 ft. apart. Provide full sun or part shade and well-draining, sandy soil. Amend with compost or humus and add a product containing saponin if soil is clayey. For containers, use a commercially available cactus mix. Stem cuttings and even single leaves propagate easily. Add 20 percent perlite to the cactus mix; keep the medium moist, but not soggy until new growth. Transplant cuttings in spring or fall.

Growing Tips
Keep soil moist, not soggy until established; thereafter, water when soil dries and withhold during winter dormancy. Use slow-release or organic granular food at planting, otherwise do not fertilize.

Advice and Care
Pruning is unnecessary except to remove damaged or dried stems, or to use as cuttings to propagate more plants. Allow cut ends to dry out for two to three days in a protected, shady spot before planting in a loose planting medium such as cactus mix. Continue to provide moisture to the planted cuttings, but don't let them get soggy. Wash off aphids and mealybugs with a strong stream of water and apply an iron phosphate bait to get rid of snails and slugs.

Companion Planting and Design
Use in rock gardens draping over stone walls or rocks, in front of borders, in water-thrifty containers, as groundcover, or to contrast with darker foliaged, drought-tolerant plants such as ceanothus, rockspray cotoneaster, and 'Zwartkop' aeonium. Pair with another easy-care and water-thrifty plant for a fire-retarding perimeter that is also deer resistant.

Try These
For borders and rock gardens, 'Autumn Joy' (18–24 in. × 18–24 in.) has clumping erect stems displaying plate-sized clusters of flowers that begin pink, morph into salmon, and end as a coppery-rose color that lasts through autumn. The 3–6-in. tall 'Angelina' has golden yellow needlelike foliage with a trailing habit. 'Lemon Coral' is taller at 6–8 in., and has a brighter yellow color with a more upright habit. 'Blue Spruce' is wide, spreading to 18 in., and is compact with small, blue-gray succulent leaves.

GLOSSARY

adventitious: Describes a structure that develops in an unusual place, such as roots that develop from a trunk's base.

aerobic bacteria: Beneficial bacteria that require oxygen to survive; they proliferate in well-draining as opposed to clayey or soggy soils; one of two kinds of soil-dwelling bacteria.

alkaline soil: Soil with a pH greater than 7.0.

allelopathic: Describes a plant that releases a toxic chemical that inhibits growth in other plants.

all-purpose fertilizer: Powdered, liquid, or granular fertilizer with three primary nutrients: nitrogen (N), potassium (P), and phosphorus (K). It is suitable for maintenance nutrition for most plants.

alternate bearing: Describes fruit or nut trees that produce heavily one year and little or not at all the next.

anaerobic bacteria: Disease-causing bacteria, such as water molds, in plants because they do not require oxygen to survive and thrive in soggy or poorly draining soils; the second kind of soil-dwelling bacteria. (See aerobic bacteria.)

annual: A plant that completes its life cycle within one year.

anther: The pollen-bearing part of a stamen.

***Bacillus thuringiensis* or *B.t.*:** A bacterium lethal to many kinds of caterpillar pests and used to control them.

backfill: The soil mixture used to surround a rootball in a planting pit.

balled and burlapped: Describes a tree or shrub grown in the field whose rootball was wrapped with protective burlap and twine when the plant was dug up to be sold or transplanted.

bare root: Describes plants that have been packaged without any soil around their roots. (Often young shrubs and trees purchased through the mail arrive with their exposed roots covered with moist peat or sphagnum moss, sawdust, or similar material, and wrapped in plastic.)

beneficial insects: Insects or their larvae that prey on pest organisms and their eggs. They may be flying insects such as ladybugs, parasitic wasps, praying mantids, and soldier bugs, or soil dwellers such as predatory nematodes, spiders, and ants.

berm: A narrow raised ring of soil around a tree, used to hold water so it will be directed to the root zone.

biennial: A plant that completes its life cycle within two years.

bipinnate: Describes a leaf that has divisions that are themselves once or several times compound.

borer: An insect or insect larva that bores into the woody parts of plants.

bract: A modified leaf structure on a plant stem near its flower that resembles a petal. Often it is more colorful and visible than the actual flower, as in bougainvillea.

brown rot gummosis: A disease characterized by the formation of patches of gum on a fruit tree, the result of insects, microorganisms, or weather; when left untreated, it causes bark to scale, fall off, and ooze from the infected site and will eventually lead to the tree's demise.

bud union: The place where the top of a plant was grafted to the rootstock; usually refers to roses.

bulb: A short, modified, underground stem surrounded by usually fleshy modified leaves that contain stored food for the shoot within. True bulbs have pointed tops, short underground stems on basal plates, and new growths, called bulblets, which form from offshoots of the parent bulbs. The term is used loosely to describe bulblike plants (such as corms, rhizomes, and tubers), as many plants are technically not true bulbs.

canopy: The overhead branching area of a tree, usually referring to its extent, including foliage.

ciliated: Edged with hairs along the margin or edge, usually forming a fringe.

cold hardiness: The ability of a perennial plant to survive the winter cold in a particular area.

color packs: Sectioned plastic containers used for growing annuals and perennials.

compost: Organic matter that has undergone progressive decomposition by microbial and macrobial activity until it is reduced to a spongy, fluffy texture. Added to soil of any type, it improves the soil's ability to hold air and water and to drain well.

corm: A structure that grows upwards and is similar to a bulb, except that each summer a new corm grows on top of the original one. As the parent corm disappears, the roots of the new corm grow downward into the hole left by the decayed corm.

corolla: The petals of a flower considered as a group or unit.

corona: A crown-shaped, funnel-shaped, or trumpet-shaped outgrowth of certain flowers, such as the daffodil or the spider lily. Also called crown.

cultivar: A CULTIvated VARiety. It is a naturally occurring form of a plant that has been identified as special or superior and is purposely selected for propagation and production.

deadhead: To remove faded flower heads from plants to improve their appearance, abort seed production, and stimulate further flowering.

deciduous plants: Unlike evergreens, these trees and shrubs lose their leaves in the fall.

desiccation: Drying out of foliage tissues, usually due to drought or wind.

dimorphic: Existing or occurring in two distinct forms.

dioecious: Having the male and female reproductive organs borne on separate individuals of the same species. Both male and female plants are needed for pollination and seed production.

disbud: To take out the center flower bud shortly after the side buds emerge so that the plant's energy is directed toward the side buds.

division: The practice of splitting apart perennial plants to create several smaller-rooted segments. The practice is useful for controlling the plant's size and for acquiring more plants; it is also essential to the health and continued flowering of certain ones.

dormancy: The period, usually winter, when perennial plants temporarily cease active growth and rest. "Go dormant" is the verb form, as used in this sentence: Some plants, like spring-blooming bulbs, go dormant in the summer.

drupe: A fleshy fruit, like a peach, plum, or cherry, with a single hard stone that encloses a seed.

drupelets: Individual bumpy, fleshy, seed-containing units that make up a whole berry.

earwig: An elongate insect of the order Dermaptera with a pair of pincerlike appendages.

epiphytes: A plant that grows on another plant upon which it depends for mechanical support but not for nutrients.

espalier: A tree or shrub that is trained to grow in a flat plane against a wall, often in a symmetrical pattern.

establishment: The point at which a newly planted tree, shrub, or flower begins to produce new growth, either foliage or stems. This is an indication that the roots have recovered from transplant shock and have begun to grow and spread.

evapotranspiration: The moving of water from the earth into the air by evaporation from soil and transpiration from plants.

evergreen: Describes perennial plants that do not lose their foliage annually with the onset of winter. Needled or broadleaf foliage will persist and continues to function on a plant through one or more winters, aging and dropping unobtrusively in cycles of three or four years or more.

Fibonacci sequence: The Fibonacci numbers are those that follow 0, 1, 1, 2, 3, 5, etc. and each subsequent number is the sum of the previous 2; Fibonacci sequences appear in plant growth such as spiral patterns in many succulents, pine cones, pineapples, sunflowers, and other plants; the total number of spirals will be a Fibonacci number.

floret: A tiny flower, usually one of many forming a cluster, that comprises a single blossom.

foliar: Of or about foliage.

frass: Sawdust-like debris that accumulates below the holes caused by insects or larvae that bore into the woody parts of plants.

freestone: Describes a fruit with flesh that separates easily from the stony pit.

germinate: To sprout; germination is a fertile seed's first stage of development.

graft (union): The point on the stem of a woody plant with sturdier roots where a stem from a highly ornamental plant (or plant with superior fruit quality) is inserted so that it will join with it. Roses and fruit trees are commonly grafted.

hardpan: A layer of hard subsoil or clay.

herbaceous: Describes plants having fleshy or soft stems that die back with frost.

holdfasts: Tendrils with disc-like suction cups or rootlets that enable a plant to attach to just about anything.

hybrid: A plant that is the result of intentional or natural cross-pollination between two or more plants of the same species or genus.

inflorescences: Flower clusters.

June drop: A common citrus malady: the sudden shedding of immature fruit, nature's way of adjusting the crop size to the tree's capability to produce good fruit.

latex: The colorless or milky sap of certain plants, that coagulates on exposure to air.

leach lines: Sewer discharge lines.

lignotuber: A swollen portion of the root flare that is just above or below the ground. It functions as a moisture and nutrient storage reservoir during times of drought. Even after a natural disaster, such as a fire, the lignotuber allows it to regenerate.

molluscicide: An agent that kills mollusks, including slugs and snails.

monocarpic: Describes plants that flower and bear fruit only once.

monocotyledon: A flowering plant, like grasses, orchids, and lilies, that has a single leaf in the seed.

mulch: A layer of material over bare soil to protect it from erosion and compaction by rain and discourage weeds. It may be inorganic (gravel, fabric) or organic (wood chips, bark, pine needles, chopped leaves).

mycorrhizal fungi: Important soil organisms that colonize plant roots, aiding in the roots' uptake of water and nutrients as well as helping in disease suppression.

naturalize: (a) To plant seeds, bulbs, or plants in a random, informal pattern as they would appear in their natural habitat; (b) to adapt to and spread throughout adopted habitats (a tendency of some nonnative plants).

nectar: The sweet fluid produced by glands on flowers that attract pollinators such as hummingbirds and honeybees.

offset: A shoot that develops at the base of a plant and may root to form a new plant.

operculum: A lid that covers each bud and pops off when its stamens unfold during its flowering period.

organic material, organic matter: Any material or debris that is derived from plants. It is carbon-based material capable of undergoing decomposition and decay.

palmate: Describes fronds that are round or semicircular in outline.

peat moss: Organic matter from peat sedges (United States) or sphagnum mosses (Canada), often used to improve soil texture.

pedicel: In a cluster of flowers, a stem bearing a single flower.

percolation: Passing or oozing through porous material, as in water passing through soil.

perennial: A flowering plant that completes its life cycle in more than two years. Many die back with frost, but their roots survive the winter and generate new shoots in spring.

petiole: The stalk by which a leaf is attached to a stem.

pH: a measurement of the relative acidity (low pH) or alkalinity (high pH) of soil or water based on a scale of 1 to 14, 7 being neutral. Individual plants require soil to be within a certain range so that nutrients can dissolve in moisture and be available to them.

pinnate: Describes fronds that are linear or oblong in outline with segments arranged like the pattern of a feather.

pollen: The yellow, powdery grains in the center of a flower. A plant's male sex cells, they are transferred to the female plant parts by means of wind or animal pollinators to fertilize them and create seeds.

pollinator: The male plant that supplies the pollen to fertilize the female plant of a dioecious pair; also called pollinizer.

pollinizer: See pollinator.

pony packs: Sectioned plastic containers used for growing annuals and perennials.

rectilinear: A shape bound by four straight lines and with 90-degree corners.

rhizome: A swollen, energy-storing stem structure, similar to a bulb, that lies horizontally in the soil.

rootbound (or potbound): The condition of a plant that has been confined in a container too long, its roots having been forced to wrap around themselves and even swell out of the container.

rootstock: The lower part of a grafted tree or rose.

russeting (or silvering): A blemishing of the rind on lemon trees, caused by mite infestations.

scion: The top part of a tree or rose that has been grafted onto a rootstock.

self-fruitful: Describes a fruit tree that pollinates itself.

semi-evergreen: Tending to be evergreen in a mild climate but deciduous in a rigorous one.

shearing: The pruning technique whereby plant stems and branches are cut uniformly with long-bladed pruning shears (hedge shears) or powered hedge trimmers. It is used when creating and maintaining hedges and topiary.

slow-release fertilizer: Fertilizer that is water insoluble and therefore releases its nutrients gradually as a function of soil temperature, moisture, and related microbial activity. Typically granular, it may be organic or synthetic.

sow bug: A small terrestrial crustacean; also known as wood louse.

spathe: A leaf or bract subtending a flower grouping.

spray: A cluster of flowers in different stages of development on a single stem.

stamen: The pollen-producing reproductive organ of a flower.

stolon: A specialized above-the-ground stem that produces roots and shoots at the nodes.

stomata: Leaf pores.

sucker: A new growing shoot. Underground plant roots produce suckers to form new stems and spread by means of these suckering roots to form large plantings, or colonies. Some plants produce root suckers or branch suckers as a result of pruning or wounding.

tillering: Sending forth shoots from its base (as grass does).

tomentose: Fuzzy in texture.

tuber: A swollen rhizome that produces pulpy, instead of scaly, stems. Tubers normally grow just below the surface of the soil and, like bulbs, store food for the plants. The buds on tubers become stems, leaves, and flowers, and clusters of roots form at the base. They multiply by division, and as they divide, the parent tuber deteriorates.

tuber: A type of underground storage structure in a plant stem, analogous to a bulb. It generates roots below and stems above ground.

umbel: A flat-topped or rounded flower cluster; the flower stalks rise from about the same point.

variegated: Having various colors or color patterns. The term usually refers to plant foliage that is streaked, edged, blotched, or mottled with a contrasting color, often green with yellow, cream, or white.

vectoring: Carrying (diseases from plant to plant).

xeriphytic: Having to do with water-conserving landscaping.

xeriscape: A landscape system designed to conserve water.

BIBLIOGRAPHY

Bailey, L. H. *A Standard Cyclopedia of Horticulture*. 3 volumes. New York, New York: The Macmillan Company, 1958.

Condit, Ira J. Ficus: *The Exotic Species*. Berkeley, California: University of California Division of Agricultural Sciences, 1969.

Graf, Alfred Byrd. *Exotica Series 3: Pictorial Cyclopedia of Exotic Plants from Tropical and Near-tropic Regions*. East Rutherford, New Jersey: Roehrs Company, Inc., 1973.

Griffiths, Mark. *Index of Garden Plants*. Portland, Oregon: Timber Press, Inc., 1994.

Pizzetti, Ippolito and Henry Cocker. *Flowers: A Guide for Your Garden*. 2 volumes. New York, New York: Harry N. Abrams, Inc., 1975.

Smiley, Beth and Ray Rogers, editors. *Ultimate Rose*. New York, New York: Dorling Kindersley Publishing, Inc., 2000.

Vavilov, N. I. *Origin and Geography of Cultivated Plants*. New York, New York: Press Syndicate of the University of Cambridge, 1994.

PHOTO CREDITS

Bill Adams: pp. 93

Bruce Asakawa: pp. 9, 92, 186, 207, 210, 214

Sharon Asakawa: pp. 13, 14, 17, 35, 38, 47, 57, 62, 73, 76, 79, 181, 182, 184, 187, 193, 209, 224

Liz Ball & Rick Ray: pp. 32, 46, 52, 107, 109, 114, 119, 155, 156, 159, 162, 167, 178, 201, 222

Cathy Barash: pp. 30

Courtesy of Phil Bergman, www.junglemusic.com: pp. 97

Tom Eltzroth: pp. 10, 33, 34, 36, 37, 39, 41, 42, 43, 44, 49, 54, 55, 56, 58, 59, 61, 65, 66, 67, 69, 71, 72, 75, 77, 78, 80, 82, 83, 84, 85, 87, 88, 90, 91, 95, 96, 98, 100, 102, 104, 105, 110, 111, 112, 113, 117, 118, 132, 133, 134, 135, 137, 139, 142, 143, 147, 149, 150, 151, 152, 153, 154, 160, 164, 166, 169, 171, 173, 179, 183, 185, 190, 191, 192, 195, 196, 197, 198, 199, 200, 202, 204, 211, 212, 213, 215, 216, 217, 218, 219, 220, 221, 222, 227

Katie Elzer-Peters: pp. 23 (both), 45

Lorenzo Gunn: pp. 64, 70, 81, 99, 101, 136, 141, 158, 163, 172, 175, 177, 194

iStock: pp. 62

Jupiter Images: pp. 68

Courtesy of Monrovia, www.monrovia.com: pp. 146, 157, 223

Jerry Pavia: pp. 40, 51, 59, 108, 115, 116, 121, 131, 138, 144, 161, 168, 174, 205, 206, 208

Proven Winners® ColorChoice®: pp. 140, 145

Felder Rushing: pp. 165

Shutterstock: pp. 6, 50, 106, 170, 180, 188

Nan Sterman: pp. 225

Danny Takao, Takao Nursery: pp. 89

Weeks Roses: pp. 124, 125, 126, 127, 128, 129

INDEX

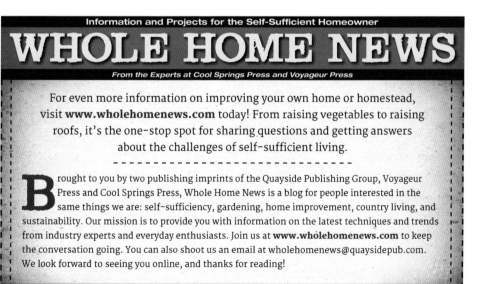

MEET BRUCE AND SHARON ASAKAWA

Bruce Asakawa has been active in the green industry, landscape design, and gardening communication most of his life. His parents founded Presidio Garden Center in 1950, which became one of the premier retail nurseries on the West Coast. Their nursery was one of the first to diversify into landscape architectural planning, landscape contracting, FTD floral designing, and koi and tropical fish sales.

Bruce graduated from Cal Poly, Pomona, with a major in landscape architecture, a field that combined his interest and talents in horticulture, art design, and nature. He developed and taught horticulture classes through the University of California Extension program. During the early 90s, Bruce hosted the *West Coast Garden Line,* a popular, live call-in radio show that aired throughout California. The program became *Garden Compass,* which was on the air until 2008.

Sharon Asakawa began working at Presidio Nursery after marrying Bruce, eventually managing both florist departments at Presidio and Bonita Garden Center, which she and Bruce owned and operated. Sharon regularly appeared with Bruce on the *Over the Hedge* television program and co-hosted the *Garden Compass* radio program with Bruce and John Bagnasco in 2000. Sharon currently co-hosts the national gardening and lifestyle radio talk show *GardenLife,* airing live every Saturday and Sunday with John Bagnasco and Bryan Main. She is content editor for *GardenLife,* the weekly online newsletter, blog, and website at www.gardenlife.com.

Several years ago, the Asakawas published their first book *Bruce and Sharon Asakawa's California Gardener's Guide* (Cool Springs Press, 2001), now in its seventh printing. They then co-authored the southwestern editions of *Jackson & Perkins Beautiful Roses Made Easy* and *Jackson & Perkins Outstanding Perennials.* With their son Eric Asakawa, their fourth book was *California Gardening Rhythms.* Bruce and Sharon's latest book is *California Gardener's Handbook.* If you'd like to touch base with Sharon, call in with your garden questions at 1-866-606-TALK every Saturday from 8-9 AM and every Sunday from 8-10 AM PST.